history from the EARTH

An introduction to archaeology

J. FORDE-JOHNSTON

history from the
EARTH

An introduction to archaeology

NEW YORK GRAPHIC SOCIETY

Frontispiece. Silhouette of a body lying on its side with legs slightly bent, found at Elp in Tumulus II, in the commune of Westerbalk, Netherlands (excavated by A. E. van Giffen, 1932). All traces of the body have disappeared, but it has left its imprint in the soil in the form of a dark colouring seen clearly against the light sand of the original ground surface.

for James, Kathleen, Richard and Andrew

International Standard Book Number 0–8212–0602–8 (Cloth)
International Standard Book Number 0–8212–0605–2 (Paper)

Library of Congress Catalog Card Number 73–91709

First published in Great Britain 1974 by Phaidon Press Limited, London.
Published in the United States of America and in Canada by New York Graphic Society Ltd., Greenwich, Connecticut 06830.

Printed in Great Britain by Hazell Watson & Viney Limited.

Contents

The Meaning of Archaeology

The word 'archaeology' means literally the study of old things, from the Greek *archaios*, old, and *logos*, knowledge or study. The literal meaning of the word, however, gives only the most general indication of what the subject is about. What is needed is a more precise definition which goes beyond the meaning of the original Greek words and defines archaeology as it is understood today, as one of the great branches of the study of Man. This last, the human aspect, is perhaps one of the most important points to establish, in formulating any extended definition of 'archaeology'. In spite of the Greek words the subject is, ultimately, concerned with people and not with things. Things obviously loom large in the subject, but the archaeologist is no mere collector of antiques. Such things as he does collect are a means and not an end; they are not so much valuable objects in themselves as important pieces of evidence relating to Man's past, and it is the attempt to tell the story of Man in the past which justifies archaeology as a branch of learning.

The recognition of archaeology as a branch of the study of Man enables one important point to be made: the subject is thereby specifically restricted to the period of Man's existence on earth. Earlier phenomena, dinosaurs, for example, which became extinct some ninety million years ago, have nothing whatsoever to do with archaeology. They are certainly 'old things', but not in the archaeological sense, since they have nothing to do with Man. Another subject popularly associated, again wrongly, with archaeology is that of fossils. Apart from occasional fossilized bones of very early Man, fossils are the concern of geologists rather than archaeologists.

Having thus excluded two groups of 'old things', it is appropriate at this stage to say something about those 'old things' which are the legitimate concern of the archaeologist. Objects which can be held in the hand, such as pots or stone implements, are often termed portable antiquities or arte-facts, and these certainly form a very important part of archaeology. However, the term artefact (literally, anything made by human skill) embraces much more than portable antiquities. In its widest sense it embraces everything made by Man, not only portable antiquities but also the whole range of structures which he erected for his accommodation, burial, worship, defence, etc. Thus a Greek temple or an Egyptian pyramid is an artefact just as much as the stone axe or bronze dagger blade on display in the local museum [1, 2]. All belong in the same category, as the products of human ingenuity, and these products are among the main raw materials of archaeology.

Artefacts account for many of the 'old things' which the archaeologist uses as evidence. There are, however, some other things, both portable and

1. Opposite: a greek temple of the fifth century BC, built in the Doric style: the temple of Hephaestus, popularly known as the Theseum, overlooking the Athenian *agora* or market-place of ancient times. This, as much as the inlaid bronze dagger blade from Mycenae [2], is an artefact, something however large and complex made by Man to meet his particular needs, in this case religious.

2. Bronze dagger blade from Mycenae, inlaid with gold, silver and niello, known from its subject as the 'Lion Hunt' dagger, found in Shaft Grave IV, 1500–1400 BC. Note the two types of shield, the figure-of-eight type and the rectangular type, known as tower shields.

3. Opposite: Glastonbury Tor, dominated by the tower which is all that remains of the medieval church of St. Michael. The terraces stepping down the sides of the hill are almost certainly the results of ploughing during the medieval period and are known as strip lynchets, to distinguish them from the lynchets of the prehistoric period, which consist of rectangular fields, usually called 'Celtic fields'. Nevertheless, both types of formation are the incidental result of ploughing for cultivation purposes.

monumental, which provide material evidence but which are not, strictly speaking, artefacts in the sense of being something deliberately made by Man. Two examples will suffice to show what is meant on the monumental side. On the slopes of the chalkland of southern England, one of the results of ploughing during the last few centuries before the Roman conquest (AD 43) was to produce a series of terraces stepping down the hillside, known as lynchets. Large numbers of these are still clearly visible on the ground and provide invaluable evidence of prehistoric Man's agricultural activity [3]. But the lynchets are not artefacts, even in the widest sense of the word; they are an incidental result of ploughing the same fields over a long period. Nonetheless they are important pieces of evidence and are classed as archaeological monuments. So also are the rubbish mounds associated with Pueblo Indian settlements in the South-western United States. Again there is no deliberate intention of building a monument; the mound is the result of dumping normal domestic refuse in a given place away from the living area. Over a period of two or three generations it grows to a considerable size and is, again, an easily recognizable feature of the landscape and an archaeological monument. Because it contains the debris of day-to-day living, always of great interest to the archaeologist, it is an invaluable source of archaeological evidence, even though it is not a deliberate piece of construction.

The same pattern holds good for portable antiquities. The bulk of these, uncovered by excavation or found accidentally, are deliberately made by Man for his own use, such as tools, weapons, and pottery, but not infrequently mixed in with these objects are others which are incidental to their production or to some other activity. For example, flint tools are normally made by striking off flakes from a parent lump of flint. What is left at the end of the process is a core of flint which shows clearly where the flakes have been struck off. Such a core is invaluable in the study of flint technology. So also are the waste flakes which result from trimming the tool to the required shape. Neither core nor waste flakes are deliberately made as such, but they are nonetheless very much the concern of the archaeologist in his search for evidence.

A third important group of 'old things' consists of objects which can best be described as the planned or intended, rather than the incidental, result of some previous activity. These include such things as animal bones (the result of stock-rearing, hunting, trapping, fishing, etc.), carbonized grain, seeds, and fruit stones (the results of crop-growing and food-gathering), and naturally occurring substances and objects (amber, shale, natural pebbles) collected in order to use as raw material or, in the case of the pebbles,

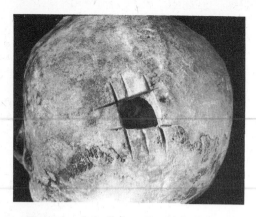

4. Trepanned skull from Lachish, Palestine. Trepanning or the removal of a portion of the skull, either before or after death, was a widespread practice and occurred in the ancient Near East, prehistoric Europe and in the British Isles. It was presumably performed for the purposes of ritual or magic.

5. Opposite: a burial, in a large jar, under a house floor in the Lebanon. This was presumably a 'foundation burial', made for ritual purposes when the home was being built to ensure the well-being of its inhabitants. Because of the practice of burying bodies, at any time, beneath the floors of houses and huts it is not always possible to distinguish true foundation burials from simple under-floor burials.

as they stand, for example, as sling stones. The importance of such remains is clear, particularly relating to food, since they can tell us so much about the diet and basic economy of the people concerned. There is, however, one way in which this whole group differs from the two previous groups. These, both deliberate artefacts and incidental products, show clear evidence of human agency, wherever they are found or whatever the circumstances. In other words, a flint tool, or the core from which it has been struck, are quite clearly pieces of archaeological evidence whether they are found buried deep in an ancient site or lying on the surface, as they sometimes do, on the chalk downs of southern England. This is not true, however, of objects in the third group. These become archaeological evidence only when they are found in an 'archaeological context', that is, either when they are found in association with objects in the first two groups, or when they are found buried within an archaeological site. For example, a stone pebble found lying on the ground has no archaeological significance whatsoever. The same pebble found with a Bronze Age burial, however, immediately assumes the role of an object utilized by early Man and is therefore a piece of archaeological evidence. The same is true of animal bones: by themselves they are of no archaeological interest, but the same bones in an archaeological context assume very great significance as evidence of diet, economy, etc.

Human, as opposed to animal, bones do not come into the third group. As the remains of Man himself they quite clearly constitute a special, self-contained fourth group. Again, much depends on the circumstances in which they are found. By themselves they are meaningless, except when very early, Old Stone Age remains are involved. In an archaeological context, on the other hand, they can, among other things, provide evidence of the stature and general appearance of the people involved as well as indicating in certain cases state of health, the presence of disease or even attempts at surgery [4]. In collective burials comparison of the skeletons can reveal resemblances indicating a family grave. Human remains can also tell us a great deal about religious beliefs and ritual practices. The finding of a skeleton under the floor of a prehistoric hut suggests the practice of 'foundation burial', a burial associated with the building of the house to ensure its prosperity. This evidence of ritual practice arises not from the skeleton itself but from the particular circumstances in which it is found, and this aspect will be returned to later [frontispiece, 5].

These four groups cover virtually everything studied by the archaeologist and can be conveniently grouped under the heading of 'material remains' of Man's past. These material remains are subject to study by archaeologists in a variety of ways which can be summarized by the sequence: fieldwork—excavation—publication, although other forms of study arise out of these and will be described in their turn.

FIELDWORK

As a form of archaeological work, fieldwork is less familiar to most people than excavation, but it is a fundamental part of archaeology. Briefly, it involves the search for, and recording of, archaeological sites and monuments without actually excavating. On grounds of cost alone, excavation can be carried out only on a very small proportion of archaeological sites. The vast majority must remain unexcavated. It is doubly important, therefore, to discover as much as possible about them by careful examination and planning of their

surface features. This is very simply archaeological evidence freely available on the ground, without involving the more complex and costly process of excavation. It is less precise than the evidence provided by the latter, but it is nonetheless an integral part of the total body of information relating to the past and as such it is not only desirable but quite essential that it should be fully recorded. A more immediate reason for this form of record is as an insurance against destruction. The demands of housing, road-building, forestry and modern farming methods, among others, are responsible for the complete destruction of many archaeological sites, and this threat does not appear to be diminishing—if anything, it is on the increase. It is therefore of paramount importance to record all the details while they are still available. Then if the site is, unhappily, destroyed, there is at least a measured plan and a written record of its features, so that it can still be evaluated as a piece of archaeological evidence.

The importance of field archaeology, however, goes far beyond the recording of a particular site. It embraces also an assessment of the total number of such sites, and their distribution. At a very simple level, the number of sites of a particular type is important as one of the physical dimensions of the problem to be tackled. Unless it is certain that all such sites are known, it is difficult to proceed to the next stage with any confidence. The total, even in isolation, is some broad indication of the significance of the type of site involved; a handful of sites is likely to be a less important aspect of a civilization than a group of several hundred. The same total, in comparison with the totals for other groups, enables some sort of judgement, however generalized, to be made about relative importance.

Numbers, whether of a single type or of several different types, assume even greater significance when studied in terms of distribution by means of a distribution map, an important device for the study of all types of antiquities, both monumental and portable [6]. Plotting the location of monuments (or portable antiquities) on a map is an indication of the geographical extent of the territory occupied by the people responsible for their construction or manufacture. A statement in words, however long, will not make the point so effectively as an outline map with a simple dot to indicate each location involved. A series of such maps showing the distribution of several different types, or a single map showing the same types plotted together, enables comparisons to be made between the geographical spread of different types of monument. Broadly speaking, where distributions coincide, it can be suggested (as a hypothesis requiring further confirmation, rather than as a definite fact) that the sites or antiquities involved are closely related, probably the work of the same people; where they only partially overlap or are entirely separate, then some other explanation is called for. Such an explanation cannot be supplied by field archaeology alone. The more particular evidence of excavation is required here, and this gives rise to the matter of field archaeology as related to excavation.

This relationship can perhaps best be illustrated by studying the basic archaeological sequences (fieldwork—excavation—publication) in a hypothetical country, previously untouched archaeologically. One of the first requirements of successful fieldwork are good base maps. Without them the making of a good distribution map is virtually impossible. However, it will be assumed in this case that good base maps are available. Probably the first move by an archaeologist contemplating a field survey would be a recon-

6. Distribution map of long barrows in England and Wales. The black dots represent long barrows with stone-built chambers, i.e. megalithic tombs; the open circles represent long barrows without chambers, or rather chambers built of wood which has not been preserved, i.e. earthen long barrows. Although the two major groups are adjacent, the map makes it quite clear that the two types occupy largely different areas.

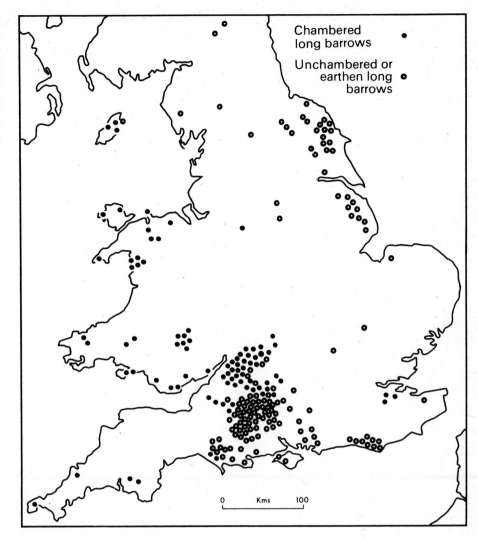

naissance trip, or a series of such, depending on the size of the country. From this he would get some idea of the size and nature of the problem to be tackled. He would know generally in what parts of the country monuments were to be found, approximately how numerous they were, and roughly how many types or groups they belonged to. He would also have begun to be familiar with the portable antiquities of the area, for almost certainly on visiting certain sites he would be able to pick up such things as pieces of pottery or stone tools, or other remains of Man's occupation, lying on the surface. Long before he is ready for excavation, these finds give him a start in studying the sort of evidence which normally is produced only by digging. They also provide the nucleus for a museum collection, another important aspect of archaeology which will be considered later.

With the completion of the reconnaissance the archaeologist is now ready for the next stage, a systematic survey and recording of all sites and monuments in the country. The first step is to record the location of every visible site or monument so that at the end of this process there is a distribution map of the country's archaeological sites which shows not only the total number of sites, but also where they are located. By the use of different symbols for different types of sites, the map can also show the number of each type and their geographical relationship to each other. The same map, with the main natural features included, can show the relationship of all these sites to rivers, lakes, mountains, etc., and, with geological features added, can show their relationship to the basic surface geology of the country. Already this is a valuable piece of archaeological evidence and a statement, even if only a very general one, about the country's history. It can tell us, for example, where people preferred to live, whether on the coast, or in the upland areas, or along the rivers; or what type of country they preferred, a clay area with heavy vegetation, or a chalk or limestone area with much lighter vegetation. In the prehistoric period, with only simple tools available, this was a very important factor, and the lighter soils tended to be settled first.

One of the great modern aids to archaeological survey work is aerial photography, both vertical and oblique. Oblique photographs are normally taken from a relatively low level (750–1000 ft.) and are usually directed at individual sites and monuments. One of their great advantages is that they give an overall view of monuments which quite often cannot be easily seen as a whole at ground level. Vertical aerial photography, although it too can be used to record individual sites, is more often concerned with coverage of a given area of countryside, by means of a continuous series of overlapping photographs. The height from which the photographs are taken is much greater. Much of the vertical cover held in the Department of the Environment's Air Photographs Library was taken (by the R.A.F.) from 16,000 ft. [7].

Both vertical and oblique aerial photography have been responsible, in the last twenty-five years, for the discovery of thousands of archaeological sites of which there was little or no trace on the ground. The evidence for these sites takes three forms: crop marks, soil marks and shadow marks. Crop marks are the result of buried archaeological features affecting the quality of the growing crop above. For example, the grass above a buried ditch, with its tendency to retain moisture, will be taller and greener than the grass on either side. Conversely, the grass above a buried wall will tend to be stunted and less green because it is thereby being deprived of moisture. Such differences are virtually impossible to see from ground examination, but from above they are often extremely clear [8, 10].

Soil marks perform a somewhat similar function where there is no covering crop, i.e., when the field or area is newly ploughed. Any previous disturbance of the soil, such as the digging of a ditch (which has subsequently been filled in and is therefore no longer visible to ground examination) will have caused some change in the soil pattern. Soil excavated from the bottom of the ditch is likely to be a different colour from that on the surface and although such differences are too small to be noticeable on the ground, from aerial examination they often show up as a clearcut pattern defining an archaeological site. On the chalklands of southern England, for example, the soil mark for a former bank derived from the excavation of a ditch will show as a band of white and the ditch itself, as a result of silting, will show as an accompanying line of black [11].

In the case of both crop marks and soil marks the sites involved have been completely flattened and it is only colour differences which give the clue to what lies beneath. In the case of shadow marks there is usually some trace left on the surface, too slight to be noticed or, if noticed, understood, at ground level, but often quite clear when viewed from the air. The technique depends on light (usually low light, in the early morning or late afternoon) catching such slight surface features as remain and showing them up as strong shadows or highlights. Apart from the time of day, quite clearly the best times for seeing such sites are spring and autumn, when the sun is relatively low on the horizon [9].

With the mapping stage of the survey complete, the next step is the planning in detail, at a suitable scale, of each individual site and the preparation of a written account of its features and peculiarities. This part of the survey can be tackled in a number of different ways. It can be tackled by regions, either arbitrary regions (e.g. by squaring off the whole country) or by natural regions (upland areas, or river valleys), surveying and planning all types of monument which fall within them. Alternatively, it can be tackled by doing a complete countrywide survey of one particular type of monument. Either way, the cumulative result of the whole survey will be an enormous amount of material consisting of maps, plans and written accounts forming a very comprehensive statement of the archaeological remains in the country. Such a statement is of enormous value and importance, not only to the archaeologists immediately concerned but also to future generations of archaeologists, since the further and more detailed investigation of the country's archaeology will need, from the cost aspect alone, to be spread over very many years.

This being so, it becomes of the greatest importance that all the results of the survey should be published so that they are permanently and easily available. As drawn, the maps and plans will be available only in one place, and readily accessible only to the people involved in the survey. Various circumstances (changes of personnel, changes of policy or interest, fire, vandalism, or simply the lapse of time) can lead to the partial or even complete destruction of this valuable body of evidence, which means that virtually all of the original effort has been wasted and the work will have to be done again. Where sites have been destroyed since the first survey even this will not be possible. Publication was mentioned earlier as one of the fundamental archaeological processes. It cannot be emphasized too strongly that evidence, once gathered, must be preserved so that it can be permanently and easily available to all who wish to make use of it. The original documents are a very precarious record. Once they are published, however, they are recorded in hundreds if not thousands of copies in books or journals which will always be available in libraries. The chances of all copies of the particular publication being destroyed are negligible.

THE EXCAVATION PROGRAMME

The completion of the survey stage paves the way for the next step in the programme: the formulation of an excavation programme. The relationship between fieldwork and such a programme is very important and needs to be presented clearly and precisely. As stated earlier, excavation is an expensive process, in terms not only of money but also of time and resources. It is not something to be lightly undertaken nor something which can easily be repeated. It is therefore of paramount importance that such money, time and resources as are available should be used to the fullest possible advantage to give the maximum archaeological return. This means the most careful selection of sites to be excavated and such a selection can be properly made only

7. Example of vertical aerial photography. The aircraft flies along a straight track and the camera takes a series of overlapping exposures to give complete coverage of the strip of territory. A series of such strips side by side, with a slight overlap, provides blanket coverage of a whole area. Unlike oblique aerial photography, which is usually done at a fairly low level (750–1000 ft.), vertical photography is normally carried out from a height of several thousand feet.

8–11. Examples of oblique aerial photography as an aid to archaeologists. Unlike vertical photography which gives blanket coverage of an area, oblique photography is usually concentrated on a particular site. Above: a circular medieval moat at Magny-sur-Tille, France; the ditch has been filled in but the filling still appears as a very much darker ring. Right: crop and shadow marks outline the plan of a small Roman villa. Below: concentric ditches and postholes are clearly visible because the additional moisture retained by their filling causes the vegetation above to grow thicker and greener than in the surrounding areas. Opposite: a soilmark north of Devizes, Wiltshire, the band of white being the remains of a chalk-built bank of earth.

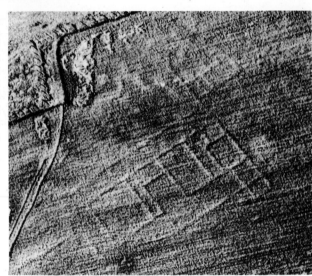

on the basis of a full and complete field survey. Without it, selection becomes
a matter of chance rather than choice, and fieldwork, quite apart from its
value as already described, is justified if for no other reason than that it
provides the only sure foundation on which an excavation programme can be
based.

What this means in practical terms can be demonstrated quite simply from
our hypothetical country. Let us assume that the survey produced a total of
2000 monuments, divided into six different types, with the following sub-
totals for each: type A (burial mounds [12]), 1000 sites; type B (circular enclosures), 400 sites; type C (undefended settlements), 200 sites; type D (defended settlements), 150 sites; type E (rectangular sites of unknown function),
50 sites; type F (isolated hut circles), 200 sites. None of these has been previously excavated and they are scattered throughout the country, some types
predominating in one area, other types in other areas. Without the survey,
any excavation programme formulated would almost certainly be unbalanced,
resulting in the excavation of too many of one type to the exclusion of others,
and this in turn would lead to an unbalanced interpretation of the country's
archaeology. On the other hand, the survey would indicate that an obvious
first stage in the excavation programme would be to excavate one example of
each of the six types. This would produce some new, more specific evidence
for each group and is, in fact, the minimum excavation programme. A fuller,
more comprehensive programme would involve a fixed percentage of sites in
each group, say five per cent, probably spread over an extended period of time,
and such a programme would depend even more on a precise knowledge of the
nature, size and distribution of each group.

The excavation programmes outlined above are based on the distribution
maps which indicate simply the number and location of different types of site.
However, an even more refined choice of sites for excavation can be made
from the detailed survey of individual sites. Within any one group, careful
examination and planning are likely to indicate which sites are, or appear to
be, the most promising from the point of view of excavation. A site which
has not been disturbed in any way, for example, is much better than one
which is riddled with rabbit burrows or one from which stones have been

removed for building purposes. A more positive reason for preferring certain sites is the prospect of uncovering in them evidence of a long period of use or occupation; the indications of this can be size, extent or complexity. Sites of different types which touch or overlap each other are also promising, since on excavation they can show which is the earlier of the two, and this can establish an important archaeological fact and greatly contribute towards settling the sequence of events in the country's history. It must be quite clear from this that a really careful selection of sites for excavation can be made only from the detailed inventory of sites and their accompanying plans. It must be equally clear that any excavation programme which is not preceded by intensive field survey is doomed to failure. Many of the shortcomings of present-day archaeology are due to the neglect of this very simple archaeological principle.

EXCAVATION

To many people excavation is synonymous with archaeology, but it is in fact only one part, admittedly a very important part, of the whole archaeological process. The previous section has indicated the importance of field archaeology, and in later sections other important processes will be described. Nevertheless, excavation is bound to figure prominently in any work which attempts to act as an introduction to archaeology. It should be made clear immediately that this section is not intended as a manual of instruction on the technique of excavation. This can be learnt only on a properly conducted excavation under an experienced director. This point cannot be emphasized too strongly. Excavation is not something which should be attempted by inexperienced people; too much invaluable evidence can thereby be destroyed. Unlike field survey, excavation cannot be repeated. Once the evidence is dug away it is destroyed for ever. It is, therefore, of the utmost importance that every last scrap of information is extracted from the site, and this can be done only by those with the proper training and experience. The purpose of this section is rather to help the beginner to understand how excavation is carried out, and why, so that he may better appreciate what the archaeologist can, and cannot, achieve by this method of investigation.

Enough has been said already about fieldwork and the formulation of an excavation programme to make it perfectly clear that digging is not a haphazard process. There must be some visible feature, or a crop or soil mark, or some other evidence of Man's former presence (such as pottery or other remains), before excavation can even be contemplated. However, the existence of a monument or the presence of pottery, etc., are not in themselves a justification for digging a site. They simply indicate where digging can take place if it is decided that excavation is necessary. This last is the crucial point—it is not enough to excavate sites 'because they are there'. Every site chosen for excavation must be chosen for a specific reason, to answer particular questions, to contribute to the solution of particular problems. Apart from rescue excavations (the excavation of a site threatened with destruction), all excavation should form part of a progressive investigation of the country's past and should be aimed at filling in a particular part of the picture. It should certainly not be done for the 'fun of digging', as, unfortunately, it sometimes is. The excavation of a site involves its destruction as a piece of archaeological evidence. This evidence can be extracted only once. Although the surface appearance of the monument may be

restored it is now of value only as an example of a particular type of structure. It is no longer susceptible to investigation by excavation. It is because excavation represents the once-and-for-all chance of obtaining evidence from a particular site that it should be undertaken only where it can be fully and completely justified.

Before describing how an excavation is conducted, the fundamental principle on which the whole practice of excavation is based must be considered. This is the principle of stratigraphy, borrowed by archaeology from the science of geology. The earth's crust is made up of a number of different layers or strata: granite, sandstone, limestone, chalk, etc., which quite clearly must have been laid in a definite sequence. Except where subsequently disturbed, by folding, for example, the lower layers or strata of rock must be earlier than the layers above, and this simple principle provides a time framework, a sequence of periods according to the number of layers involved. The lowest layer in any sequence is thus Period 1, the next layer above Period 2 and so on. It follows from this that anything found in the lowest layer (Period 1) is earlier than anything found in the next layer (Period 2) and so on, so that there is a very simple way of establishing the relative ages of all the things found in the different layers.

This simple but quite fundamental principle has been adopted by archaeology to govern the practice of excavation. The layers or strata used by the excavator are on a much smaller scale than geological layers, but the same principle applies: the lowest layers or strata, and everything in them, are earlier than the layers above. The archaeologist's strata consist of the remains of the buildings constructed (and reconstructed) by early Man and the debris of his day-to-day living, together with the effects of nature on these in the form of silting, erosion, and the growth of turf lines. The nature of archaeological stratigraphy will become clear from the examples to be given later, but it is the establishing of a clear and well-defined stratigraphical

12. Aerial view of the long barrow at West Kennet, Wiltshire. This is a stone-built, megalithic, chambered tomb set in a large, trapeze-shaped mound c. 330 ft. long. It has five burial chambers reached by a passage which enters the broad end of the mound. Although it was dug into a century ago, the major excavation of the site was carried out in 1955–6 by Professor Stuart Piggott.

13. Excavated section across the filling at one end of an original ditch at the eastern entrance at Maiden Castle, Dorset. The stratigraphical sequence is clearly visible here: above the man standing at the bottom of the ditch is the turf-line over natural silting, and immediately above this can be seen the artificial filling inserted in the second phase of the entrance. The thin line over the filling is the layer of the hut-floors of Iron Age B and C, and on top of this is the superimposed dump of the Roman period.

sequence that is one of the major aims of archaeological excavation [13]. This is the evidence which the excavator seeks, not the buried treasure of popular imagination. A magnificent piece of jewellery will by itself tell him very little about the past. The same piece of jewellery, carefully recorded as being from a particular layer, can with certainty be associated in time with all the other material from the same layer, and is quite clearly earlier than the material from the layers above and later than the material from the layers below. These associations and relationships, the precise archaeological context of all the finds and structures in the various layers, constitute the real evidence and represent the main aim of any serious excavator.

From the great importance accorded above to the principle of stratigraphy, two cardinal rules governing all excavation follow: very careful digging and very full and precise recording. The way in which these two rules are obeyed will become clear when the successive stages of an excavation are described, but briefly, unless the actual digging is done with the greatest care, the various layers, which can sometimes look very much alike, will not be distinguished and the main purpose of excavation is thereby nullified; equally, even if the excavation is meticulously conducted, unless a full and very exact record is made at the time, the whole exercise is a waste of time and money, because the information uncovered is lost to human knowledge almost immediately. The excavator's memory is no substitute for a written account, supported by measured plans, sections and photographs.

Once an excavation has been decided on (justified in accordance with the principles outlined earlier), the first step is a careful examination of the site and the drawing of a detailed plan, if this has not been done already as part of the field survey. Whether a site is being completely or only partially excavated, the placing of the trenches to be dug is a matter of some importance. Although it is always difficult to decide just what lies beneath the surface, some parts of a site are likely to yield more information than others. This is a matter of experience on the part of the director, but briefly he will be looking for areas free of tree roots, rabbit holes, quarrying, etc., so as to avoid any disturbance of the stratigraphy; for parts of the site which are better preserved than the rest so as to get the longest possible stratigraphy; and, finally, for parts of the site which are more complex than the rest because these are likely to give evidence of the relationships of the various structures and layers involved. Well-placed trenches can make a tremendous saving in time and effort and can produce much better evidence than those placed without due forethought and attention. In considering the location of his trenches, the excavator will also give an eye to the position of the spoil heap or dump. An excavation may well involve the moving of hundreds of tons of earth, and quite clearly the placing of this calls for the most careful consideration. One thing that must be avoided is the placing of the dump in an area which, at a later stage, it becomes necessary to excavate. This means that the whole dump has to be moved and this is a great waste of resources. In most excavations the earth excavated has to be replaced, usually by the people participating. For this reason a spoil heap on a downward slope should be avoided; it is very convenient during the dumping stage, but when it comes to refilling the trenches everything has to be carried uphill and this can take much longer than expected and badly affect time schedules, etc., as well as being very tiring work for people who have probably already had several weeks of unaccustomed manual labour. Happily, the refilling of trenches and the general restoration of the site to its former appearance are matters which are nowadays increasingly being carried out by contractors rather than the 'dig' personnel.

Having decided on the location of the trenches, the next step is to mark them out clearly and precisely on the ground so that digging can begin. This is done by means of wooden or metal pegs or pins in the ground with string stretched between them to indicate exactly where the edges of the trench are to come. The actual pattern of trenches will depend on the type of site being dug, and this will be considered later, but the trenches themselves will be normally either rectangular or square, of given dimensions and with right-angled corners. Dimensions and exact shape are important because these have to be drawn to scale on the plan as part of the record of what has been done. This is of the greatest importance for future excavators who may wish to continue previous work, so that they will know exactly what has and what has not been done already. Without a precise record they could well waste their time by digging part of the site which had been dug already, perhaps ten or twenty years before. The laying out of the trench with pegs and string also re-emphasizes the point made earlier about careful digging. Even on a chosen part of a known archaeological site there is much more to excavation than simply digging a hole in the ground to uncover what lies below. Care and precision start with the marking out of the trench and continue to the bottom, until the last traces of human activity have been excavated.

Before taking off the turf, there is one other step the excavator takes in the interests of exact recording. This is the placing of a series of wooden pegs alongside his trenches at fixed intervals and at an exact distance back from the edge. These are usually 2×2 in. in cross-section and about 18 in. long, 12 in. being hammered into the ground. Each peg is given a separate number or letter, clearly marked on it, and the position of each is marked on the site plan. These marked pegs provide a grid of fixed points on the site, from which the position of any find or feature can be exactly measured and plotted to scale on the site plan. If the dig is conducted over several seasons a number of key pegs can be hammered flush with the ground at the end of each session, from which the whole system of recording pegs can be re-established in the following session, so that there is no confusion as to what has already been excavated and what remains to be done.

With these preparations made the first stage of actual digging, the removal of the turf, can begin. As pointed out earlier, in many cases a site has to be restored to its original state after the completion of the excavation, so that it is imperative that the turf is taken off in regular portions and stored in a convenient place ready for replacing when the filling in is complete. With the aid of a turf-cutter, the edges of the trench are cut, following closely the line of the string. Once this has been done the string and its pegs can be removed. The space inside the trench limits is then cut both lengthwise and across, dividing the whole area to be excavated into a grid of rectangles. There is no set size for these but dimensions of $18 \times 12 \times 3$ in. thick produce a turf or sod which can be lifted on a spade without too much difficulty. Once all the cutting has been done the turves can be lifted one by one and stacked to one side.

With the turf removed excavation proper can begin. As stated earlier, this section is not written as a manual of instruction for intending excavators.

This being so, the broad aims rather than the precise technique of digging will be described, and briefly the aim is to dig in accordance with the stratigraphy, removing the layers involved one by one, obviously in the reverse order to that in which they were laid down. This means removing the whole of the first layer over the full extent of the trench, and recording and preserving everything therein, before beginning on the second layer, and so on down to the lowest layer, below which should be virgin or undisturbed soil, or chalk, or rock, depending on the local geology. In most cases a trench will be dug by a team of two or three people, using picks, shovels and wheelbarrows. In spite of the prominence given in newspapers and television to more delicate work involving the use of spoons, brushes and penknives, most archaeological excavation is still carried out with the aid of the heavy equipment mentioned above. Delicate work is sometimes called for [14], but the bulk of archaeological excavation is hard manual labour. It is obviously more than just that, but this side of the picture must be set against 'the glamour of excavation' so often invoked when archaeology is being discussed. One hot, sweaty day, or one cold, wet day, at the bottom of a trench will rapidly dissipate the glamour, although for those with the right attitude of mind the interest will always remain.

The general sequence of digging is begun by the pickman, who loosens the earth to a given depth, say 6 in., over a given area, say, the first 4 ft. of the trench from one end, across its full width, perhaps 6 ft. In spite of its size and weight, and its association with 'navvies', the pick, in the right hands, can be quite a delicate implement. On an archaeological excavation it should certainly never be used 'navvy' fashion to hack out the largest possible quantity of earth in the shortest possible time. While the earth is being loosened, both the pickman and the shovelman will be watching carefully for any artefacts (pottery, flint, metal objects) which may be exposed and for any sign of buried structures. The procedure for dealing with these will be described in a moment, but when they have been disposed of, it is the turn of the shovelman to clear away the remaining loose earth. It is very important that this is cleared away completely before any more picking is begun. The watchword of archaeological excavation is tidiness, and no dig would remain tidy very long if heaps of loose earth were allowed to accumulate in trenches. The earth is placed on one side of the trench (the opposite side to the pegs), but always sufficiently far away (usually about two feet) to prevent it slipping back into the trench. This must never be allowed to happen since it could 'contaminate' lower layers with material from the top of the trench. Where the soil is dumped in this way a team of two is sufficient until the trench gets too deep to throw the earth on to the dump. Then a third man with a bucket is required to haul it up and dispose of it. Where the earth is being dumped at a distance away, a third man is needed at the start, using a wheelbarrow to transport the earth.

Work proceeds in this way until the whole area of the trench has been cleared to a depth of six inches or such other depth as has been decided on. Then the whole process is repeated, going down another six, or more, inches. At some stage in this process the top of the next layer will be exposed. At this point, regardless of the agreed depth, work is confined to clearing out the remainder of the first layer over the whole area of the trench. Until layer one has been completely cleared and recorded no work can begin on layer two. When this has been done, work on the second layer can begin in the

14. Opposite: an archaeologist clears a double burial with a brush. Most archaeological excavation is still done with a pick and shovel, but occasionally it is necessary to resort to more refined techniques. Careful brushing will allow the whole of both skeletons to be exposed (so that they can be recorded photographically) without disturbing the soil between and beneath the bones which keeps the whole of each skeleton in place.

same way as on the first, until the top of the third layer is reached, and so on until all remains of human occupation or activity have been removed from the trench. If the work has been properly carried out, there should now exist a complete record (in various forms, to be described next) of the stratification of the trench and of the contents of, and structures associated with, each layer. If such records have not been kept, the whole effort of digging the trench has been wasted. It will now be readily understood that when the trench is refilled at the end of the dig it will simply be refilled with a mass of earth from the dump. The layers, and their contents, of this particular trench have been destroyed for ever, and for this reason full recording of the work is of the utmost importance.

So far only the purely mechanical part of digging has been described. The various devices which are used by the archaeologist to record the evidence he has uncovered take the form of plans, sections, notebooks, labels, photographs, etc., each of which has a particular function in the total excavation record. Perhaps the most important item in the recording equipment is the site notebook, which contains the basic written account of all the work done and of all the features uncovered. On a small dig there may be only a single notebook, kept by the director, covering the one or more trenches involved. On a large excavation, perhaps in the Middle East, there may well be a separate notebook for each trench, although the trenches will probably be much larger, and deeper, than the average trench in Britain. The primary purpose of the site notebook is to give a full account of each layer, beginning with its number (say, layer 2) and a brief description of the soil or other material involved (e.g. dark brown, stony). The account should also include details of small finds (pottery, tools, ornaments, etc.) and of any structures occurring in the layer. Briefly, the notebook should be the next best thing to the trench itself, and with the contents of the latter removed it should take its place as the primary evidence of the excavation.

Let us assume that a separate notebook is being kept for each trench on a site. The first thing is to write on the front the name of the site (it is surprising how often this basic piece of information is omitted), and the identification of the trench (say trench B, or trench III, etc.). The site name should also be accompanied by a code letter or letters which will be a means of identifying objects from the site. For example, a site called Sutton Hall Farm (Cheshire), the site of a Bronze Age barrow, could have the identification letters SHF, which can be used as a means of identification for all material from the site. Thus SHF/B will indicate all material from trench B at Sutton Hall Farm. The first working page of the notebook will be concerned with the topmost layer, layer 1, and in the top right-hand corner will have the full identification of layer, trench and site, thus: SHF/B/1. This will continue for as many pages as are required to record layer 1. When this is finally completed then the following pages can be designated SHF/B/2 for the second layer. This process is repeated for all the layers to the bottom, so that each one has a unique identification code and a separate section in the notebook containing all the written evidence relevant to that layer. This sort of clear identification is of the utmost importance when the excavator comes to write his report, because he will rely heavily on what is in the site notebook for his factual evidence.

The use of the identification letters is not confined to the notebook. They are used, in fact, to link together clearly every other form of recorded

evidence and all the finds from the layers. As each layer is being dug there will be a metal tray at the side of the trench with a label in it recording the site, trench and layer, i.e. corresponding exactly with the relevant pages in the notebook. In this tray are placed all small finds from that particular layer, and that layer only. Before the next layer is begun, all the finds are removed and a new label is placed in the tray with the appropriate identification letters. The small finds removed are normally placed in bags with the label inside, and the same information is then repeated on the outside of the bag. This is a precaution against the loss of the label or the obliteration of the writing on the outside. One or the other will survive. The link between the notebook and the finds provided by the identification letters enables the excavator, again when working on his report, to go from a particular layer in a particular trench in his notebook to the actual finds from that layer, so that the written evidence can be placed quickly and easily, and with certainty, alongside the material evidence.

This is the basis of the standard method of recording small finds. Quite clearly some other method is called for when it comes to recording structures. This takes the form of a trench plan or plans on a much larger scale than the general site plan, something around one inch, or half an inch to one foot, depending on the size of the trench. Again the plan will record the site designation, the trench, and the layer. On it will be planned to scale any structures associated with that layer, so that when the excavator comes to

15. Surveyors recording the remains of the Roman temple of Mithras in the City of London (note the measuring staff being placed in position on the left). The temple was uncovered in 1952 during clearance work preparatory to the building of Bucklersbury House, an office block. The cult of the god Mithras was at one time a rival to Christianity and, because of its severe initiation ceremonies, had a special appeal for soldiers. For the same reasons, however, it failed to become popular with the people at large and eventually died out.

the appropriate section in his notebook he can quickly turn up a measured plan of the structures described. Where structures are associated with each layer then the ideal is to have separate plans for each layer, although sometimes successive structures are superimposed on a single plan.

In addition to measured plans, all structures uncovered should be recorded photographically. A good archaeological photograph can be as good a record as a measured plan, and in some instances better. A crucial piece of evidence recorded photographically is more likely to be accepted as an objective record than the same evidence recorded by means of a plan or section drawing, where the human factor is involved. The importance attached to a good photographic record can be gauged from the time spent in preparing the site to be photographed, which can amount in some cases to a matter of hours or even the best part of a day. The work involved is mostly that of brushing down all surfaces, stones and other visible features so that they are clean, clearcut and stand out sharply. What this means in practical terms can be learnt only on an excavation but in this undertaking preparation is everything. Taking the photograph may be a matter of seconds, but the quality and value of the finished print depend almost entirely on the patience and hard work which have been put into the very necessary preparatory work. The inclusion of a scale (e.g. a surveyor's pole marked in metres or feet) is an important part of the photographic record; without it there is no way of relating what appears in the photograph to its actual size [15].

The last of the major forms of record, the section drawing, can be carried out only when the excavation of the trench is complete. After the site notebook, the section drawings are probably the most vital of all the dig records. They do visually what the site notebook does in words, record the stratigraphy layer by layer from top to bottom, again carefully noting site and trench identification on the drawing (SHF/B), as well as layer numbers on each layer, and indicating which of the four faces or sides of the trench is being recorded, thus: 'SHF/B/north face'. The ideal, of course, is to record all four faces, but more often than not only one is recorded, usually one of the longer sides of the trench. As with the trench plans, the section drawing is done to a much larger scale than the overall plan, often the same scale as the trench plan, perhaps an inch or half an inch to the foot. The procedure is first of all to establish a base or datum line, a length of string stretched tightly along the section to be drawn, usually midway between top and bottom, and adjusted exactly to the horizontal by means of a spirit or surveyor's level; a measuring tape is stretched along just below. Using squared paper the datum line is drawn to scale on the sheet and then the actual drawing of the section can begin. This is done by measuring up and down from the datum line at fixed intervals along the trench, say every 3 ft. starting from one end and working along to the other. The features measured in each case are, from the top, modern ground surface, and then the line between each layer, right down to the bottom of the trench. These measurements are plotted to scale on the drawings, producing a vertical line of dots. This is repeated, say, every 3 ft., or at closer intervals where greater detail is required, and so on until the end of the trench is reached. Then, by joining the corresponding dots, a complete visual record of the stratigraphy is produced. The layer number and brief description (dark brown, stony soil, for example) should then be clearly marked on each layer, producing a record which can be directly linked with the entries in the site notebook. When it comes to the

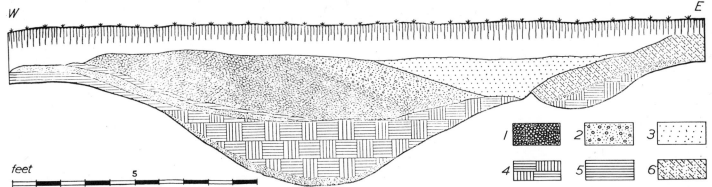

feet   5

1	2	3
4	5	6

matter of publication, this section drawing is the only satisfactory means of explaining the stratigraphical pattern; no amount of descriptive writing, however clear, can by itself do the job so well [16].

Enough has been said by now to make clear the basic aims and methods of archaeological excavation. The whole dig may consist of no more than the single trench, involving only half a dozen people over two or three weeks. It may, on the other hand, entail the investigation of a whole ancient city, over a period of years, with a labour force of several hundred. But however large or small an excavation is, it consists basically of one or more trenches, precisely laid out, carefully dug and meticulously recorded in accordance with the methods described above. The size of the dig does not matter; the basic principles remain the same and must be applied whether there is one trench or fifty.

It will be readily understood, in view of the wide range of archaeological sites and monuments which exist in the world, that no simple rule can be laid down as to how a particular site should be tackled. Each one must be considered on its merits by the director of the dig and this, of course, is where his experience is displayed. However, there are certain standard methods of tackling particular kinds of site which can usefully be considered here. The term trench suggests something long and relatively narrow. As used in archaeology it applies to an excavation of any shape, long and narrow, square, or even, in certain circumstances, triangular. One of the standard patterns is, in fact, a relatively narrow trench (6–10 ft. wide) and anything from fifty to several hundred feet in length, according to the requirements of the site. This is the sort of trench which would be used to obtain the cross-section of any sort of linear work, i.e. a work which cannot be totally excavated by reason of its length, often a matter of many miles. It becomes, therefore, a question of investigating it by means of one or more trenches dug at right angles to its length. Sites excavated in this way would include Roman roads, frontier works of the bank-and-ditch variety, and enclosures where the total circuit is too long to make total excavation feasible [17].

The cross-section excavation just described provides what is inevitably a relatively small sample of the whole site. A much larger sample, and sometimes complete excavation, can be provided by what is often termed area excavation. This consists of a grid of rectangular trenches (10, 15 or 20 ft. square), separated by undug baulks 2 or 3 ft. wide. This can be extended as required to cover the whole site, time and money permitting. This technique is particularly useful on flat sites where there is little or no surface contour to dictate the placing of trenches, and where the existence of the site may be

16. Section drawing of the inner and outer ditches of a Bronze Age round barrow at Cassington, Oxon. The later, outer ditch on the left has cut through and partly destroyed the outer edge of the earlier, inner ditch and its filling. Such a drawn section is the standard method of recording what has been excavated in a particular trench. Key: 1, clean gravel; 2, earthy gravel; 3, fine sandy silt; 4, fine reddish silt; 5, brown soil; 6, gravelly soil.

known only from aerial photography. Usually no great depths are involved in such sites; baulks only 2 ft. wide would become dangerous beyond 6 or 7 ft. and where depths greater than this are involved the baulks have to be removed, or lowered, or some other method of approach adopted [18].

The last method to be considered here is the quadrant method of investigating round burial and other mounds. Burial mounds are found in many parts of the world and can be regarded as an almost universal type, so that any method of tackling them could be of very wide application. In fact, there are other methods of dealing with them, although the quadrant technique is the most common. This consists of dividing the mound into quarters with a baulk, usually 2 ft. thick, between each, forming a cross in plan view. Each quarter is tackled as a separate trench. Only at the end are the baulks removed, thus achieving total excavation of the site. This method provides two complete drawn sections across the mound, by means of the baulks, at right angles to each other. Two more sections can be provided by a star-shaped arrangement of eight baulks dividing the mound into eight equal, triangular trenches. A less common method of tackling a circular mound is the slice technique. In this the mound is divided into a series of strips running in one direction across the surface. The alternate strips are excavated, leaving the intermediate strips as baulks, thus providing a series of parallel sections across the full width of the mound. The last stage is again the removal of the baulks to achieve total excavation of the site.

PUBLICATION

For the director, the aftermath of an excavation is much more arduous and long-drawn out than the dig itself. When the digging and recording have been completed, when the trenches have been refilled and the turf replaced, when

18. Part of the eastern entrance at Maiden Castle, Dorset, in course of excavation. This shows the grid technique of excavating a large area in a series of regular squares with baulks of undug ground between. At a later stage the baulks themselves are carefully removed as a last step in the complete excavation of the area.

17. Opposite: cutting through the inner rampart, Maiden Castle, Dorset. This illustrates one of the standard techniques of excavating large earthworks such as hillforts, where a complete excavation would be quite impossible because of the size of the site.

 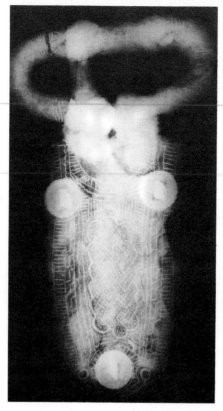 

19. Belt buckle from the Merovingian cemetery of Lutlommel, Limbourg: left, as found; centre, X-ray photograph; right, after laboratory treatment. Late-fifth to early-seventh century AD. The Merovingians, the first kings of France, named after Merovech, ruled from some time before AD 481 to AD 639, when they were succeeded by the Carolingians.

the site has been cleared of every trace of excavation and the last helper has left, then the director's work is only just beginning. A dig lasting perhaps two months will keep him fully occupied for several years to come. His ultimate aim must be the publication of a full report on his work and an assessment of its significance for the particular archaeological field to which it belongs, but before he can achieve this there are many things to be done both by the excavator himself and by specialists in various fields on his behalf.

Already during the progress of the dig the director, out of his knowledge and experience, will have begun to assess the significance of certain finds or structures and to draw some tentative conclusions. This is simply the beginning of a process which must be carried on, but now much more intensively, when the dig is over. It is the excavator's task to study in detail all the small finds from the dig and, by means of the records (notebooks, plans, sections, photographs, etc.), all the structures, so that he can fully understand them and relate them to the stratigraphy in order to produce a comprehensive picture of the site throughout its history. Comparison with other sites is an important part of the process; for this, the excavator will draw on his existing knowledge and also on the published accounts of other excavations, hence one of the reasons why all excavations must be published. Such comparisons enable the site to be placed in its proper relationship to other sites, and this process is as important as giving a full account of the site actually dug. There are many people who can dig neatly, in accordance with the principles outlined earlier; there are fewer people who can fully understand and report on what they have done; and fewer again who have the wide background knowledge of the period and area involved to be able to assess and comment on the significance of the new evidence uncovered by the excavation. This, in a sense, is the essence of the excavation process, not the actual digging, and is one of the reasons why an excavation should take place only under the direction of a qualified director, someone with the knowledge and experience to report on the work in the terms just outlined.

At the end of the dig, all the finds and all the records will be removed by the director to wherever he will be undertaking the job of writing the report, perhaps in a university or museum department of archaeology. One of the first tasks to be tackled is the examination of all the finds, one by one, to see, among other things, if they need any treatment to preserve them. A certain amount of treatment will already have taken place on the site, but only on those objects which could not otherwise be removed. The basic, permanent treatment of everything which needs it will be undertaken either in the department or, where very special treatment is called for, in a museum laboratory [19]. One of the reasons for such treatment is to enable the finds to be handled without causing them any damage. Both during study in connection with the excavation report and subsequently they are likely to be handled a great deal, and it would be unfortunate if they disintegrated after a couple of months or even a couple of years. As evidence which has taken a lot of time, money and effort to produce they are worth taking some trouble to preserve in perpetuity. As primary, irreplaceable evidence, all finds must be preserved so that in cases of doubt or dispute, perhaps fifty or more years hence, archaeologists can turn to them when the published report, as it must sometimes do, proves insufficient by itself.

The facility of examining excavation finds subsequent to their publication depends on two factors, both very much part of the whole archaeological process. The first of these is the ability to tell exactly where any particular find comes from on a site. To enable this to be done it needs to be marked permanently with the site code, the trench number, and the layer number, as described earlier; thus a sherd of pottery from layer 3 of trench B at Sutton Hall Farm will be marked SHF/B/3 in some form in which it will not wear off, and every other sherd from that layer, even if several hundred are involved, must be marked in the same way. Thus every find from a site is permanently linked with the site, the trench and the layer from which it came. In some cases, good quality pottery (Roman samian, for example) can be marked on the site, but in most others the marking has to await the move to the department. This is why it is so important to include a label with full details in the bag as well as putting the same information on the outside, as described earlier. There may be dozens, if not hundreds, of bags of pottery and other finds in the department concerned, from this and other excavations, and the possibilities of mix-up and confusion can be imagined. It is therefore of the utmost importance that every find should be permanently marked with its code as soon as possible. Until this is done it is dangerous to have the finds out of their bags or to separate one from its group. Once they are suitably marked, however, they can be freely handled and sorted in different ways without any danger of confusion [20].

The second factor is the accessibility of the finds after the completion of the reports. It is most important that they should be housed where they will be permanently preserved and where they are easily accessible, and this means in a museum. The question of the disposal of finds is one which should be settled before the excavation is begun and is a matter which is, or should be,

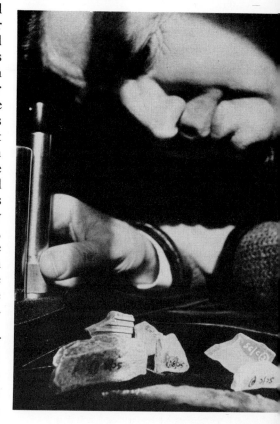

20. Professor Leslie Alcock, director of excavations at Cadbury Castle, Somerset, examines a sixth-century knife and pottery sherds on which can be seen the site/trench/layer code letters and numbers clearly marked on each piece.

very much part of the overall excavation plan. The final, permanent location of the finds, and the dig records, should be stated in the published report, so that anyone consulting it, perhaps thirty or forty years afterwards, will know immediately where all the relevant material is. The retention of excavated material in private hands is something which should be avoided at all costs. Quite apart from the greater difficulty of access, even if the location is known, the chances of the material being properly housed and cared for, and, most important of all, permanently preserved, are far less than in a museum, which, let it be repeated, is the only satisfactory repository for excavated finds and records.

Already, during the progress of the excavation, a certain amount of sorting of finds will have taken place. For example, in a layer containing quantities of both pottery sherds and animal bones the two will have been placed in separate bags, suitably marked as to contents, in addition to the layer, trench and site code. After the dig is over there will be a sorting out on a much larger scale. Basically the division, into two main groups, is between material which will be dealt with on the spot by the director and any assistants he may have, and material which will be sent away for a specialist report. Animal bones are a case in point, particularly where they occur in quantity. They will normally be sent off to a zoologist, after each one has been marked with its appropriate code. The zoologist, armed with the basic information about the site, will study the bones in detail, giving attention to such aspects as types of animal present, whether wild or domestic, the relative quantities of each, the proportion of old to young animals, the stature, etc. Eventually he will produce a written report for the excavator. This will form an important part of the final published report and will usually appear, exactly as written by the zoologist, as an appendix to it. The same will happen to other groups of specialized material and the final report may incorporate half a dozen, a dozen, or even more specialist reports. One of the excavator's tasks in writing his report is to draw the appropriate conclusions from all of these separate reports and incorporate them in the final story of the site.

The types of specialist reports required will obviously vary considerably from area to area—from sites on the chalk downland of England to sites in Egypt and the Near East—but a few of the more common ones can be mentioned here. Animal bones have been considered already. Human bones form another very important group and are likely to occur on archaeological sites anywhere. Probably the commonest finds in any part of the world are broken pieces of pottery. Certain types of pottery were made in such quantity that only someone who has specialized in that particular field is competent to comment on them, and the excavator will ask him for a report on his finds. Among such types are Roman red-glazed ware (Samian), Greek black- and red-figure pottery [21], medieval pottery and Pueblo black-on-white pottery of the South-western United States, of which over two hundred different varieties are known. Coins also were produced in great quantities in certain periods and in most cases call for the attention of an experienced numismatist. In the Near East inscriptions, giving valuable written information about people and events, are not infrequent finds, on clay tablets and on scarabs, and such finds will be submitted to an epigraphist for a report. These are just a few examples of some of the commoner finds for which the excavator calls on the services of specialists. There are many others. No subject is excluded. If there is any find from the excavation which the excavator does

1. Opposite: the bee pendant, from Mallia, Crete, 1700–1550 BC, height 1¾ in., an example of Minoan jewellery and goldwork. The details of the two bees and the honey cake between them are picked out in filigree wire and granulation.

not understand or cannot identify, then he must make every effort to find out by consulting the appropriate specialists. Such a find may turn out to be of crucial importance.

One type of specialist report which deserves particular attention is the one that attempts to deal with the date or age in actual years of a particular find. Advances in recent years have produced techniques for dating by scientific means and some of the dates produced have necessitated drastic re-adjustments of chronology, particularly in the prehistoric field. The whole question of chronology is of great importance to the archaeologist, for it provides the time framework within which he can write his account of the site. Without it, the site is floating in time and difficult to fit into the overall picture of the area or period. In dealing with specialist dating techniques, therefore, the whole question of chronology will be considered, albeit briefly.

CHRONOLOGY

There are, in fact, two forms of archaeological dating, relative and absolute. Absolute dates are dates in actual years, whether precise (e.g. AD 43) or more general (late second millenium BC). However, it is relative dating which needs to be considered first, since this provides the basic chronological framework to which such absolute dates as can be obtained are applied. The two main forms of relative dating are by stratigraphy and by typology. Although stratigraphy by itself does not yield absolute dates, by means of its different, superimposed layers, it does provide a sequence, a succession of objects and structures, from the earliest to the latest, with a clear and firmly established time relationship between them. Of any two objects or structures from a stratified site it can be said, according to the layers in which they were found, that one is earlier than the other, or contemporary with it, or later than it, and this is the time relationship or relative chronology of the two objects. The same principle holds good for any number of objects from any number of stratified layers. The pattern of time relationships is more complex in that the terms later and earlier can now be qualified: the objects from layers 2–7, for example, are all earlier than those from layer 1, but those from layer 5 are obviously very much earlier than those from layer 2, but still not so early as those from layer 7. In spite of the absence of any dates in years, this is already a very useful piece of archaeological evidence which can be used beyond the limits of the excavation from which it comes. It may, for example, establish the relative chronology of similar, but unstratified, objects in a museum collection and this in turn may help to establish a firm typological sequence.

The essential contribution of stratigraphy is the sequence provided by all the layers in the site, each of unknown duration, but each clearly marked off from the preceding and succeeding layers, thus forming a timetable of events for the particular site. This timetable provides the framework into which the more precise dates yielded by absolute chronology can be fitted. At this stage the whole stratigraphical sequence is still 'floating' in time. It could be of any date or any duration (50 years or 500 years); to fit it, and therefore the whole site, into the full archaeological picture it needs to be 'anchored' at as many points as possible by dates in actual years obtained from the material from the various layers. The ideal, of course, is dating evidence from every layer so that not only can the duration of the site be calculated, but also the duration of each separate stage in its development.

II. Opposite: part of Hadrian's Wall at Milecastle, near Cawfields, Northumberland.

33

The second form of relative dating is by typological sequence. Typology is, briefly, the study of the variations in appearance (size, proportions, decoration, etc.) within a particular group of objects, say, bronze axes or bronze pins. Some of these variations are simply regional, i.e. the differences are due to the objects being made at more or less the same time in different places, and this is one of the limitations of the typological method. However, other changes are the result of a natural development over a period of time, perhaps a matter of centuries. When the same basic type of object, say a bronze axe, is manufactured over such a period, it is unlikely to remain exactly the same from beginning to end. Small changes will occur which tend to conform to a recognizable pattern. The axes can be placed in a 'typological sequence' in which each small change is illustrated by a particular type of axe. Such a sequence (if correct) establishes relative dates for the axes in it in the same way as a stratigraphical sequence. There is one important difference, however. In the case of a stratigraphical sequence there is no doubt as to the 'direction' of the sequence; material from the lower layers is earlier than material from the upper layers and nothing can alter this. The danger of a typological sequence, formulated from visual examination of, in this case, a group of bronze axes in a museum collection, is that it can be reversed. The series of small changes observed between one axe and another could, in fact, operate in either direction. There is quite clearly a development from one end of the sequence to the other but, as yet, no way of determining which is the 'early' end and which the 'late' end. Until this is done, any attempt to date by typological means is suspect. One of the ways in which the 'direction' can be established was referred to above, namely by means of similar objects found in a stratified sequence. If one stage of the typological sequence can be shown by this means to be later than another, then the direction of the sequence and thus the relative chronology of the objects is established. Like the stratigraphical sequence, it is still floating in time until absolute dates can be applied to it. Once the duration of the whole sequence, and the dates of the various stages, are established, however, then they can be used in turn to provide absolute dates for an archaeological sequence. If any object from a stratified layer can be identified with one from a well-established and dated typological sequence, the layer can then be dated, in years, in accordance with the known date from typology. By the same token unstratified objects, found casually in digging or ploughing, can be dated in years if they can be identified with a particular stage of an established typological series.

Before dealing with absolute dating methods there is one other form of dating, cross-dating, which in a sense falls somewhere between relative and absolute chronology. Cross-dating can be used when one or more objects from a stratified layer is recognizably from some other area or civilization with a well-established chronology, for example a Greek coin, or a piece of Greek metalwork, found (as a result of trading in antiquity) stratified in an Iron Age site in central Europe. This would establish a date for the particular layer and provide the beginnings of an absolute chronology for the site. In this case, the cross-date is absolute because a great deal is known about Greek chronology. In other cases, however, the cross-date is only a relative date. This happens when the object or objects recognized are known to belong to a particular period in a well-established, but as yet undated, sequence elsewhere. For example, a few pieces of painted pottery found in the bottom layer

21. Opposite: detail of a Greek amphora or wine-jar in the black-figure style, typical of the Late Archaic period (see p. 213), showing Ajax and Achilles playing draughts, painted by Exekias, c. 550–40 BC. On general typological grounds the excavator would place such a pot, and all associated material, within the sixth century BC, the period when the black-figure style flourished. The same vessel, submitted to a specialist in the black-figure style, would produce a much more precise date, based either on a well-established typological sequence or, when his name is known, as here, the period during which the artist worked.

(Period 1) of a site could be recognized as the main type of pottery in Period 3 of an area perhaps several hundred miles away. Although no absolute dates are known in either case, a relationship has been established which is a useful piece of archaeological evidence. At a later stage the discovery of a date in years for one will enable the other to be dated also, so that the cross-dating will move from relative to absolute [22].

Of all the absolute dating methods, probably none has made a greater impact than that of the Carbon-14 (C-14) process, particularly in the more refined form resulting from its application to the older method of tree-ring dating. Before dealing with these two, the other main methods of absolute dating will be described.

One of the older techniques, dating by varved-clay, is mainly limited to Scandinavia and to the period from 10,000 BC on. As such, it has been of most use in the study of the Mesolithic period (see below, pp. 79–82). In the much colder conditions prevailing in the period in question, the spring thaw produced a great increase in the flow of rivers, so that a great quantity of silt was carried along and deposited in the lakes and estuaries where the rivers terminated. This silt settled gradually at the bottom, forming a horizontal bed or varve, hence the name of the technique. This process was repeated year after year so that gradually a whole series of superimposed layers was produced, each representing a particular year. Because of normal variations in weather conditions the thickness of the varves varied from year to year and this enables a sequence of varves from one area to be correlated with those from other areas. By means of overlapping sequences, an overall picture for the whole of Scandinavia was gradually built up. In 1910 Baron de Geer was able to publish a dated sequence for the area going back to 10,000 BC. The events covered by this sequence, however, are geological rather than archaeological, so that for it to be of any use, a site has to be clearly related to a geological feature before any absolute date can be read off. This is a limitation over and above the limitation of the technique to a particular area and to a particular period, but nonetheless the varved-clay method has its uses.

Another method which covers the same period but a much wider area (northern Europe) is that of pollen-analysis. The pollen grains produced by trees and flowers do not decay, even over very long periods, and the species of trees and flowers, and their relative quantities, can be established by pollen analysis of a soil sample. In the post-Glacial period (from *c.* 10,000 BC onwards) there were considerable variations in the vegetation of northern Europe, beginning, *c.* 10,000 BC with virtually no forest at all. Fluctuations in climatic conditions produced corresponding fluctuations in the forest growth and these fluctuations now form a known sequence of (vegetational) events, into which the sample from a particular site can be fitted and dated, even if only very approximately. With the aid of the Carbon-14 process, dates in years have now been added to this sequence so that samples can be much more clearly and securely dated. This technique is valuable not only for dating purposes but also for what it can reveal about Man's environment at the time and place represented by the pollen sample.

In recent years, dating techniques based on modern scientific discoveries have been developed. These, which will not be described here, include potassium-argon dating, obsidian dating and dating by thermo-luminescence and archeomagnetism. Some of these are limited in their application: potassium-argon dating, for example, to samples of not much less than a million years old. In spite of any limitations, however, these techniques have thrown invaluable light on areas and periods which were formerly obscure, if not completely blank. No doubt future scientific progress will throw up new and more refined techniques of dating the past.

The last two, now closely related, dating techniques to be described are tree-ring dating (dendrochronology) and Carbon-14 dating. Dendrochronology was developed in the Pueblo area (see pp. 156–62) of the South-western United States, where timber was used extensively in building and, more importantly, where it has been preserved in great quantity by the hot, dry climate. In a not dissimilar way to the varved-clays of Scandinavia, the annual growth rings of a tree reflect annual variations in climatic conditions, although this happens only when such variations are fairly well-marked. Any piece of preserved timber from a Pueblo site will provide a sequence of growth rings, long or short according to its size. This sequence can be correlated with sequences from other pieces of preserved timber, and by correlation and over-lapping, the sequence has been gradually extended until a full series of growth rings reaching back from the present day, each representing a calendar year, has been obtained. The growth rings of a newly excavated piece of timber need only be matched with the correct section of the established and dated sequence to provide its date in actual years. The main limitation of the method is that it can be used only in areas where the climate is such as to cause well-marked variations in the sequence of growth-rings. In Britain, for example, growth-rings from year to year would tend to be so alike that correlation with other timbers would be very difficult and any master sequence suspect. One of the great advantages of the technique, particularly in relation to Carbon-14 dating, is that it is based on a sequence of separate rings, each representing a year, which can be counted individually back from the present day, and it is therefore almost foolproof.

The technique of dating by radioactive carbon was pioneered by Professor W. F. Libby of Chicago in 1946, since when it has revolutionized chronology in many parts of the world. The basis of the method is the carbon which all organic matter contains; organic matter (either animal or vegetable) is matter which grows, such as bone, or wood. The carbon is, in fact, of two kinds, Carbon-14 which is radioactive, and Carbon-12 which is inert. In the atmosphere, and in organic matter still in growth, the proportion of C-14 to C-12 is constant. When the material ceases to grow (for example, through the death of the body in the case of bone, through felling in the case of a tree), then the radioactive carbon (C-14) begins gradually to diminish in quantity while the inert carbon (C-12) remains static. Fortunately, from the point of view of dating, the radioactive carbon reduces at a constant rate, based on what is known as the half-life period. This means that in a given period the quantity of Carbon-14 is reduced to half, and that in a succeeding period of the same length the remainder is reduced to half again, and so on. By determining the proportion of the diminishing Carbon-14 to the constant Carbon-12 in the light of the half-life period, it is possible to calculate the length of time which has elapsed since the growth process ceased, and this produces what is known as the C-14 date of the specimen. The half-life period used so far is one of 5,568 years, but it is now clear that this is too low. One of 5,730 has been suggested but so far there is no universal agreement on this.

Unlike other dating methods described, which are limited to given areas or given periods, the great advantage of C-14 dating is that it is capable of

22. The obverse and reverse of a tetra-drachm of the Greek city of Naxos, in Sicily, c. 460 BC. The well-established date of such a coin is invaluable dating evidence when found stratified in an archaeological site elsewhere, say in Iron Age Europe. It would indicate clearly that any buildings, pottery, etc., associated with it were later than 460 BC, and thus provide the beginnings of an established chronology for the site.

universal application. The chemical properties of matter are constant throughout the world and are not limited or affected by such things as climate. This means that in the course of time it will be possible to build up a large series of absolute dates which will provide a secure chronological framework for the whole world. Within this framework the archaeologist will be able to work with a degree of confidence which he has hitherto not enjoyed and will be able to devote more of his time to non-chronological matters such as the social, political, and economic aspects of the past. The C-14 dating method is not perfected yet. There are still problems to be solved, such as the duration of the half-life period, but there is no doubt as to the basic value of the method. Once these difficulties are ironed out the archaeologist will have in his hands the key to the fundamental problem of the past—its chronology [23].

The new dates provided by the C-14 method began to make their impact in the early 1950s. As far as the British Isles were concerned, their main effect was to push back certain accepted dates by something like a thousand years. The period most affected was the Neolithic. Prior to C-14, the generally accepted date for the beginning of the Neolithic period was, in round figures, 2500 BC. It soon became clear from early C-14 dates that this was much too low and now, with many more C-14 dates available, a date of around 3500 BC seems probable, with the duration of the period increased accordingly. This new date represents a fundamental change in the whole pattern of British prehistory and necessitated a re-assessment of all our ideas about the prehistoric past. The new C-14 dates produced similar revolutionary changes in accepted chronology in many parts of Europe and the Near East.

The latest development in the C-14 method has been to combine it with the older method of tree-ring dating, which provides a cross-check on the accuracy of the dates produced. With the aid of the Californian bristle-cone pine (*pinus aristata*), it has been possible to produce a sequence of growth rings stretching back 6,500 years from the present. By using the C-14 technique on a portion of the actual growth ring it has been possible to obtain a C-14 date which can be compared with the date achieved by counting back from the present, which must be an accurate date. In fact, comparison of the two series of dates has revealed some marked discrepancies. In many cases the C-14 dates have proved to be too low, necessitating a further extension backwards of many chronologies, over and above that caused by C-14 dates alone. The discrepancies suggest that at certain times in the past the proportion of C-14 to C-12 may have been variable rather than constant. Together with the duration of the half-life period, this is another problem which needs to be solved before C-14 dating can be perfected. In spite of this, it still offers the most satisfactory and universally applicable solution to the problem of dating the past. The variation between C-14 dates and tree-ring dates can best be seen by means of a graph. This also allows a C-14 date to be adjusted to a date in calendar years by reading off the corresponding tree-ring date, although this is not the final answer to the problem of discrepancy.

MUSEUM WORK

Thus far two major areas of archaeological work have been considered: fieldwork and excavation, together with all the subsequent activities that they entail such as research and publication. These latter activities, however, are involved in other forms of archaeological work, such as that which takes

23. Opposite: the village of Jarlshof, Shetland, the occupation of which, in its different periods, spans some 3000 years, from *c.* 1500 BC to *c.* AD 1600. Apart from some slight evidence of Late Stone Age occupation *c.* 1500 BC, there are well-documented Late Bronze Age and Iron Age settlements, the latter continuing down to AD 750. Norse and medieval settlements occupy the years between *c.* AD 750 and 1300 and the final episode is the building of the Laird's house at the end of the sixteenth century (not shown in this view).

place in museums. One of the archaeological functions of a museum, the treatment of material from a dig, has been touched on already. Because of the need to have a conservation laboratory to look after their existing archaeological and ethnological collections, most large museums are well-equipped to undertake preservation and restoration work on excavated material.

Over and above these laboratory activities, however, and not directly connected with any particular excavation, is the work which is carried out on museum archaeological collections. Although the more recent acquisitions, either from excavation or casual finds, will be, or ought to be, fully recorded, the older, and larger, part of the collection will probably have little or no documentation. This generalization holds good not only for Britain but also for Europe as a whole and arises out of the history of the subject, particularly in the nineteenth century. A great part of museum archaeological collections was acquired before the standards of excavation and recording outlined earlier were in operation. Not infrequently the only information is the name of the site from which the object came, and sometimes even this is not known. This shortage of basic information makes it doubly difficult to fit the material into the overall archaeological picture, but equally it is the reason why it needs such intensive study. Its sheer bulk is too great for it to be ignored. In a sense, the archaeologist working on these collections is attempting to do the job which should have been done when the material was first discovered, perhaps a hundred or more years before. Anything he can achieve and, again, publish goes some way towards redressing the imbalance between the undocumented and documented parts of the museum's collections.

Some archaeologists operate in all three of the major forms of archaeological activity (fieldwork, excavation and museum study), although most engage in only one or two. Thus there are professional archaeologists who do not undertake excavation but who are nevertheless fully occupied in the subject. There is more than enough to do in the other two types of archaeological work to keep them fully occupied for the whole of their professional working lives. Within the confines of a single museum, the work (possibly undertaken by an archaeologist on the museum staff) may consist of the cataloguing of the whole of the museum's archaeological collection. This is an important body of archaeological evidence which needs to be published to make it available to other archaeologists, and it is just the sort of record an excavator would need to consult in searching for parallels for his finds when he is writing his report. Without it, the parallel is not drawn or else the excavator is involved in time-consuming and expensive visits to a large number of museums. Most museums have a catalogue of their collections in the form of a card index, but this can be consulted only in the museum itself. Regrettably, far fewer museums have any sort of published catalogue, but this evidence demands publication just as much as the most recent excavation. Without publication, the collections virtually do not exist and cannot play their part in filling out the picture of the area or period involved.

Another type of catalogue or corpus involves the listing and study of all objects of a particular type (Beaker pottery, for example, see pp. 199, 200), regardless of where they occur. Such works when published are of immense value to other archaeologists. Quite apart from the conclusions which can be drawn from such an all-embracing survey, their existence means that a newly-excavated Beaker can be very quickly compared with every other known Beaker and its importance immediately assessed. The alternative is a

laborious search through dozens if not hundreds of books and journals with, at the end, no real assurance that all the ground has been covered. The Beaker catalogue is an example of the sort of work that needs to be done, but it is only a beginning. There is enough work of this type to keep dozens of archaeologists busy all their lives without ever recording a field monument or lifting a spade. Fortunately, after generations of neglect, this aspect of archaeological work is now receiving some of the attention it deserves.

Apart from work at the corpus level, many archaeologists work on a smaller scale in studying particular kinds of artefacts, without actually making a complete corpus. Such work is usually published as a paper in an archaeological journal and often involves a suggested typological sequence; typology is also inevitably involved in any corpus of archaeological material. There is a two-way traffic between typology and excavation: stratigraphy can confirm the validity of a suggested typological sequence; a well-established typological sequence can, in return, be of the greatest assistance in dating a stratigraphical sequence. The study and publication of museum collections, in all of the ways described so far, is quite clearly a very important part of the whole archaeological process. Such collections still represent a very large proportion of our archaeological evidence, and unless they are brought fully into the body of available information the resultant archaeological picture will be woefully incomplete.

SYNTHESIS

There is one last, very important archaeological process to be described, that of synthesizing all that we know about a particular period or area. All

24. Aerial view of the white horse at Uffington, Berkshire, the oldest of the hill figures, dating to the Iron Age, and probably having some religious significance.

of the archaeological processes described so far have, by their very nature, been concerned with the details rather than the whole picture: with field monuments of a particular type or area; with the excavation of a particular site; or with the study of a particular group of artefacts. But these, by themselves, however well published, can never tell the whole story. The publication of all the work relating, for example, to prehistoric Britain (the field surveys, the excavations, the museum collections), does not by itself tell a coherent story of British prehistory; it simply makes all the evidence thereto available. The story as such has still to be written and it is the writing of this story, the process of synthesis, which forms a specialized field of archaeological endeavour. It calls for qualities of high scholarship, wide knowledge and deep comprehension, for someone who can stand back and survey, and understand, the whole scene without being too much influenced by any particular aspect. The process in a sense is one of digestion. An enormous amount of evidence is available, probably amounting to millions of words in published form, but still, in spite of its length, not telling a coherent or readable story. Quite apart from its value in summarizing all the existing evidence, a synthesis is an invaluable stimulus to research. It can indicate the direction of future work by pointing to areas or periods where information is inadequate, and by proposing hypotheses which can then be tested by further excavation. The late Professor Gordon Childe was a brilliant exponent of this form of archaeological work. His *Prehistoric Communities of the British Isles* (first published in 1940 and now inevitably out of date) was the first synthesis of the prehistory of these islands from earliest times down to the Roman conquest; not only the first, but also the last. A vast amount of evidence has accumulated in recent years which urgently needs the process of digestion, and the resultant comprehensive account, which someone like Gordon Childe was so qualified to give. Around the same time Professor Christopher Hawkes' *Prehistoric Foundations of Europe down to the Mycenaean Age* was a synthesis of European prehistory (also now out of date). More recently Professor Graham Clark has provided the same service on a world basis in his *World Prehistory, A New Outline* (2nd ed., 1969).

Synthesis is the last stage in the archaeological process as described here; but it is last only in a relative, not an absolute sense. The whole process is a continuous one. As one synthesis is being published more evidence is accumulating from all the other forms of archaeological work which in a year or two (in some cases even less) will cause some of the conclusions therein to be questioned, so that the process is one of continuous development with more and more detail becoming visible as work progresses. Ultimately the picture will be full and complete in all its details, although for most branches of archaeology this stage is still a very long way off.

This completes the survey of the various ways in which the archaeologist studies the past. It was, in effect, an extended definition of the Greek *logos* mentioned at the beginning of the chapter. For many people this definition is limited to the process of excavation, but it should now be clear that excavation is only one side of a many-sided approach to the problems of the past. By itself, it is as incapable of providing all the answers as any other exclusive approach. All of the forms of study described are inter-dependent. There are, in fact, no 'separate' approaches; there is only one all-embracing approach to the study of the past which takes in everything described in this chapter.

2

The Growth and Development of Archaeology

It will be clear from what was said in the last chapter that certain present-day archaeological problems (the recording of museum collections, for example) arise out of events which occurred in the last century and sometimes earlier. Quite apart from its own intrinsic interest, it is important to be familiar with the history of the subject, if only in broad outline, in order to be aware of the range of problems faced by the archaeologist and thereby to understand some of his attitudes. The history, perhaps more so than in other branches of learning, is very much part of the subject.

The history of archaeology is composed of many diverse elements which, at first sight, appear to have no obvious connection: the Renaissance, the Industrial Revolution, Napoleon's invasion of Egypt, Darwin's *Origin of Species*, and many more. To these must be added the many outstanding personalities who have emerged at different times to provide the stimulus and impetus necessary for the subject's further development: Champollion, Rawlinson, Layard [25], Boucher de Perthes, Petrie, Pitt-Rivers, and many others. Between them, men and events tell a story which is of the greatest relevance to the understanding of archaeology in its widest sense.

25. Sir Austin Henry Layard and his servant, wearing the costume of the Lurisans, a nomadic tribe of the Syrian border region.

For practical purposes the story begins with the Renaissance, the re-birth of learning which took place in Italy during the fourteenth century, and which spread through Europe during the following centuries. The Renaissance marked the end of the medieval world, dominated by Gothic art and architecture, and a revival of interest in the Classical world, particularly in Classical literature. But in the birthplace of the movement, Italy, many of the remains of the Classical world were still visible as ruins, so that there was a very direct archaeological as well as a literary link with the ancient past. Inevitably, the study of the Classical world came to include not only the ancient writers, so long neglected, but also the material remains of the same era. Monuments were described, sites were excavated (although in nothing like the modern sense of the word) and antiquities were gathered to form private collections. In these activities there is a link, however tenuous, with the present-day archaeological practices of fieldwork, excavation, and museum collection. In fact, the so-called excavation was simply haphazard digging for the purpose of finding new antiquities for private collectors. Nonetheless, the seeds of archaeology, the study of the past by means of its material remains, are quite clearly there, rooted in Renaissance learning, even if they still needed four centuries of careful cultivation by many different hands before they blossomed into full maturity.

This re-awakened interest in the material remains of Greece and Rome marks the beginning of Classical archaeology, but it also provided the first stimulus in prehistoric archaeology, although this was to prove the most intractable and controversial of all the branches of the subject and was not firmly established until the second half of the nineteenth century. Alongside the study of the Classical world, there developed in northern and western Europe a growing interest in the less spectacular but much more numerous monuments to be observed in the countryside. The works of many Classical writers included descriptions of, or references to, the barbarian peoples of these areas, and such references caused a great deal of speculation among local scholars. They had no written records of such a remote period and it was, in fact, a complete blank to them. Inevitably they began, tentatively at first, to try to connect these shadowy figures with another source of endless speculation, the earthworks and stone monuments scattered about the landscape. Neither literary references nor actual monuments fitted into what they knew of their own history. It seemed not unreasonable to assume that these two unknown quantities were part and parcel of the same puzzle. In this attempt to see the past in terms of its material remains lies one of the roots of prehistoric archaeology.

Another form of stimulus was more direct. Very simply, the study of Classical ruins prompted the study of monuments closer to home, not only earthworks and other structures of unknown origin, but monuments of more recent periods, both ruined and otherwise. The dissolution of the monasteries by Henry VIII in 1540 and their subsequent decay, for example, provided a rich field of antiquarian interest and study. A number of factors were involved in this new-found interest in native monuments: national pride for one—the desire to show that beyond the bounds of the Classical world there were monuments which, in their own way, were as striking as anything in Greece or Italy. For those who had made the journey to these countries there was the desire to continue the study of the past when they returned home, and the native monuments were readily available. For many the journey to Greece and Rome could never be repeated, difficulties of travel being what they were, and for many others such a journey could not even be contemplated. In such cases the study of national antiquities was a natural substitute for the more fashionable tour of Greek and Roman remains. Such antiquarian studies embraced a wide range of subjects, including place names, family histories, and architectural history, as well as the earthworks which represent the beginnings of prehistoric archaeology [26]. However, it is not the wide range of topics which is so important as the curiosity which prompted their study, and it is this curiosity about the past, particularly the remote past, beyond the era of written records, that eventually produced the subject of prehistoric archaeology.

In England, during the sixteenth century, antiquarian studies produced such outstanding names as William Camden and John Leland. The latter held the title of King's Antiquary and toured widely in England and Wales. William Camden produced one of the great landmarks in antiquarian publication: his *Britannia*, published in 1586. The outstanding figures in the seventeenth century were John Aubrey and Edward Llwyd. Aubrey described Stonehenge and Avebury in detail and with great perception suggested that they were religious in function. Aubrey was a great field archaeologist and so also, in the eighteenth century, was William Stukeley (1687–1755). His *Itinerarium Curiosum*, published in 1724, contained descriptions of monuments based on his own observations. In the two and a half centuries

from c. 1500 to Stukeley's death in 1755, the great British tradition of field archaeology (i.e. observation and recording) was established, particularly in the persons of Aubrey and Stukeley, and it is a tradition which is probably unrivalled anywhere in the world.

The writing of county histories also flourished during the seventeenth and eighteenth centuries and these too were important, for in most cases they included accounts of antiquarian remains in the county. Among such works were those of William Dugdale on Warwickshire, Robert Plot on Stafford-shire, William Hutchins on Dorset and Samuel and Daniel Lysons on Gloucestershire. But during the eighteenth century a new trend began, bring-ing antiquarian studies somewhat closer to the modern interpretation of archaeology. Such things as place-names and family histories became less prominent and there was much more concentration on the purely material remains. These were now looked upon as subjects worthy of study in their own right rather than simply as an incidental part of some county history. The change was not dramatic, but it was nonetheless important in the develop-ment of archaeology, for it marked a narrowing of focus and increased attention on the present concern of archaeologists—material remains.

This trend is observable about the middle of the century (1750) and there were a number of developments in the second half of the century, in both the British and Classical fields, that must be considered next. As far as Britain was concerned, the earlier revival of interest in the Classical world had been almost entirely literary. The difficulties and dangers of travelling to Greece and Italy in the sixteenth century can be imagined, and the number of people who could have taken advantage of the opportunity to do so would have been relatively small. By the second half of the eighteenth century,

26. Earthwork at Burrough-on-the-Hill, Leicestershire. This, and many others like it, we now know to be Iron Age hillforts but in the early days of archaeology, during the sixteenth and seventeenth centuries, such remains, and those of other types and other periods, were causes of endless speculation and discussion, and in this curiosity lay the seeds of modern archae-ology.

however, both social structure and travel conditions had altered considerably and the journey to view the remains of the Classical world could be contemplated as a perfectly feasible proposition by very many more people. But apart from touring Greece and Italy as a cultural exercise, this period also saw the first serious published academic works on Classical remains. Scholars were now making careful written records and measured drawings of the visible remains—and publishing their work. James Stuart and Nicholas Revett published their *Antiquities of Athens* between 1762 and 1816. The *Antiquities of Ionia* by Nicholas Revett, Richard Chandler and William Parr appeared between 1769 and 1797, and the *Ruins of Palmyra* and the *Ruins of Baalbec* by Robert Wood in 1753 and 1757 respectively. Publication made the remains of the Classical world familiar to a much wider public and this in turn had its effect on a growing leisured class. Apart from written records and measured drawings, many travellers brought back with them examples of the more portable antiquities for their private collections. Such collections were a foretaste of the museum aspect of archaeology, and indeed many such collections eventually found their way into, and formed the nucleus of, the permanent museums which were established in Britain in the nineteenth century, just as the earlier Italian collections of the fifteenth and sixteenth centuries eventually found their way into various European museums. Probably the most famous collection brought back to Britain was that by Lord Elgin in 1816. This consisted of the sculpture from the frieze, pediments and metopes (see p. 218) of the Parthenon in Athens. The Elgin Marbles, as they are known, are now housed in the British Museum [27].

As in the earlier Classical revival, interest in Greece and Rome had its effect on developments at home. In spite of the greater ease of travel not everyone who wished could travel abroad. As a substitute they turned to their native monuments where the ground was already well prepared. The works of the county historians, for example, had made known the existence, if not the precise details, of a whole range of monuments. The more intensive study of these monuments for their own sake was almost certainly inspired, in part at least, by the study of Classical monuments on the ground and perhaps more particularly by the publication of the written records and measured plans mentioned in the previous paragraph. Such intensive studies led almost inevitably to another important stage in the development of British archaeology: excavation. Recorded history gave virtually no information about the earthworks and stone monuments which were such a prominent feature of the landscape. The only answers seemed likely to come from the monuments themselves, and in trying to obtain these answers the first, necessarily crude, attempts at excavation on a large scale were made. In the second half of the eighteenth century the Rev. Bryan Faussett excavated a series of burial mounds in Kent (published in *Inventorum Sepulchrale* in 1856), and in the first half of the nineteenth century Charles Warne did likewise in Dorset, publishing the results in his *Celtic Tumuli of Dorset* in 1866. These are only two, admittedly outstanding, examples of a growing practice of trying to make good the lack of written records by resort to the monuments themselves to see what excavation could reveal of their history. The methods were crude, but the first seeds of modern excavation were quite clearly present.

Many of the great steps forward in archaeology, including branches not so far mentioned, were made in the nineteenth century which is, in many ways, the watershed of the subject. There was a world of difference between

27. Sculptured relief of horsemen from the north frieze of the temple of Athena Parthenos (the Parthenon) in Athens, 447–38 BC. This panel is a part of the Elgin Marbles, sculptures from the Parthenon brought back to England by Lord Elgin in 1816.

archaeology pre-1800 and archaeology post-1900. However, before dealing with the nineteenth century there are certain aspects of the preceding half century (1750–1800) which need to be considered. The Industrial Revolution, the Romantic movement and a growing interest in natural history all had a bearing on what was to follow. One of the effects of the Industrial Revolution was to produce a new leisured class. There had always, of course, been people of leisure, but now they existed in larger numbers and were, moreover, concentrated in the growing towns and cities. This combination of numbers, affluence, and leisure led almost inevitably in the succeeding century to the formation of societies, both national and regional, in all sorts of subjects, for the dissemination of knowledge. These included archaeology and natural history societies, both of which had an important role in the development of the subject. The archaeological societies, under a variety of names, included most of the existing county and regional societies. These are and always have been important for many reasons, but for one in particular, their annual journals, they are invaluable. These have provided a large number of outlets for archaeological work which could not otherwise have been published. The nineteenth century also saw the formation of such national societies as the Royal Archaeological Institute and the British Archaeological Association from the same eighteenth-century roots in the Industrial Revolution.

The greatly increased interest in natural history also had an important role to play. This had been of long-standing interest to country dwellers with the necessary leisure (clergymen for example), and with the emergence of the new urban leisured class the subject was taken up with great alacrity. It was, and still is, combined with archaeology in certain cases (the Dorset

Natural History and Archaeological Society, for example), but it had a particular importance in the development of prehistoric archaeology. Before any progress could be made in this field, the antiquity of Man, and the various stages of his advancement, had to be demonstrated from sources other than written records. These said nothing about the earlier stages of human existence, and it needed the great advances in the science of geology made in the nineteenth century to provide the key to this chapter of life on earth; and these advances grew out of the eighteenth century and the (originally) countryman's pursuit of natural history.

Paradoxically, the Romantic movement in literature was making its effects felt in archaeology at the same time as the developments in the natural sciences just mentioned. The antiquities in the countryside (the barrows, hillforts, stone circles, etc.) provided the focus for the romantic imagination which the movement provoked. Classical remains could be peopled with figures and events from recorded history and Classical legend. Influenced strongly by the Romantic movement, antiquaries in the northern countries began to look at their native monuments and see them in terms of national events and detailed happenings in the lives of the Druids and the Celts. In spite of the romantic licence involved, this development did have the effect of focusing even greater attention on the monuments themselves. Inevitably, in the midst of any such imaginative exercise, the desire for confirmation, or otherwise, of the suppositions arose—and in this questioning were the seeds of further progress. The beginnings of excavation mentioned earlier no doubt owed something to the Romantic movement.

The nineteenth century witnessed enormous progress in the archaeological field, so much so that by the end of the century it was barely recognizable as the same subject. It saw also a broadening out, beyond Europe and the Classical World, into such fields as Egyptian, Near-eastern, and American archaeology. Before describing these developments, something must be said about the still largely unsolved problems of prehistoric archaeology and the moves which were made to try to solve them. There were two basic problems. First of all, there was no proof as yet of the antiquity of Man's existence on earth, beyond the earliest written record. Archbishop Ussher's date of 4004 BC for the Creation was still widely believed, and in the absence of any convincing proof to the contrary it was difficult to get any general acceptance of the concept of prehistoric archaeology. The second problem was that of arranging the existing artefacts in some sort of coherent sequence; stone tools, bronzes, and iron remains were all quite clearly pre-Roman, but beyond that there was no proof that they represented any particular chronological sequence. They could be described as ancient British or prehistoric but beyond that it was not possible to specify any particular part, whether early or late, of the prehistoric period, and without some sort of secure chronological framework there was little hope of significant progress.

The final acceptance of the proof of the antiquity of Man was not to come until 1859, but the solution to the chronological sequence was provided early in the century, even though it took some considerable time to find acceptance everywhere. The pioneer work was carried out in Denmark in the second decade of the nineteenth century and involved the creation of what is known as the Three-age system. This was based on the hypothesis that the earliest tools were made of stone, to be succeeded by tools of bronze, and these in turn by tools and weapons of iron. In fact, the idea of three successive

technological ages was known to the ancient Greeks, but only as a philosophical concept. The idea was first demonstrated in a practical way in the Danish National Museum, in Copenhagen, in 1819 by C. J. Thomsen, who arranged the extensive prehistoric collections there in three groups on this basis. However, the original idea was not Thomsen's but that of a Danish historian, Vedel-Simonsen, who first published it in 1813; but it was Thomsen's use of the Three-age system in the Copenhagen museum which gave it the wide publicity that it deserved.

In spite of its obvious advantages in classifying museum material and in interpreting the prehistoric past, it was half a century before the Danish Three-age system was fully accepted. It was in use in Scandinavia and Germany in the first half of the nineteenth century, but even by 1850 it had not been accepted in Britain. It was not until 1871 that the then-published *Guide to the Exhibition Rooms of the British Museum* acknowledged the existence of Stone, Bronze, and Iron Ages in accordance with the Scandinavian system. By this time there had been a breakthrough on the other major problem, that of the antiquity of Man. As the Three-age system spread throughout Europe and was applied to different collections, it became clear that further sub-divisions were not only possible but very necessary to further progress. In particular it became clear that the Stone Age as originally distinguished in Scandinavia was in fact only the latest part of a much longer Stone Age which was well-represented in western Europe, particularly in France. However, the eventual solution to the problem of the antiquity of Man was provided by geology, and to see how this was done it is necessary to look at developments in the earlier part of the century.

During the late eighteenth and early nineteenth centuries there had been occasional finds of what we now know to be Old Stone Age tools associated in geological layers with the bones of extinct animals. A few perceptive scholars saw this as sufficient proof of the great antiquity of Man on earth, but their voices were ignored. For many, the stone implements were not man-made at all but thunderbolts or other unlikely alternatives. Many questioned the validity of the associations, saying that they were simply accidental, due to the disturbance of the ground, by animal burrowing for example. The greatest stumbling block was the lack of understanding of the basic geology of the earth's crust. Most geologists still saw the formation of the various layers or strata of rocks in terms of a great catastrophe which had deposited them all in a very short, and fairly recent, period of time. Until such views were abandoned and there was a general acceptance of geological principles, little progress could be looked for.

Already at the end of the eighteenth century there were the beginnings of a movement against the catastrophic theory of geology. One or two pioneers argued that the geological strata had been laid down in an orderly fashion over a very long period of time. But the greatest step forward was the publication of Charles Lyell's *Principles of Geology* between 1830 and 1833. He argued that geological stratification could be correctly understood only by abandoning the simplistic catastrophe theory and accepting the fact that the various layers were formed in sequence and at a rate similar to modern geological formations. For example, we know something of the infinitely slow rate of formation of stalactites and stalagmites and the same rates must have applied in the past. If, therefore, human bones or man-made tools occur below a thick layer of stalagmite, it argues convincingly for a very great

IV. Opposite: Upper Palaeolithic cave-painting at Lascaux, south-western France, showing a wounded bison, a 'man', and a bird.

28. Sir William Flinders Petrie.

29. Opposite: the Rosetta stone, a basalt slab discovered in the foundations of a fortress at Rosetta, at the western mouth of the Nile, bearing a trilingual inscription in Egyptian hieroglyphic (top), Egyptian Demotic (middle) and Greek' (bottom). From the Greek portion it was clear that the inscription was a decree in honour of King Ptolemy V (203–180 BC). The fact that in the hieroglyphic version, the King's name, following normal Egyptian practice, was enclosed in a ring or cartouche enabled some of the symbols to be identified, and in this lay the beginnings of the decipherment of Egyptian hieroglyphic which had for so long been considered insoluble.

antiquity. Although Lyell's ideas were not fully accepted until the second half of the century, they marked a very important stage in the understanding of the formation of the earth's crust and provided the essential base for progress in establishing the antiquity of Man.

General acceptance of the proof of the antiquity of Man came in 1859, largely through the work of Boucher de Perthes, in the Somme valley in France, and of William Pengelly at Brixham in Devon. In fact, clear associations of human bones or man-made tools with the bones of extinct animals had been noted and published on a number of occasions during the late eighteenth and early nineteenth centuries, but they were largely ignored. In the prevailing state of opinion such ideas were considered at best foolish and at worst blasphemous. Pengelly excavated at Windmill Hill Cave, Brixham, in 1858 and 1859 and proved a clear association between man-made tools and the bones of extinct animals beneath a thick sheet of stalagmite, three to eight inches thick; the time needed for such a layer to form can be imagined. The work of Boucher de Perthes was accepted at the same time. Boucher de Perthes, a French customs officer, had for many years been collecting stone tools associated with extinct animals in the gravels of the Somme valley. In 1858 his work was noted by the English geologist Falconer, and in 1859 Sir Joseph Prestwich gave a lecture describing it and relating it to some of the earlier, derided, discoveries noted above. Although these two pieces of proof were not accepted immediately by everyone, they did signpost a significant change in the general climate of opinion. The catastrophists and those who scoffed at the antiquity of Man were on the defensive; the tide now moved slowly but decisively against them.

The year 1859 was significant also for another reason, for it saw the publication of Darwin's *Origin of Species*. This, as published, made no direct reference to the antiquity of Man, but it was important in shaping the general climate of opinion in the direction of accepting the idea that present-day species of animals were the result of a selective and long-drawn out evolutionary process. Just as geologists had demonstrated the antiquity of the earth's crust, so Darwin demonstrated the antiquity of the animal kingdom, and both made the idea of the great antiquity of Man much more readily acceptable. They provided a logical framework, a reasoned scheme of events into which it was feasible to fit the existence of Man over a much longer period than had hitherto been visualized.

The events just described (from the new ideas in geology to Darwin's *Origin of Species*) occupied the last few years of the eighteenth and first six decades of the nineteenth centuries. In the meantime, very important developments were taking place in areas which had previously been virtually unknown archaeologically. Napoleon's invasion of Egypt in 1798, quite apart from its military and political importance, had important and long-term consequences for Egyptian archaeology. The invasion force included scholars and draughtsmen whose purpose was to look at and record the topography and monuments of Egypt and in this event is a very clear beginning for Egyptian archaeology. The results of the survey were published between 1809 and 1813 in a series of volumes, the *Déscription de l'Egypte*. In addition to recording monuments, the French expedition also made a collection of portable antiquities, including the famous Rosetta stone, which was of crucial importance in the decipherment of hieroglyphic writing [29]. When the French withdrew from Egypt in 1801, the collection fell into British hands

30–31. Major-General Sir Henry Creswicke Rawlinson and, opposite, the cliff at Behistun with the cuneiform inscription of Darius of which he made a complete copy, and a complete translation, in the years from 1837 to 1846.

and the Rosetta stone and all the other antiquities ended up in the British Museum. There were further important surveys of Egyptian antiquities in 1828 and 1840, and by 1850 virtually all the major monuments of ancient Egypt had been recorded and this, added to the decipherment of hieroglyphic writing, placed the subject on a fairly secure foundation.

Thereafter, probably the most important developments in Egyptian archaeology were the work of Mariette and of Petrie, although the important work of Vyse and Perring on the Great Pyramid in 1837–8 deserves mention. Mariette, sent out to Egypt by the Louvre in 1850, spent thirty years there, most of them as head of the Egyptian Antiquities Service. With him begins the first systematic excavation of Egyptian sites, even though his methods left much to be desired. Nonetheless, by his authority and strict control he brought some sort of order to what had previously been a chaotic situation. During his time in Egypt he excavated over thirty major sites, representing a substantial advance in our knowledge of Egyptian archaeology

The work of probably the most distinguished Egyptologist who has ever lived, Sir William Flinders Petrie [28], began in the same year as Mariette died—1881. It is difficult to overestimate Petrie's contribution not only to Egyptology but also to archaeology as a whole, particularly in the realm of excavation technique. He established new and very high standards of excavation, insisting on meticulous care in digging and the most scrupulous recording of all objects found and all structures uncovered. He crowned all this painstaking work with full and very quick publication, so that the new evidence was available to all in the shortest possible time. This was in marked contrast to many earlier excavations where the digging was often haphazard, inadequately supervised and frequently unpublished—or if published, only after a long delay. Apart from the technique of digging, probably Petrie's major contribution to Egyptian archaeology was the discovery and elucidation of the pre-dynastic period in Egyptian history. Written history in Egypt begins with dynasty I around 3000 BC. Petrie's work at Naquada and other early sites uncovered remains which were quite clearly earlier than dynasty I and represented the prehistoric or pre-dynastic period in Egyptian archaeology. Although Petrie started work in the last two decades of the Victorian era, and was then a contemporary of such quasi-legendary nineteenth-century figures as Schliemann and Pitt-Rivers, he remained active in archaeology until well into the twentieth century, publishing his *Seventy Years in Archaeology* in 1931.

The history of Near-eastern archaeology begins effectively, about the same time as that of Egyptian archaeology, with Claudius James Rich who was appointed British Resident in Baghdad in 1808 and who died of cholera in 1820. In the intervening twelve years he visited and surveyed many of the ancient Near-eastern sites and collected the more portable antiquities. His work on Babylon was particularly important and was published in his *Memoir on the Ruins of Babylon* in 1815 and *Second Memoir on Babylon* in 1818. After his death his collections were purchased by the British Museum.

Mesopotamian excavation began in the 1840s with the work of the Frenchman Paul-Émile Botta and the Englishman (later Sir) Austen Henry Layard [25]. Botta began work in 1842 on a mound identified by Rich as Nineveh, one of the ancient capitals of Assyria. In 1843 he switched his attention to Khorsabad and, because of his spectacular finds there, decided that this was in fact Nineveh and not the first mound. Layard's work began at Nimrud

in 1845, although he is chiefly remembered for his work at Nineveh and a popular account, *Nineveh and its Remains*, was published in 1848. This proved to be a bestseller. Layard had at first assumed that Nimrud was Nineveh. But both he and Botta were wrong. The original Nineveh was, in fact, the mound identified as such by Rich many years before. Confirmation of this was provided through the advances made in the decipherment of cuneiform writing, largely through the work of (later Sir) Henry Creswicke Rawlinson [30].

Rawlinson's major work, which he began in 1837, was the copying and decipherment of the famous trilingual inscription at Behistun. Quite apart from the decipherment, the sheer difficulties of copying the inscription have become a legend. It is carved in a rock face 400 ft. above the ground and is virtually inaccessible [31]. To have produced a complete copy of the inscription was in itself a very considerable achievement, but by 1846 he was also able to publish a complete translation of it. This new-found key to the language enabled many other cuneiform inscriptions to be read and was of immense help in the identification of sites, in particular Nineveh.

The work of Botta, Layard, and Rawlinson stimulated a great deal of further work in the early 1850s and many now-famous sites were identified and partially excavated. However, the Crimean War which started in 1855 caused a halt to further work in the Near East and it was only in the last two or three decades of the century that it was resumed on any scale [32, 33].

In America, the story begins in the 1840s with the work of Stephens and Catherwood on the ruins of the cities of the Maya civilization of Mexico and Honduras, and with the work of other scholars on the monuments and remains in North America. Stephens and Catherwood published their work in two classic accounts, *Incidents of Travel in Central America, Chiapas and Yucatan* (1841) and *Incidents of Travel in Yucatan* (1843). The work of recording the visible antiquities in the various states of North America was a similar process to that which had gone on in Britain a century or more before. For a while difficulties of travel inhibited any further work on the Maya remains, but great steps forward were made by the work of Sir Alfred Maudslay between 1881 and 1894, published in his *Biologia Centrali-Americana*. By the turn of the century, access to the Maya remains was very much easier and work has continued since then in both Central and South America, where spectacular Aztec, Maya and Inca remains have been uncovered.

This necessarily brief account of the development of archaeology will not be carried beyond the early years of the twentieth century and can be concluded by considering the work of three men: Pitt-Rivers, Schliemann, and Evans. There have, of course, been many advances during the present century, particularly in the realms of chronology, but by the turn of the century, or shortly thereafter, the broad outlines of the subject of archaeology as a whole were fairly well established, except in such areas as India and China where noticeable progress came only in the 1920s.

General Pitt-Rivers is known chiefly for his extensive excavations of Cranbourne Chase, Dorset, which he inherited in 1880. By then a wealthy man, he was able to carry out a series of now-famous excavations at a standard of unheard-of precision. With an enormous talent for organization, he dug with painstaking care and thoroughness, meticulously recording everything, even the smallest and most insignificant finds, and publishing the full and

32, 33. Above: the great death-pit at Ur during excavation. From the remains excavated by Sir Leonard Woolley in 1922–9, it is quite clear that when a king, or queen, of Ur died all the members of the court died with them. In the great death-pit (*c.* 37 × 24 ft. at the bottom) there were the bodies of six menservants and sixty-eight women, richly dressed and showing no signs of reluctance or resistance, as far as one can judge from the ordered layout of the bodies. Right: a plan of the death-pit showing the arrangement of the bodies and also the bull-headed lyres to the left.

RAMP

ENTRANCE

34. Bastion projecting from the wall of the sixth city of Troy. Heinrich Schliemann, who rediscovered Troy and carried out extensive excavations there between 1871 and 1890, thought that the second city (Troy II) was the Troy of the Trojan wars and Homeric legend, but it is now known that this city was, in fact, Troy VI and Troy VIIa, dating to the fourteenth and thirteenth centuries BC.

detailed results in four thick volumes, *Excavations in Cranbourne Chase* (1887–98). Even today the standard of work represented by his excavations would stand out; at the end of the nineteenth century it represented a revolutionary advance over the current standards of work. Among other things he stressed the importance of commonplace rather than spectacular finds, which had too often been the objective of excavators. He realized that a handful of broken pottery, properly studied, could reveal far more about a site than the most splendid single find and to this end he made a careful note of all stratigraphy and recorded all finds, even those he did not understand, in detail. His practices are now the routine of excavation but it must be recalled that at the time they could not have been further removed from the crude digging of holes in the ground which then passed for archaeological excavation.

The work of Heinrich Schliemann was roughly contemporary with that of Petrie and Pitt-Rivers but in a field about which little has been said, that of Classical archaeology. This was last considered, as far as Britain was concerned, in the period from about 1750 on when detailed publications on the Classical remains first appeared. Interest continued into the succeeding century, but in this particular branch of archaeology German scholarship was to be pre-eminent and during the nineteenth century it came to dominate the whole of the Classical field. It was thus appropriate, and perhaps inevitable, that it was a German, Heinrich Schliemann, who, by his discoveries at Troy, Tiryns and Mycenae, gave substance to the world depicted by Homer which forms the essential background to the more familiar Greek world of the seventh century BC onwards. Schliemann had been excited by Homer's account of the siege of Troy ever since his childhood and it became his life's ambition to prove that Troy had actually existed and was not simply a creation of Homer's imagination. The fulfilment of his ambition had to await the end of a very successful business career in which he amassed a fortune which gave him the freedom to follow his own inclinations. After

35. Opposite: Grave Circle A at Mycenae, enclosing the famous Shaft Graves, presumed to be the burials of the Royal House of Mycenae, *c.* 1600 BC. The graves stand just inside the walls of the main citadel, near the Lion Gate [170], and the circle of upright slabs surrounding them was, in fact, a later feature, added only when the citadel was built, *c.* 1400 BC.

a period of study and travel he came to the conclusion that the original city of Troy lay buried under a mound or tell at Hissarlik in the extreme north-west of Asia Minor. He began excavations there in 1871 and continued at intervals until his death in 1890. The excavation was important for a number of reasons. When Schliemann began work there was no visible monument on the surface; he was simply digging a mound or 'tell' and this was the first time this had been done. Hitherto excavation had been concentrated exclusively on monumental remains. In digging through the mound, moreover, he was careful to distinguish the different stratigraphical levels, and although the principle of stratigraphy was already known, it had not previously been demonstrated on such a large scale. And, of course, the excavation was important because it achieved Schliemann's ambition: it discovered Troy, and in doing so opened up a whole new prehistoric era, stretching back long before the Troy of the Homeric poems. Schliemann distinguished seven levels or cities (I–VII) and concluded that Troy II was the Troy of Homer and the Trojan war. Subsequently it was proved that Homeric Troy was in fact Troy VI [34], so that there were five previous settlements stretching back over a then unknown but undoubtedly very great length of time. This brought an entirely new dimension into the archaeology of the Aegean area. The world of Troy VI was the Mycenaean world as described by Homer and, in addition to his excavations at Troy, Schliemann dug very successfully at both Mycenae and Tiryns—two of the great strongholds of the Mycenaean princes [35].

These three major excavations illuminated the Mycenaean civilization which stood behind the Greek Dark Age (1100–700 BC) and which occupied the centuries between roughly 1500 and 1100 BC. But what lay behind Mycenaean civilization? Somewhere, either in Greece or in the surrounding areas, there had to be a source from which it had developed and this was the great problem posed by Schliemann's discoveries. In the last twenty years of the nineteenth century a number of people turned their attention to this problem and such clues as there were seemed to point in the direction of the island of Crete, particularly to Kephala (which we now know as Knossos) where pottery similar to Mycenaean pottery had been found as early as 1878. One of the participants in this great debate was Sir Arthur Evans [36]. He was convinced of the Cretan origin of Mycenaean civilization and in 1899 he began digging at Kephala to test his theories. Within a matter of weeks he was proved right. His excavation uncovered the remains of an enormous palace building, nearly three acres in area, and this and other impressive architectural remains proved to be part of a whole civilization (which he called the Minoan, after the legendary King Minos), which was quite clearly earlier than the Mycenaean civilization of mainland Greece [37]. In fact, it became clear that the Mycenaean civilization began, c. 1500 BC, only when the great period of Minoan civilization was at an end, so that the beginnings of the Minoan civilization had to be placed very much earlier than 1500 BC. Evans eventually showed that Minoan civilization began c. 2500 BC, thus extending the prehistoric background of Greek civilization by a thousand years at a stroke. In fact, at Knossos, he extended it beyond the beginnings of the Minoan Bronze Age civilization back to the Neolithic, or New Stone Age, period which, on recent Carbon-14 evidence, had begun in Crete by 5000 BC. Leaving this to one side, Schliemann and Evans between them had filled in virtually the whole background of Greek civilization as

36. Sir Arthur Evans. The work of Heinrich Schliemann at Troy, Tiryns and Mycenae had thrown new light on early Greek civilization in the Mycenaean period. Evans was convinced that behind the Mycenaean civilization lay a still earlier culture, probably in the island of Crete. In 1899 he began work at Kephala (which we now know as Knossos) and very quickly uncovered the remains of the first of the great Cretan palaces.

represented by the Classic remains of the seventh to fourth centuries BC. There was now a well-established sequence, starting *c.* 2500 BC with the Early Minoan period (*c.* 2500–2000 BC) and running through Middle Minoan (*c.* 2000–1500 BC), Late Minoan and Mycenaean (*c.* 1500–1100 BC), the Greek Dark Age (*c.* 1100–700 BC) to the Archaic period (700–500 BC) and the fully developed Greek civilization of the fifth century BC.

The work of Evans at Knossos brings the story of archaeological development well into the twentieth century. There was still much to happen in the branches of the subject already considered, not to mention developments in such places as India and China, but limitations of space prevent any further consideration of this aspect of archaeology. In any case, although many refinements were still to be added, the main lines of the major branches of the subject were now fairly well established so that in a sense the essential history has already been fully dealt with. Although the story has been pursued along the lines of the separate branches of the subject, it is essentially one story, that of the rediscovery of the past. Evans' work on the Cretan Neolithic and Bronze Ages, for example, provided firm links between the Classical world and prehistoric Europe, and other work (notably Petrie's) had forged links in the opposite direction with the ancient Near East, so that the whole process of archaeological development is that of creating a single picture from the many pieces of a jigsaw puzzle. Developments in recent years, particularly in the field of chronology, have enabled us to see the whole of the ancient Near East, the Classical World and prehistoric Europe as a single coherent picture, both in space and in time. There are, and probably always will be, some gaps, but more and more the separate scenes are being linked to form part of one single picture which portrays all the aspects of Man's antiquity on earth.

37. Remains of the palace of Minos at Knossos in Crete. The excavation of this, the greatest of all the Minoan palaces, represented the life's work of Sir Arthur Evans, whose name will always be associated with the rediscovery of the whole Minoan civilization in the early part of this century. Three other palaces are known in Crete: Phaistos, Mallia and Kato Zakro [167–9].

3

The Beginning: the Palaeolithic Period

The whole period of Man's existence can be divided into two major phases: prehistoric and historic. The historic period is relatively short (*c.* 5000 years at most) and can be defined as that part of Man's history covered by written records, while the prehistoric period covers everything prior to that, from Man's first appearance on earth. The date when prehistoric changes to historic varies according to area but the earliest date is *c.* 3000 BC in the ancient Near East, at the beginning of the dynastic periods in both Mesopotamia and Egypt. In the greater part of Europe the prehistoric phase persists for another 3000 years, until the time of the Roman conquest, and in other parts of the world it lasts even longer—until comparatively recent times in places such as Africa, South America, and New Guinea.

In the historic period the major events are known from written documents so that the archaeologist working, for example, on ancient Egypt, already has a well-defined framework within which to work. In particular, in the field of chronology or dating (always of prime concern to archaeologists), he is relieved of an enormous burden in that he knows, often to the precise year, when certain events took place. This is in marked contrast to the prehistoric period when events can frequently be dated only to the nearest century, and sometimes not even as closely as that. The absence of written records means that the whole story of prehistoric Man has to be built up solely from the material remains as defined in Chapter 1. There is no other source of information. There are no documents to provide dates or details of events, or the names of people involved in them. The prehistoric archaeologist starts with nothing but such remains of Man's material culture as have survived and proceeds as best he can from there.

As compared with the 5000 years (maximum) duration of the historic period, the prehistoric period is immensely long, beginning possibly as early as 1,750,000 years ago. This enormous span of time is sub-divided (in the prehistory of Europe, Asia and Africa) into five periods: Palaeolithic (Old Stone Age), Mesolithic (Middle Stone Age), Neolithic (New Stone Age), Bronze Age, and Iron Age, although not all of these periods are represented everywhere. In the greater part of Africa, for example, there is no Bronze Age, the Iron Age following directly on from the Neolithic. The span of time covered by the four most recent periods (Mesolithic to Iron Age) is, like the historic period, relatively short, with the Mesolithic beginning in round figures *c.* 10,000 BC. This means that the immense length of the prehistoric period referred to above is almost entirely accounted for by the Palaeolithic or Old Stone Age period in which Man must have emerged and in which tool-making first began. As such it provides the broad background against which

38. Opposite: the cave of Lascaux, in south-west France, discovered only in 1940, with multicoloured paintings on the ceiling dating to the final phase of the Upper Palaeolithic period, the Magdalenian, *c.* 15,000–10,000 BC. In recent years the cave has been closed to the public while investigations have been carried out into a growth which is in danger of obscuring the paintings.

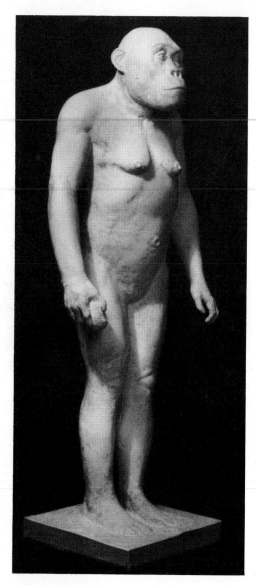

39. *Australopithecus,* tool-making hominid, *c.* 4 ft. high. Restoration by Maurice Wilson based on a female skeleton from Sterkfontein, Transvaal. *Australopithecus* may be as early as 2,500,000 BC.

all subsequent developments took place and it is appropriate therefore to use this chapter on the Palaeolithic as the introduction to all subsequent chapters, bringing the story from the beginning up to the threshold of *c.* 10,000 BC, from which point later developments can be most conveniently considered on a geographical basis.

The Palaeolithic (Greek *palaeos,* old; *lithos,* stone) phase of human existence took place against the background of the Glacial period. Although we speak of the Ice Age or Glacial period in the singular, it would be wrong to assume that it consisted of a single event, a single advance and retreat of the northern ice cap. In fact, there were both glacial and interglacial periods within the million or so years that the Ice Age lasted. For many years the established pattern consisted of four glacial periods—Günz, Mindel, Riss, and Würm— representing maximum advances of the ice across northern Europe, separated by three interglacial periods which represented periods when the ice retreated and climatic conditions became correspondingly less severe. More recently, the sequence has been extended backwards by the inclusion of the Donau glaciation and the consequent Donau/Günz interglacial period. The most likely explanation of this long series of glacial fluctuations is probably to be found in corresponding fluctuations in the sun's radiation, and some larger variation in the latter may possibly provide the reason for the whole phenomenon of glaciation.

Dates for the various glacial and interglacial episodes can only be approximate but the following timetable of events provides a chronological framework within which the Old Stone Age period can be discussed:

Donau Glaciation ⎫	1,000,000 BC
Donau/Günz interglacial ⎭	to 600,000 BC
Günz Glaciation	begins 600,000 BC
Günz/Mindel interglacial	550,000 BC
Mindel Glaciation	475,000 BC
Mindel/Riss interglacial (The Great Interglacial)	435,000 BC
Riss Glaciation	230,000 BC
Riss/Würm interglacial	190,000 BC
Würm Glaciation	120,000 BC
End of glacial period	10,000 BC

By any standards the periods of time involved are enormous and emphasize the painfully slow development of Man during the Palaeolithic period. Accustomed as we are to dates in terms of the Christian era, which have not yet reached 2000 years, the dates for the Great Interglacial, for example, (435,000–230,000 BC—over 200,000 years) are very hard to comprehend, especially when it is seen that virtually one type of tool was in use for the whole of this period.

EARLY MAN

Although there is no difficulty in distinguishing between Man and modern apes, the broad similarities make it quite certain that a relationship exists in the form of a common ancestor. However, because of the still very marked differences between the skeletal remains of even very early Man and apes, it looks as if this common ancestry is of great antiquity, dating possibly from as long as twenty million years ago, from which time the apes on the one hand

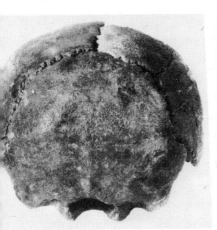

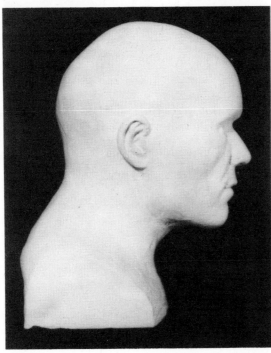

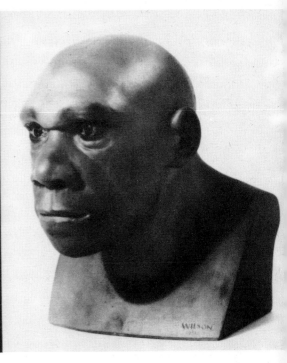

and the ancestors of Man on the other developed on progressively divergent lines. It is, therefore, perhaps more correct to say that Man is a distant cousin of the apes rather than a direct descendant of the family.

The development stages during these twenty-or-so million years are virtually unknown, but at some time during this period an upright posture must have been adopted, because it is as a long-established two-legged creature that Man eventually emerges into the light of our archaeological knowledge. The upright posture may reflect the environment in which he lived, which may, in turn, provide the basic reason why he diverged from the apes. The normal habitat of the latter is the forest where the long, muscular forelimbs are necessary for easy movement. In a different environment, however, in more open country, where survival might well depend on speed, the best form of locomotion would probably be by means of two (rear) limbs rather than four. This would lead eventually to the development of the rear limbs as the exclusive means of movement, leaving the forelimbs free for handling and holding tasks, and, eventually, for tool-making. The availability of two hands would mean that the projecting jaw and teeth would be less used and this and similar changes would lead to progressively greater differentiation between the apes and what was to become Man.

The hypothetical, but nevertheless probable, developments just outlined are followed by the actual fossil remains of Man and Man-like creatures, grouped under the heading of *hominids*; these are divided into two main groups, *Australopithecus* and *Homo*. The *Australopithecines*, who may date from as early as 2,500,000 BC were very small (*c.* 4 ft. tall) and had brains of similar size to apes, but they had an erect posture and walked on two legs [39]. They also showed other features (jaw, teeth, and forehead, for example) which place them much closer to Man than to the apes. All the other fossil remains of early Man, from *c.* 500,000 BC on, are now grouped under the

40–42. Above left: the Swanscombe skull (viewed from the back), from the 100 ft. gravel terrace of the Thames at Swanscombe, Kent: *Homo erectus*. Above right: Neanderthal Man, *Homo sapiens*. Above centre: *Homo sapiens sapiens*.

63

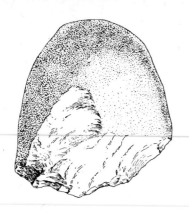

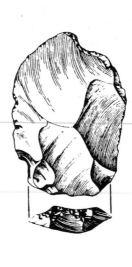

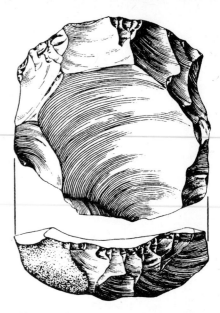

heading *Homo* (Latin—man), and are sub-divided into three groups: *Homo erectus*, *Homo sapiens*, and *Homo sapiens sapiens*.

Homo erectus, who probably emerged about half a million years ago, was a capable tool-maker but still noticeably different from modern Man. In particular, he had a low, receding forehead, massive eyebrow ridges, and a strongly projecting mouth and jaw [40]. *Homo sapiens*, who almost certainly developed from this stock, emerged during the last (Riss-Würm) inter-glacial, probably between 150,000 and 100,000 BC. The most notable feature of the *Homo sapiens* group was the increased brain capacity, which was very close to that of modern Man, and this development of the brain quite clearly represents a very important advance. The *Homo sapiens* group includes one of the best-known types of prehistoric Man, the Neanderthal, and in spite of all the popular misconceptions it is interesting to note that he belongs to the group that is directly ancestral to modern Man [42]. The third group, *Homo sapiens sapiens*, developed directly from the previous group, at a date of between 40,000 and 35,000 BC, i.e. during the last (Würm) glaciation. There is little doubt that all the modern races of Man are direct descendents of the *Homo sapiens sapiens* type, who in stature, mental capacity and general appearance was little or no different from present-day human beings [41].

LOWER PALAEOLITHIC PERIOD
The Palaeolithic period is normally divided into three stages: Lower, Middle, and Upper, each characterized by different forms of tool-making. The Lower Palaeolithic may have begun as early as 1,750,000 BC and lasted until about 190,000 BC. The dominant tool type in the later part of the Lower Palaeolithic (from *c*. 475,000 BC on) is the hand-axe, but there is an earlier type (the work of *Australopithecus*) from which it probably developed known as a 'chopper-tool'. Choppers were made by striking off a few flakes from one side of a stone so that some sort of cutting or chopping edge was produced. It is difficult to imagine anything simpler or cruder in the way of equipment, but chopper-tools are nonetheless significant in human history because, as objects needing experience, forethought, and manual dexterity to produce, they separate Man decisively from the animal kingdom [43].

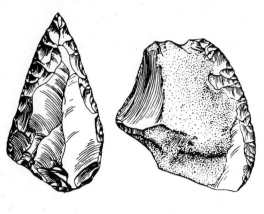

43–46. Opposite, far left: chopper tool of the Oldowan culture, eastern Africa. These very simple chopping implements are earlier than the long series of Lower Palaeolithic hand-axes and may be the form from which the latter developed. Opposite, left: Levalloisian flake and tortoise-shaped core. The Middle Palaeolithic period is noted chiefly for the development of the flake technique of manufacturing stone tools, in contrast to the earlier, Lower Palaeolithic core method. Above: further examples of the Middle Palaeolithic flake technique: a Mousterian point and side-scraper. (All the above tools have been reduced to about half their size.) Right: an Acheulean hand-axe of the Lower Palaeolithic period, indicating the actual size and probable method of gripping the implement.

The hand-axe was almost certainly developed from the chopper and is, in a sense, simply a refined version of it. The selected stone or pebble was flaked over most if not all of its surface to produce a tool which was more or less pear-shaped, with an oval cross-section. This was presumably meant to be held in the hand by the broader end, using the pointed end as the business part of the tool or weapon. Two main stages are distinguished in the production of hand-axes: Abbevillian (formerly Chellean) and Acheulian (after the French sites at Abbeville and St. Acheul) [46]. Abbevillian hand-axes are relatively crude in shape and rather thick; they tend to have some of the original pebble surface left unflaked at the broader end. Acheulian hand-axes show much finer flaking, a more regular shape and are rather thinner in cross-section. Hand-axes are found widely in Europe, Africa, the Middle East and India. Beyond, in the Far East, the chopper-tool remained the dominant type; nor did it go entirely out of use in the hand-axe territory, being found alongside the latter in a number of localities.

Lower Palaeolithic man *(Homo erectus)* was a great meat-eater and hunted a wide variety of animals (elephant, rhinoceros, hippopotamus, zebra, buffalo, gazelle, pig, and horse) with the aid of wooden spears, hardened at the tip by fire. In addition to meat, the animals killed also supplied skins for clothing and shelter, and bones and horn for making tools other than those of stone. Hand-axes must have constituted the main tool of *Homo erectus* for well over 250,000 years, an immensely long time, indicating an infinitely slow rate of change. Moreover, they continued to be used during the following period alongside the new types of stone tool which were introduced then.

MIDDLE PALAEOLITHIC PERIOD

Hand-axes are classed as core-tools, that is, tools formed by removing flakes from a suitable stone so that the core left at the end is the finished tool. In the Middle Palaeolithic period flake-tools were introduced, that is, tools made by striking flakes from a block of flint, the flake and not the remaining core forming the desired tool. Two main variations of the flake technique are known, both, again, named after French sites: Levallois and Le Moustier. Levalloisian-Mousterian tools belong to the period of the third (Riss-Würm) interglacial and the early part of the Würm glaciation, occupying the years from *c.* 190,000 to *c.* 40,000 BC, and coinciding broadly with *Homo sapiens,* the successor of *Homo erectus* of the Lower Palaeolithic. These Middle Palaeolithic tools occur in a great east-west band on both sides of the Mediterranean, from the Atlantic to western Asia, and many of them are found in caves, perhaps indicating the onset of cold conditions at the beginning of the final, Würm, glaciation [44, 45].

The animals hunted appear to be the same as in the previous period, as do the methods of hunting. The presence of flint scrapers, for cleaning animal skins, suggests a need for clothing, perhaps another hint of cold conditions. There is also, for the first time, some evidence of deliberate burial of the dead. In Lower Palaeolithic times there is clear evidence of cannibalism, and this continues into the Middle Palaeolithic period, but there are now also examples of bodies buried deliberately in a crouched position, in specially-cut graves in the floors of caves and other habitation sites. Such burials do, perhaps, suggest that Middle Palaeolithic Man was beginning to justify his title of *Homo sapiens.*

THE UPPER PALAEOLITHIC PERIOD

The Upper Palaeolithic period began some 40,000 years ago, that is, during the second half of the last (Würm) glaciation. It was characterized by flint tools based on what is known as the blade technique. This is a refinement or development of the preceding Middle Palaeolithic flake technique, involving a much greater degree of control over the final product which is, in fact, a flake of flint in the form of a (relatively) long, parallel-sided blade. This, in turn, served as the basis, or blank, from which a whole series of other tools were made. For many years it was believed that the Upper Palaeolithic blade tools marked a complete break with the preceding flake tools, just as Upper Palaeolithic Man was supposed to be radically different from, and far in advance of, Neanderthal Man, the dominant type of the Middle Palaeolithic period. As pointed out earlier, however, Neanderthal Man belonged to the group which was directly ancestral to Upper Palaeolithic Man *(Homo sapiens sapiens)*, and a similar link is now recognized in the flint industry. Although by the sheer volume of their production they constitute the distinguishing feature of the Upper Palaeolithic period, blade tools were already present, if only in small numbers, in the Middle Palaeolithic Mousterian culture. There is, therefore, no decisive break between the two periods. The seeds of the Upper Palaeolithic technique were, in fact, planted

47. Upper Palaeolithic family group. Reconstruction of the rock-shelter home of Magdalenian hunters in south-western France at the close of the Ice Age, *c.* 10,000 BC.

earlier, in the Middle Palaeolithic. It is the rapid and widespread exploitation of the blade technique, rather than its initial discovery, that is the characteristic feature of the Upper Palaeolithic culture.

As compared with earlier periods, the Upper Palaeolithic was one of rapid development. In the 25–30,000 years during which the period lasted there were (at least in western Europe) no less than five major sub-periods, each with its own clearcut characteristics and achievements. These achievements included not only an expanded range of flint tools, but tools and equipment in other materials as well, most notably animal bone. To a population which lived mainly by hunting, bone had always been available as a raw material, but it was only the range and quality of the flint tools developed during the Upper Palaeolithic which enabled it to be utilized for the first time on a large scale. This, in turn, led to other advances. Bone needles, for example, must have caused a virtual revolution in the manufacture of clothing, adding greatly to the quality of life, the more so in the harsh environment of late glacial times.

More or less coincidental with these technological developments was the emergence of the direct ancestor of modern Man *(Homo sapiens sapiens)*, frequently described as Cro-magnon Man, from the name of a well-known site in France where good skeletal remains of the type have been found [41]. Unlike earlier periods, such skeletal material is of relatively frequent occurrence, so that the picture of Upper Palaeolithic Man is fairly clear. In fact, physically, Upper Palaeolithic Man differed little from modern Man. He was of slim build with a high forehead, small eyebrow ridges, small teeth and a pointed chin [47]. Suitably dressed, shaved, etc., it would be difficult to pick him out of a group of similarly dressed modern men! From this stock developed all the modern races of Man throughout the world. Non-skeletal features (colour of skin, type of hair, etc.) are largely a result of adaptations to the wide variety of climatic and environmental conditions encountered in the progressive expansion of world population which began in the Upper Palaeolithic period. Upper Palaeolithic tools and weapons have been found over an enormous territory, covering great parts of Europe, Africa and Asia, including India, Burma, China, Japan and Siberia. In the New World, moreover, it seems likely that the stone industry first carried into North America via the Bering Straits was of a general Upper Palaeolithic type.

The sub-divisions of the Upper Palaeolithic are again based on the names of particular French sites, although it is now known that the European sequence was later, by several thousand years, than the sequence in western Asia. Five main stages are distinguished: Châtelperronian, Aurignacian, Gravettian, Solutrean, and Magdalenian. With the aid of Carbon-14 determinations it is now possible to indicate broad dates for each of these periods (in Europe), starting with the most recent:

Magdalenian:	10,000–15,000 BC
Solutrean:	15,000–20,000 BC
Gravettian:	20,000–26,000 BC
Aurignacian:	26,000–32,000 BC
Châtelperronian:	32,000–35,000 BC

THE CHÂTELPERRONIAN CULTURE (35–32,000 BC)
In earlier works the Châtelperronian is called the Lower Aurignacian because it was originally thought to have been ancestral to the second stage

48. Some of the main tool types of the Châtelperronian culture, the first phase of the European Upper Palaeolithic period. The period was characterized by the blade technique of tool manufacture in which blade-like flakes were struck off a parent core of flint and then used as the 'blanks' for a whole range of different implements: knife-blades, scrapers, boring and engraving tools, etc. (reduced to *c.* ⅜).

of Upper Palaeolithic culture, the Middle Aurignacian, here called simply Aurignacian. However, it is now recognized that no such close relationship exists, hence the revised terminology. The Châtelperronian immediately succeeds the Mousterian in western Europe and may well have been derived, at least in part, from it, perhaps under the influence of new ideas from some outside source. Whatever its origins there is no doubt about its main types of flint tools, which are markedly in advance of anything produced by the Mousterians [48]. The three main types are backed blades, scrapers, and burins. A backed blade is one which can be used for cutting purposes in much the same way as a penknife blade. It consists of a parallel-sided blade, two or three inches long, with one of the two sharp edges deliberately blunted or backed so that pressure can be applied. In use the blade is held between the thumb and the second finger and pressure is applied to the 'backed' edge by the forefinger. The late L.S.B. Leakey records that as an experiment he skinned and cut up a gazelle in a very short time using a single backed blade less than two inches long, and this is the sort of function for which the Châtelperronian people no doubt used them. Apart from food, the most useful products of the kill were undoubtedly the bones and the skin, and for treating the latter the end scraper was the chosen tool. It consists of a blade, again about two or three inches long, with one end rounded by steep flaking to provide a good scraping edge for cleaning the animal skins on the inside as part of their conversion into clothing. The remainder of the blade acts as a sort of built-in handle held between the thumb, on top, and the remaining fingers beneath. The third main Châtelperronian tool type, the burin, was used, among other purposes, in the working of bone. It consisted, again, of a blade, one end of which had been fashioned like a chisel, giving it the sharp but also strong cutting edge necessary for cutting hard materials such as bone. Burins had been made in earlier periods but it was only in the Upper Palaeolithic that they were produced in the numbers and variety which transformed the utilization of hard materials.

The Châtelperronian appears, on present evidence, to be confined to western Europe and not a great deal is known about its origins. It is clearly a much more localized development than the succeeding Aurignacian culture.

THE AURIGNACIAN CULTURE (32–26,000 BC in western Europe, but probably *c.* 5000 years earlier in western Asia.)
The Aurignacian culture (formerly called Middle Aurignacian) is found over a wide territory from western Europe to Afghanistan. It may well have originated in Palestine, or at least somewhere in the surrounding area, where there appears to be an early phase, pre-dating the full Aurignacian phase and representing its beginnings. From the Near East the fully developed Aurignacian was carried in one direction into Europe (reaching western Europe *c.* 32,000 BC), and in another further into Asia, reaching Afghanistan and possibly India as well. In many parts of Europe the Aurignacian follows directly on from the Mousterian, and there are indications that some features were inherited.

Although the Aurignacian people made and used backed blades these were less common than they had been in the Châtelperronian period. They now made use of plain blades (i.e. without backing) and these must have required some sort of handle or binding to allow them to be held whilst in use. However, the main Aurignacian tool types were the burin and the scraper,

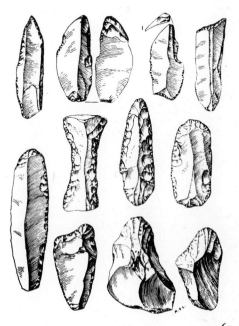

49. Tool types of the second phase of the Upper Palaeolithic period, the Aurignacian culture (formerly called Middle Aurignacian), showing a further development of the blade technique of tool manufacture (reduced to $\frac{3}{8}$).

50. Tool types of the Gravettian and Magdalenian cultures. In these, the two major final phases of the Upper Palaeolithic period, the range of blade-tools reaches its peak and very small (microlithic) implements make their appearance. The microlith becomes the characteristic form of the succeeding Mesolithic period (reduced to $c.\frac{7}{8}$).

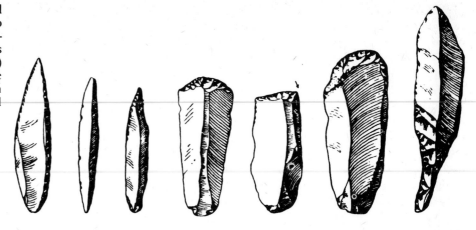

the latter in several different forms and techniques. End and hollow (i.e. concave) scrapers were common, as well as much heavier scrapers based not on the blade technique, but on the older core technique (p. 66). The predominance of scrapers suggests a great deal of activity in connection with the treatment of animal skins for clothing, but also possibly for other purposes as well. The wide variety of burins is evidence of a greatly increased use of animal bone as a raw material in the Aurignacian period [49].

THE GRAVETTIAN CULTURE (26–20,000 BC in western Europe, but again almost certainly earlier by several thousand years in Russia.)
In many ways the Gravettian is the most significant of all Upper Palaeolithic cultures, particularly in the fields of art and architecture, albeit of a very primitive kind. As found in France, the Gravettian bears some resemblance to the earlier Châtelperronian but this is probably a purely local feature. There is little doubt that the Gravettian originated somewhere in eastern Europe, possibly in south Russia, and spread to western Europe only at a relatively late date. The flint equipment included backed blades, some of them of small size, suggesting that they were used not so much separately but as part of larger, composite tools, perhaps in the form of a wooden handle with a series of small flints mounted in it. Other backed blades, with pointed ends, were so slender that they could well have been used as awls for leather and other materials. The remaining tools included a variety of burins and end scrapers [50].

It is not so much for its flint technology as for its art and its architecture that the Gravettian culture is noteworthy. Upper Palaeolithic art generally will be considered later; here attention will be concentrated on Gravettian achievement in building. In much of Europe, Upper Palaeolithic habitation sites seem to have been in caves and rock shelters, although this impression may be due to the greater chances of survival in such locations as compared with open-air sites. However, in the great Gravettian province of south Russia, the local geology does not provide the range of caves available elsewhere, so that it may have been of necessity that habitation was in man-made open-air sites rather than in naturally formed caves. The commonest form of dwelling seems to have been an irregularly shaped pit or hollow sunk into the ground and covered by a tent-like structure of skins sewn together, supported internally by posts and weighed down externally by stones, mammoth bones and tusks. Such a form would allow the most valuable part of the structure, the skin cover, to be transported as required to another site, where a new hollow could be excavated. There is also some evidence of more elaborate dwellings with low mud walls and sloping roofs supported by internal posts. The most recent discovery (1972) is of a large oval dwelling near Berdyzh in Byelorussia, dated to *c.* 21,000 BC by Russian archaeologists, i.e., almost certainly belonging to the Gravettian culture. The builders had used mammoth bones for the foundations and walls, and had also made use of mammoth tusks up to thirteen feet long. A settlement seems to have consisted of a few (perhaps half a dozen) separate establishments, each housing a single family group. Such settlements probably represent the sort of numbers required for successful communal hunting, essential where very large game, such as the mammoth, is involved.

Apart from its flint tools and its settlements, the Gravettian culture is notable also for a variety of products in other materials—bone, antler and ivory, all of course by-products of the hunt. These included objects for personal adornment (such as ivory bracelets), perforated bone needles and awls, antler clubs, and bone harpoon heads with barbs.

In eastern Europe the Gravettian, or direct developments of it, persisted to the end of the Palaeolithic period. In western Europe, however, particularly in France and Spain, there were two further Upper Palaeolithic stages not represented elsewhere, the Solutrean and the Magdalenian.

THE SOLUTREAN CULTURE (*c.* 20,000–15,000 BC)

The outstanding product of the Solutrean culture was the leaf-shaped point, carefully flaked on both faces and very thin in cross-section. The smaller examples, up to two or three inches long, were probably arrowheads, but the larger ones were presumably spear- or javelin-heads [51]. Very large examples, some of which appear too thin for practical use, may have been used for ritual purposes. One such leaf-shaped point was nearly fourteen inches long, but only a quarter of an inch thick. In addition to the (smaller) leaf-shaped arrowheads, the Solutrean people also made points with a shank or tang for attachment to a shaft and these also would appear to have been used as arrowheads. The other stone equipment included backed blades, burins and scrapers.

THE MAGDALENIAN CULTURE (15,000–10,000 BC)

Like the Solutrean culture, the Magdalenian culture in its early phases was confined to a limited part of western Europe, although later it spread eastwards as far as southern Germany. One of the most notable pieces of Magdalenian equipment was the spear-thrower, a device for increasing the range and velocity of spears, obviously a great advantage in the hunt. The spear-thrower, up to two feet long, acted as an extension of the arm and was provided with a lug or projection at the end which engaged in the end of the spear. In practice spear and spear-thrower were held together in the hand with the arm drawn back and the lug of the thrower engaged in the base of the spear. As the arm was thrown forward the spear, but not the spear-thrower, was released so that the effect was that of a throw by a very long arm, producing much greater initial velocity than would otherwise have been achieved. The Magdalenian culture was notable also for its fine range of bone harpoon heads with barbs on one or both sides. The flint work em-

51. One of the most unusual of all Upper Palaeolithic tool types is the leaf-shaped blade of the Solutrean culture, in many cases with careful flaking on not only one but both faces of the implement. The larger tools, up to six inches long, are too big to have been used as arrowheads and must have been intended as spear- or javelin-heads.

52. Spear-thrower representing a bison licking its flank, from the cave of La Madeleine, Dordogne, France. A spear-thrower is a device for increasing the launching velocity of a spear. It consists basically of a stick or rod about 2 ft. long with a hook or lug at one end. The other end is held in the hand, together with the spear, and the hook or lug is engaged in the back end of the spear shaft. The spear-thrower, in effect, acts as an extension of the arm, so that the spear is thrown with much greater force and over a longer distance.

braced the types encountered already in the Upper Palaeolithic—backed blades, burins, scrapers, etc.—but there was also a noticeable increase in microlithic flints which were to become the hallmark of the succeeding Mesolithic cultures.

UPPER PALAEOLITHIC ART

As with other aspects of Palaeolithic archaeology the subject of art tends to be dominated by the spectacular cave-paintings of France and Spain because so many of the early discoveries were made there. More recent discoveries, however, in the last few decades, have shown not only that Palaeolithic art is geographically much more widely based than hitherto assumed, but also that it is earlier than the Magdalenian period with which it has been traditionally associated. It has, in fact, been clearly demonstrated that the Gravettians played a very important part in the development of art in the Upper Palaeolithic period, and it is with the Gravettian, and the succeeding Solutrean and Magdalenian phases, that the story is chiefly concerned, a period of some 20,000 years.

The artistic endeavour of Upper Palaeolithic people took a number of different forms, some of them better represented in one phase than another. They ranged from small-scale carvings on such utilitarian objects as spear-throwers, etc., to large-scale multicolour paintings on cave walls, possibly the best known of all the forms involved [52]. The whole output can be considered under three headings: Engraving, Sculpture (in-the-round and in relief), and Painting.

Engraving is, in a sense, the simplest and most direct form of artistic expression (at least in a prehistoric context) and may well have preceded the other forms listed above, although this has not been proved. The principal tool used was the burin, mentioned earlier as one of the main achievements of Upper Palaeolithic tool manufacture. Engravings were executed not only on a relatively large scale, on cave walls, but also on a much smaller scale on utilitarian objects and on pieces of stone, ivory, etc., apparently without any particular function. It has been suggested that these latter, or some of them, may have been in the nature of artists' sketches, drawn out-of-doors from life, to be used later by the artist when drawing on a much bigger scale in the remote recesses of a cave. Although painting belongs on the whole to the later stages of the Upper Palaeolithic, it did not replace engraving which endured through the Gravettian, Solutrean and Magdalenian periods. During the latter period, indeed, engraving reached its peak artistically with fine naturalistic drawings of a wide range of animals [53].

Sculpture (which involves both carving in stone and other materials, and modelling in clay) represents an important aspect of Upper Palaeolithic art. Sculpture was produced in two forms: in-the-round, i.e. free-standing, and in relief, i.e. carved or modelled on a wall surface. In the field of free-standing or portable sculpture the so-called 'Venus' figures are among the most striking of all the artistic output in the Upper Palaeolithic period. Not the least interesting is their distribution, a great east–west band from southern Russia to the Franco-Spanish border some 2,000 miles away, coinciding closely with the distribution of the Gravettian culture and effectively disposing of the long-held assumption that Upper Palaeolithic art was centred exclusively on western Europe. The figures, usually only a few inches long, were either carved (in stone or ivory) or modelled (in clay, subsequently baked hard), and appear to have been connected with a fertility cult [54, 55].

53. Engraving of a reindeer on a schist plaque. As compared with the bulk of Upper Palaeolithic art, on the walls and roofs of dark caves, drawings such as this are easily portable. It has been suggested, therefore, that they acted as artists' sketches, made out-of-doors from life, to help them to work more easily in the remoter parts of the cave.

Breasts and buttocks were heavily emphasized at the expense of other parts of the anatomy and many such figures were pregnant. In addition to these, the Gravettians also carved or modelled a wide variety of animal figures (mammoth, lion, bear, wolf, reindeer, bison, etc.) in stone, chalk, ivory, clay, and probably in wood as well, although, unfortunately, nothing in the latter has survived.

For practical reasons, relief sculpture and modelling tended to be on a larger scale than figures-in-the-round. Only two famous examples will be quoted here. From the Cap Blanc rock shelter in the Dordogne, France, there is a magnificent frieze of horses carved in the rock in a fine, naturalistic style and dated to the Magdalenian period. Presumably some sort of stone pick, harder than the rock being carved, was used to rough out the shape, the final modelling and details being executed with flint burins. Relief modelling, as opposed to carving, is represented by the equally famous group of bison, fashioned in clay, in the Tuc d'Audoubert cave, also in France [56].

Painting (on cave walls) is the medium most popularly associated with Upper Palaeolithic art—understandably so, since the multicolour paintings produced in western Europe during the Magdalenian period probably represent the peak of Upper Palaeolithic artistic achievement. However, it is quite certain that painting began much earlier, in the Gravettian period, and was produced in many other areas as well, including Italy and Russia. Some so-called paintings appear not to be true paintings at all (i.e., carried out with liquid paint), but colour drawings executed with a crayon-like piece of some dry mineral colouring material. However, these are in a minority. The bulk of the cave-paintings were carried out with liquid paints applied in a variety of ways. The paint was the same sort of dry mineral colouring matter just mentioned, ground to a fine powder and mixed with fat, the juice of certain plants, or water. This mixture was applied in some cases with the finger tip and in others, almost certainly, with the point of a stick or a simple brush made from animal fur. A spraying technique also seems to have been used, with the paint sprayed, presumably, by mouth. The clearest examples of this are the 'negative' or 'reserve' hands, in which the artist has placed his hand on a flat rock surface and sprayed both hand and surrounding rock, leaving the shape of the hand outlined by the splash of paint. Close examination shows that some of the finest multicolour paintings were executed in this way.

The classic area for Upper Palaeolithic cave-painting is the Franco-Cantabrian region (south-west France and north-east Spain) where cave sites display a wide range of paintings, as well as artistic works in other techniques (engraving, sculpture, modelling). Several dozen sites are known (and there are probably many more awaiting discovery), but six in particular are generally considered to be of outstanding interest. These are: Altamira (Spain, the first discovery of cave art in 1879), Lascaux (discovered in 1940), Font de Gaume, Les Combarelles, Les Trois Frères and Niaux (all in France). In the use of colour and in lifelike rendering, Upper Palaeolithic painting reached its peak in the Franco-Cantabrian region and during the Magdalenian period, that is, during the last four or five thousand years of the Palaeolithic period as a whole, between c. 15,000 and 10,000 BC. Bison and horses, often in groups or friezes, and rendered in rich colours with a striking degree of realism, are among the main subjects depicted [38].

54, 55. Two Venus figurines: above, steatite figurine from Grimaldi, northern Italy; right, female statuette modelled in a mixture of clay and powdered bone, from Dolni Věstonice, Moravia. Such figurines are found over a wide area from south Russia to western Europe and are presumably part of some widespread fertility cult during the greater part of the Upper Palaeolithic period.

56. Figures of bison modelled in clay and set firmly against the sloping ground. From Le Tuc d'Audoubert, France. These are among the finest sculptures that have come down to us from the Upper Palaeolithic period.

One question which inevitably arises with regard to the whole subject of prehistoric art is the reason or purpose behind it. Quite clearly there is no single or simple answer to this; we can never know for certain what was in the mind of a prehistoric artist when he was carving a piece of ivory or painting on a cave wall. However, certain limited speculations are permissible. In many cases the art would appear to have been purely decorative, with no magical or religious significance. This is probably true of practical objects, such as spear-throwers, for example, where the carving of an animal head may have been simply to enhance its appearance. Whether this decorative approach extended beyond the sphere of portable objects (as far as cave-paintings, for example) it is impossible to say. The function of the 'Venus' figures, indicated by the emphasis of certain parts of the anatomy, has been suggested already. The major questions arise with regard to the cave art, the paintings, engravings and sculptures of the whole range of animals then in existence. It has been suggested that they are simply a form of prehistoric wallpaper, the embellishment of Upper Palaeolithic Man's domestic establishment. This may well be so, particularly in the later periods when the traditions and practice of cave art were already well established and an artist might be simply exercising his skill. However, this cannot account for all of the works known to exist. In many cases the paintings, etc., are in very remote parts of the caves, well away from the living areas and well away from daylight; even to see them must have required artificial light and the same must have been true for the artist executing them. In fact, the remains of simple lamps, made of hollowed-out stones, presumably filled with fat and lighted by a moss wick, have been found in a number of caves. If they were not merely wall decoration, then what was the reason for executing (in many cases) elaborate works of art where they could rarely be seen? There is room for endless speculation but here attention will be confined to two possible magico-religious explanations. In a number of cases spear-marks have been found on the animal figures depicted, as if someone had stabbed a spear at the drawing itself. This may have formed part of a cere-mony or ritual designed to ensure successful hunting. Having had a picture of the desired quarry drawn by an artist, possibly in a 'reserved' remote part of the cave, the hunters then went through all the motions of a hunt, including piercing the animal with their spears, thereby hoping through sympathetic magic to ensure an equally successful result to a forthcoming hunting trip. Since the hunting of game formed the whole basis of their livelihood, it is understandable that they would invoke all the help they could get to ensure its success.

The second explanation is also connected with the hunt. Some of the animals depicted can be seen to have been wounded. It has been suggested that this is a method of reserving or safeguarding the animal for a hunter who, having wounded an animal, has had to break off the pursuit for some reason, the approach of night, for example. By having it drawn in its wounded state, in a remote part of the cave, away from other eyes, he would ensure that it was safeguarded from other hunters and other animals until he could resume the pursuit himself the next day and complete the kill.

The Magdalenian period concludes the Palaeolithic stage of Man's exist-ence and brings the story down to *c.* 10,000 BC, from which point it will be resumed in each of the succeeding chapters.

4

Near-eastern Archaeology

The end of the Palaeolithic period, *c.* 10,000 BC, ushered in the Mesolithic phase, which is of particular importance in the Near East because it witnessed there a fundamental change in Man's way of life—from hunting and food-gathering to food-producing through the medium of domesticated animals and cultivated plants. The achievement of these new methods of securing the food supply has in the past been termed the 'Neolithic Revolution', but it is now clear that the essential steps were, in fact, taken in the pre-ceding Mesolithic phase, and were, moreover, spread over a much longer period of time (*c.* 3000 years) than is implied by the term 'revolution', with its suggestion of a single dramatic event. The term Mesolithic is more commonly used than Middle Stone Age, because the latter term has a rather different meaning in Africa south of the Sahara and might cause confusion.

Although the relationship of European glacial periods to African pluvial periods (i.e. periods of much greater rainfall than at present) has still to be established, it is likely that during the last glaciation at least, there was rather more rainfall in North Africa and the Near East than there is at present. The withdrawal of the ice cap would have drawn the rain-bearing westerly winds back to their normal track across Europe, leaving the areas just mentioned a prey to increasingly dry conditions from 10,000 BC on. Recent research has shown that it was in the Near East that the domestication of animals and the cultivation of plants began, shortly after 10,000 BC, and it may well be that the diminishing supply of game, following the climatic change, had not a little to do with Man's efforts to control his food supply.

·The methods by which Mesolithic Man converted wild species into domestic types are a matter for speculation but the process may have started with specialized hunting, the concentration of the chase on one particular species. In this way, the hunters would acquire a special knowledge of its habits and seasonal movements which would make its pursuit very much easier. Such a close relationship is a very probable first step in the process of domestication. With their whole livelihood bound up with one particular species or herd, it would be a logical next step not only to protect it, but also to get it ever more firmly under their control, and in such precautions are further possible stages in the process. Complete domestication would almost certainly be a matter of generations, perhaps centuries, rather than years, but the 3000 years between 10,000 and 7000 BC would be ample time for the whole process to be carried through and for domesticated animals to be well established at the beginning of the Neolithic period.

The other aspect of farming, cultivated plants, also had its origins in the Near East. These likewise were developed from wild prototypes by methods

57. Opposite: bronze head of an Akkadian king, probably Naram-Sin, builder of the royal palace at Tell Brak. Height: 14⅛ in. The Akkadian period lasted from *c.* 2400 BC until *c.* 2200 BC.

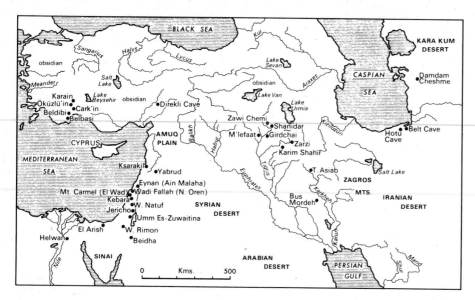

58. Left: distribution map of sites during the Mesolithic and proto-Neolithic periods in the ancient Near East, i.e. from *c.* 10,000 BC until *c.* 7000 BC, when the full Neolithic began.

59. Opposite: Neolithic portrait head from Jericho with features of plaster on a human skull. The eyes are inserted cowrie shells. Pre-pottery Neolithic B period, Jericho, from 7000 BC on. ▶

which can only be guessed at. There is archaeological evidence that wild cereals were regularly harvested by hunting peoples in the Near East. In a deteriorating climate the natural stands of such cereals would almost certainly shrink in area, and an attempt to make good the loss by planting and caring for some of the seeds seems a very likely move. Another possible development is the collection of seed to provide a portable food reserve should other (i.e. hunting) sources fail. However achieved, by *c.* 7000 BC, Neolithic peoples of the Near East were fully equipped with a range of domesticated cereal species.

The achievement of a mixed-farming economy between 10,000 and 7000 BC had enormous implications for the further development of the human race. The assurance of a regular food supply removed the necessity for nomadic existence and made possible settlement in one place; the cycle of cultivation in any case made it necessary to stay near the sown fields. Man could now build permanent houses, grouped in villages, and develop heavier domestic equipment than had been possible under nomadic conditions. Successful farming produced a surplus of food which enabled part of the population to earn a living by specialization, i.e. by concentrating on a particular activity. This led in turn to the development of a wide range of skills and these to the great artistic and technical achievements of the Near-eastern civilizations. The centres where such skills were concentrated were no longer villages but cities, much smaller than anything we would call a city today but nonetheless cities in the social, economic, and political sense of the word, and this very early development of urban life foreshadows similar developments over much of the Old World during the next six thousand years.

For archaeological purposes, the Near East can be divided into three regions: Mesopotamia, Anatolia, and Palestine. Each of these will be considered in turn from *c.* 4500 BC onwards. For the period prior to this, however, the Near East will be treated as a whole in a separate introductory section.

THE EARLY PERIOD (10,000–4500 BC)

The earlier part of this period, the Mesolithic (10,000–7000 BC), now tends to be divided into two parts: a Mesolithic proper (10,000–9000 BC), and a

second period (9000–7000 BC) during which the so-called Neolithic Revolution took place, now more commonly termed proto-Neolithic (i.e. about-to-be Neolithic). Various Mesolithic groups are known in Syria, Palestine, southwest Anatolia, the Zagros mountains, and the area south of the Caspian Sea, but these will not be considered here.

During the proto-Neolithic period (9000–7000 BC) and in the area under discussion, the fundamental discoveries of agriculture and stock-breeding were made, bringing in their train many other important changes [58]. In the Zagros mountains in northern Iraq, half a dozen sites illustrate the proto-Neolithic stage, two of the most important being Shanidar and Zawi Chemi. Already in the earliest levels (c. 9000 BC) at the latter site there were domesticated sheep, and the stone equipment included grinding-stones, possibly for the processing of cereal grains. For occupation, caves were used, but there were also villages or hamlets of circular huts with stone foundations and a lighter superstructure. In both caves and villages there were storage (later rubbish) pits dug into the ground. At Shanidar there was a cemetery of twenty-eight burials, indicating a considerable regard for the disposal of the dead. The material equipment included flint axes, knives and sickle blades, stone beads and pendants, and bone rings, awls and pins.

Some 600 miles west of the Zagros group, in Palestine, another group of sites illustrates the proto-Neolithic phase in the form of the Natufian culture. Like the Zagros group, the Natufian people lived in both caves and villages of up to fifty circular huts with numerous storage pits. The huts were built of a substructure of stone, covered with plaster, with a light, possibly conical, superstructure supported by a centre post. There is as yet no evidence of domestic animals, but the presence of sickle blades and grinding-stones suggests a knowledge of cultivation or at least the practice of reaping wild cereals and therefore the first steps in such knowledge. However, much of the food supply still came from hunting and fishing. Again, there is evidence of careful disposal of the dead, including what appears to be a chieftain's burial at the village of Eynan. The material equipment of the Natufians included bone awls, needles and spatulae, and stone fishing-net sinkers, polishing tools, bowls, and beakers.

Among the proto-Neolithic sites in Palestine was Jericho, where there was a Natufian village around 8500 BC. Around 8000 BC this small village was replaced by what can only be described as a town, some ten acres in extent. Pottery was still unknown and this phase, from c. 8000 to 7000 BC, is known as Pre-Pottery Neolithic A, to be followed later (after 7000 BC) by Pre-Pottery Neolithic B [59]. The Pre-Pottery Neolithic A settlement consisted of round houses, 12–16 ft. in diameter, with mud-brick walls on stone foundations, and domed roofs. The floors, below outside ground level, were covered with mud plaster. At a later stage, the town was impressively fortified with a rock-cut ditch, a stone-built wall and at least one circular stone tower. The population is estimated to have been at least two thousand people. This rapid emergence of a thriving urban centre was almost certainly due to two factors: a well-developed agriculture, based on wheat and barley (domestic animals there have not yet been proved), and trade. The finds from the site indicate long-distance contacts with such places as Sinai, the Red Sea, and Anatolia, and are probably the result of a trade in which Jericho was the main market. Other Palestinian sites of the same period are Wadi Fallah, Abu Suwan, and Beidha.

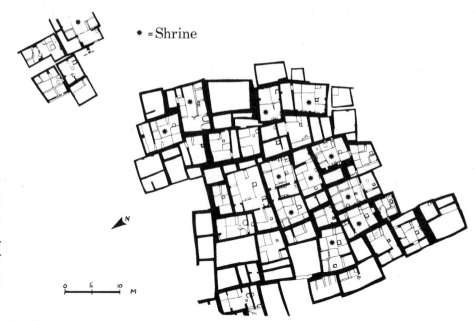

* = Shrine

60, 61. Right: plan of level VIB at Çatal Hüyük, *c.* 6000 BC. This shows very clearly the 'agglutinative' character of ancient Near-eastern building. In Europe, throughout the prehistoric period, buildings remained free-standing. In the Near East they tended to fuse into a single mass of rooms with communication by means of courtyards and, presumably, across the roofs. Below: a reconstruction drawing by Alan Sorrell of a funerary rite in Shrine E, level VII.

0 5 10 M

Around 7000 BC new settlers arrived in the Jordan valley from the north and at Jericho mark the beginning of the Pre-Pottery Neolithic B period. One of the main changes is architectural. The separate round huts of the preceding period are replaced by a mass of rectangular rooms side-by-side with communication, in the absence of streets, by means of a series of courtyards. Buildings were constructed of long, cigar-shaped mud bricks on stone foundations and walls and floors were carefully plastered and painted. The settlement as a whole was larger than its predecessor and was not at first defended. Among the smaller remains are fine tanged flint arrowheads (suggesting that hunting was still important), oval querns (for grinding grain), limestone bowls and platters and coiled, round floor mats for use in the home. This Pre-Pottery Neolithic B phase is also well represented at Beidha, where in addition to living quarters there are remains of many workshops, suggesting that the town was a considerable commercial centre.

One other Pre-Pottery Neolithic site remains to be described: Haçilar in Anatolia. The village of Haçilar was founded around 7000 BC, about the same time as Pre-Pottery Neolithic B at Jericho to which it is a comparable phase. It consisted of rectangular rooms of mud brick on stone foundations, with carefully plastered walls and floors. Agriculture was known but there was no proof of the domestication of animals except for the dog. The material equipment included bone awls, sickle blades, and stone axes. There was no pottery, but there were remains of marble bowls, and probably other containers were made of wood or leather.

The next phase in Anatolia (c. 6500–5500 BC) is represented by Çatal Hüyük, covering some thirty-two acres, for its date an extremely large site and quite clearly very different from the village settlement of Haçilar. Only about an acre of the site has been excavated and this area consists of houses and shrines, rectangular in shape and built of mud brick [60]. These were of one storey only, forming a solid mass of rooms, except for occasional open courts. Access was otherwise through the flat roof. Like Jericho in the Pre-Pottery Neolithic B phase, the economy was based on mixed farming and trade, which was particularly well developed in obsidian, sea-shells, special stones, ochres and other paints. Quite clearly Çatal Hüyük owed not a little of its pre-eminence to trade [61].

The late Neolithic in Anatolia is represented by the upper layers at Haçilar, notably Level VI, where remains of some very substantial houses were found [62]. These were over 30 ft. long and nearly 20 ft. wide, with mud-brick walls some 3 ft. thick on stone foundations, and with evidence of an upper floor, no doubt of lighter construction. The houses consisted largely of a single main room, with an oven as a regular feature, and some sub-division by means of screen walls constructed of post and plaster. Haçilar VI was destroyed c. 5600 BC and the remaining layers, V–I, take the story down to c. 5000 BC.

In northern Mesopotamia sites such as Shanidar, Zawi Chemi, and Karim Shahir are succeeded c. 6500 BC by the village of Qal'at Jarmo, with about twenty to twenty-five houses and no less than sixteen stratigraphical layers. In the upper five layers pottery appeared; in the earlier periods stone bowls, skins, and bitumen-lined baskets were probably used instead. There is now clear evidence of agriculture in the form of wheat, barley, peas, and lentils, and dogs and goats at least were domesticated. Other species (pig, sheep, gazelle, and wild cattle) were hunted. The stone equipment included

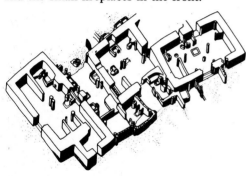

62. Isometric drawing of a group of houses from Haçilar VI, c. 5600 BC. Note the horseshoe-shaped ovens in the back walls and the small fireplaces in the front.

63. Map of ancient Mesopotamia.

axes with polished edges, querns, mortars, mace-heads, bracelets and cups and bowls for which carefully selected, veined stones were used.

A further stage in Mesopotamian development is represented by Hassuna and the Hassuna culture. Both architecture and pottery showed great advances at the site of Hassuna itself. In its developed phase (layers II–IV) it had well-planned, rectangular houses with several rooms and hearths, ovens, and storage pits. The pottery included one form of painted ware, red-on-cream, and in the later stages (from level IV onwards, *c.* 5500 BC) another, known as Samarra ware, which included painted animal and human figures. In both the Hassuna and Samarra cultures, settlements were established in areas where irrigation would have been necessary to carry on agriculture, and this is the beginning of a long Mesopotamian tradition.

The last phase of this early period is the Halaf culture which covered a great east–west band across northern Mesopotamia as far as north Syria and south-east Asia Minor. Its outstanding products were its polychrome painted pottery and its architecture. The decoration on the pottery is largely geometric and is carried out in red or black paint (sometimes both) on a cream or apricot background, with a degree of precision and sophistication that is surprising for so early a period. The architecture is equally unusual. The houses consisted of two rooms: a circular, domed inner room and a long rectangular room with a gabled roof attached to one side of it. The circular room could be as much as 20 or 30 ft. in diameter, and the rectangular room up to 60 ft. long, both with walls 6–7 ft. thick, so that quite clearly these were very considerable buildings. They formed villages set along paved roads. The Halaf villagers grew wheat, barley, and flax and kept cattle, goats, sheep, and dogs, and the diet was further supplemented by hunting. Trade was well developed with contacts from the Mediterranean to the Persian Gulf.

The Halaf culture began *c.* 5400 BC and came to an end *c.* 4500 BC, to be replaced by the Ubaid culture, which leads directly on to the Sumerian culture of the next section.

85

MESOPOTAMIA

Mesopotamia, the 'Land of the Two Rivers' (Tigris and Euphrates), embraces successively the civilizations of the Sumerians, Akkadians, Babylonians and Assyrians [63]. The Sumerian dynastic period begins *c.* 3000 BC, but prior to this is a period of about 1500 years, when the foundations of Sumerian civilization were laid.

THE UBAID PERIOD

About 4500 BC or shortly thereafter, the widespread Halaf culture was replaced by the Ubaid culture and this is in a sense the first phase of Sumerian civilization. The Ubaid culture represents the first move into the fertile alluvial valleys of the Tigris and Euphrates and, presumably, the practice of well-organized irrigation. Earlier cultures had been concentrated on higher ground overlooking the valley proper. The site of Ubaid itself, which gives its name to the whole culture, was a relatively humble agricultural village, but other sites of the same period (Tell Shahrein, Ur, and Tepe Gawra) show that there were much larger settlements, towns built of mud brick, the most outstanding monuments of which were large and elaborate temples. The Ubaid culture also saw the beginnings of metallurgy in cast copper axes and other objects. At Tell Shahrein (ancient Eridu) there is a long sequence of superimposed temples which is invaluable for the early chronology of Sumeria. By Ubaid times the standard temple plan was tripartite: a long, narrow central room with a row of smaller rooms on either side. However, the most spectacular architectural achievements were the temples of level XIII at Tepe Gawra which were ranged round three sides of an open court, the sheer scale of the whole complex marking a decisive shift from village to urban life [64].

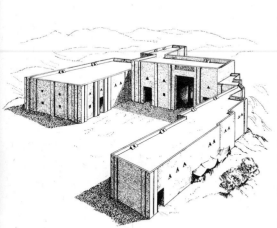

64. Reconstruction of the temple complex of the end of the Ubaid period (*c.* 4500–3800 BC) from level XIII at Tepe Gawra. Nothing more effectively demonstrates the advance of the Ubaid people from village to city life than this temple group, which would have been far beyond the resources of any purely agricultural village community.

THE URUK PERIOD

The Ubaid stage lasted for about 700 years (4500–3800 BC). It was succeeded by the Uruk (modern Warka) phase, from 3800 to 3200 BC. Architecturally, the outstanding monument is the White Temple at Uruk itself. This is the culmination of a long series of successively rebuilt temples on the same site and on the traditional tripartite plan of a long central room or hall with two rows of smaller rooms on either side. The temple measured 70 × 60 ft. and stood on a great mud-brick platform 45 ft. high, an early example of the later practice of placing temples on the top of stepped mounds or ziggurats. Apart from architecture, there were important developments in other fields. Uruk pottery was made for the first time on the wheel and not by hand and was therefore presumably now a specialist and not a domestic craft. Writing, still of a simple type, appeared on baked clay tablets, and seals, first stamp and later cylinder seals, came into use as a means of stamping or impressing the owner's mark on to his property.

THE JEMDET NASR PERIOD

The last, relatively short, phase before the Sumerian dynastic period is the Jemdet Nasr period, named after a small site between Baghdad and Babylon where the pottery which distinguishes the phase (painted designs in black and red on buff-coloured pots) was first discovered. At Uruk, the Jemdet Nasr phase is marked by a whole complex of buildings surrounding the main feature, a raised terrace, on which presumably a temple stood. The

buildings were in groups, each surrounding an open court, and included houses (presumably for priests and officials) and administrative offices. More generally, the Jemdet Nasr phase saw a further development in writing, from the evidence of temple accounts, the signs now becoming more conventionalized and less pictographic. Vessels of copper and silver were now in use and there is clear evidence of large-scale sculpture. Human and animal figures, near life-size in a number of cases, were carved in marble and limestone with eyes sometimes inlaid with shell.

THE EARLY DYNASTIC PERIOD

Shortly after 3000 BC and following the Jemdet Nasr period, the dynastic period of Sumerian civilization began. The dynastic world was one of city states, about a dozen of which are known, including Ur, Uruk, Kish, Larsa and Nippur. The emergence of dynastic kings or leaders in the separate cities after the Jemdet Nasr period marks a change in the status of the priest and of the temple. In the formative period of Sumerian civilization (4500–3000 BC) the temple formed the nucleus of the developing urban centres, with the leadership of the community as a whole exercised by the priests, at least in times of peace. But increasing prosperity led to rivalry and war between the separate cities, and between them and the poorer nomadic peoples of the highlands and the desert, so that (at first temporary) war leaders were required. Inevitably such leadership came to be wielded in times of peace as well and in this transfer of power lay the beginnings of dynastic Sumeria, each city having its own petty dynasty.

These changes are reflected in the temple architecture of the dynastic period, for example in the temple dedicated to the moon god Sin at Khafaje, about seventy miles north-east of Baghdad. In the Jemdet Nasr period the temple was a fairly normal tripartite structure. Gradually, however, the

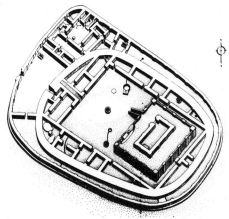

65, 66. The Temple Oval at Khafaje: aerial view and isometric restoration.

87

range of rooms on one side was suppressed and an irregular courtyard was added on the other with subsidiary buildings around its edges. By dynastic times the whole layout had been revised and there was now a clearcut temple complex cut off from the rest of the city by strong walls, indicating the withdrawal of the priesthood in favour of secular leaders. The cella or main cult room is still long and narrow with the cult platform at one end, but now with only a single entrance at the other. Access to the whole complex is via a staircase and an entrance hall immediately inside the enclosure wall. This gives access to a courtyard around which all the buildings are grouped. From the courtyard access to the cella is via a large vestibule, so that altogether the main cult room is as withdrawn and remote from the rest of the city as it possibly could be. The remaining rooms around the court were for the priests and for offices connected with the service of the temple. Instead of being a free-standing, easily accessible building, the temple had now become somewhat remote, with presumably controlled and limited access, withdrawn behind its enclosing wall in the manner of a medieval monastery. This courtyard style is found also in the Abu temple at Tell Asmar (ancient Eshnunna), a short distance to the north-east of Khafaje. In Jemdet Nasr times this was very irregular in plan, but by the dynastic period it had assumed a rectangular plan with no less than three long, rectangular cult rooms, a priest's room and an entrance vestibule, all grouped around a square courtyard, the whole complex contained within a strong enclosing wall with a single entrance.

The Sin temple at Khafaje and the Abu temple at Tell Asmar were still somewhat irregular in plan and were built on a modest scale. The Shara temple at Tell Agrab, on the other hand, was a vast and carefully planned complex within a massive, fortress-like enclosing wall (over 200 ft. square and c. 12 ft. thick), reinforced with buttresses, and with a single entrance near the eastern corner. Within was a whole series of connected courtyards with various buildings opening from them. The entrance courtyard gave access to the priest's quarters (to the west) and, to the north, to another courtyard, with rooms, possibly administrative offices, grouped around it. This second court gave direct access to two other courts and indirect access, via one of them, to a third, making five interconnected courtyards in all. The south court led to a vestibule and this in turn to the cella or main cult room, 60 ft. long with the platform at the north end. There were two smaller shrines beyond, in the west angle of the enclosure. In its size and its regular, rectangular layout, the Shara temple foreshadows the large and complex temples of later periods of Mesopotamian civilization [67].

The same elements of great size (325 × 250 ft.) and powerful enclosing walls are evident in the so-called Temple Oval at Khafaje, although it is a mixture of the new, rectilinear planning and older, more irregular layout [65, 66]. The cella, some 50 ft. long, stands on a rectangular platform, about 100 ft. long, 85 ft. wide and 19 ft. high, standing within a rectangular enclosure 190 × 125 ft. This in turn is contained within a great oval encircling wall, c. 12 ft. thick, with a second, smaller wall beyond. Between the two ovals and adjacent to the entrance were the priests' quarters, similar in layout to those at the Shara temple. There is a slightly smaller oval enclosing wall (275 × 235 ft.) around the High Temple at Al Ubaid.

In addition to walls enclosing temples, there were now also city walls, made necessary no doubt by the inter-city rivalry which produced the secular

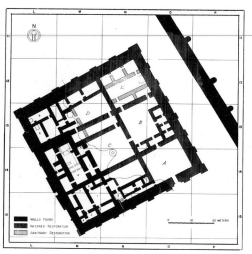

67. Reconstructed plan of the main level of the Shara temple at Tell Agrab.

leaders. The city wall at Uruk was some six miles in circumference and between 14 and 16 ft. thick, with semi-circular towers and entrances with rectangular towers.

With the emergence of secular as opposed to religious leaders, palaces to accommodate them inevitably appeared. One such is known from this period at Kish, and is a model of the rectangular, carefully planned architecture. It consists of two rectangular blocks, the more massive northern block having been built first, the southern block being a later addition. The northern block (c. 310 × 175 ft.) is surrounded by an enormous enclosing wall some 14 ft. thick. There is an impressive entrance block flanked by towers beyond the eastern end and an open court at the west around which are grouped the principal rooms. The southern block, less massively built (230 × 120 ft.), has two very large rooms at the western end, one of which may have had a row of pillars down the middle to support the roof.

Among the outstanding monuments of the period, apart from temples and palaces, are the Royal Tombs of the first dynasty of the city of Ur which enjoyed its initial great period of prosperity at this time [32, 33].

In the field of sculpture, the outstanding products of the Sumerian early dynastic period are the worshippers, male or female standing or seated figures with hands clasped across the chest, placed in the temples as a substitute for the worshipper himself. The male figures, a foot or so in height, are usually shown bearded and are naked above the waist [68]. The lower part of the figure consists of a skirt with heavy tufted decoration in horizontal rows, with the ankles and feet just visible below. In the female figures the garment is carried up over one shoulder, covering the breasts. Limestone, gypsum, and alabaster were the main materials used.

The early dynastic period was brought to an end by the invasion or infiltration of Semitic-speaking peoples among the non-Semitic Sumerians around 2400 BC. Under Sargon, ruler of Agade or Akkad, a city as yet unidentified but near Babylon, the separate city states were welded, at least for a period, into a single political unit. Henceforward this northern part of Sumer was known as Akkad and the new language and the period as Akkadian.

THE AKKADIAN PERIOD

Under Sargon and his successors, the kingdom of Akkad extended not only over southern Mesopotamia (Sumer and Akkad) but also over the northern area (later to be known as Assyria), as well as parts of Syria and Anatolia. Unfortunately, the principal city of the Akkadians, Akkad (or Agade) itself (founded c. 2370 BC), although known by name, has not yet been discovered on the ground, so that information on Akkadian architecture is meagre. Many existing Sumerian buildings were added-to during the period, but of purely Akkadian architecture there is a noticeable shortage. There are, however, remains of two palaces, at Tell Brak and Ashur (later capital of the Assyrian empire), which indicate how important the royal residence had become as compared with the temple. Both buildings are clearly the result of very careful and very regular planning. The Tell Brak palace, erected by the Akkadian king, Naram-Sin, was contained within an enormous, rectangular perimeter wall (320 × 290 ft., c. 31 ft. thick), entered through a single, monumental gatehouse [69]. This gave access to the main courtyard (125 ft. square), surrounded by a range of long, very narrow rooms.

68. Gypsum statuette of a man, from Tell Asmar, early dynastic period (c. 3000–2400 BC), one of the worshippers, so-called because they were placed in temples as a substitute for the worshipper himself. Height: 19⅛ in.

89

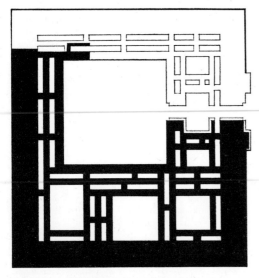

69. Plan of the palace of Naram-Sin, king of Akkad, at Tell Brak. Note the very regular planning and the massive surrounding wall (*c*. 31 ft. thick). The main courtyard was 125 ft. square and the whole structure was 320 ft. long and 290 ft. wide.

Three smaller courtyards were similarly surrounded. The so-called Old Palace at Ashur is built on very similar lines, although its perimeter wall (345 × 310 ft.) is less massive, *c*. 12 ft. thick. It has a large main courtyard (115 × 100 ft.) into which the entrance led, and a whole range of smaller courtyards, each surrounded by small rooms. The Akkadian Palace at Eshnunna (Tell Asmar) is on a much smaller scale and is in any case the result of adding-to an existing building. Because of this it lacks the careful, Akkadian layout of the two buildings just considered, and may, in fact, be simply a large dwelling-house rather than a royal palace.

Of Akkadian sculpture only two important works will be mentioned here. One is a magnificent life-size bronze head of a king, probably Naram-Sin himself, which is eloquent testimony of the Akkadian's complete mastery of the techniques of hollow-casting and chasing in the fine detail [57]. The other is a stone stele, also of Naram-Sin, celebrating a victory over the Lullubi tribe on the Iranian plateau. The slab is about 7 ft. high and 3 ft. wide and shows Naram-Sin at the head of his army advancing into the mountains and tramping his enemy underfoot. Action and movement are the keynotes of the scene and the setting is conveyed by the stepped arrangement, the trees, the mountain, and the stars, however schematically these are represented.

The Akkadian period lasted about a century and a half, until *c*. 2200 BC, when it, in turn, was overthrown by the invasion of the Guti, a tribe from the Iranian plateau, an ever-present source of danger to any dynasty in the Tigris/Euphrates valley. The southern part of the country, the original Sumer, was relatively unaffected and there was a Sumerian revival there, but one which inevitably incorporated the results of a century and a half of Akkadian domination, so that the period is best described as Sumero-Akkadian or neo-Sumerian. Further north, the Guti remained in control until they were expelled by Utu-Legal of Uruk.

THE SUMERO–AKKADIAN PERIOD

This was a period of great building activity in all the cities of Mesopotamia— in temples, palaces and tombs. It was also the period when, for a while, the city of Ur, under its third dynasty, was the capital of Sumeria. In the field of temple-building there were two main developments. The platforms on which many temples stood were probably the result of continual rebuilding on the same site. In the Sumero-Akkadian period this platform achieved the ziggurat form, the high, stepped structures so closely associated with Meso-potamian archaeology. One of the finest examples of this form, and one of the best preserved, is the ziggurat of Ur-Nammu at Ur [70, 71]. It owes its preservation mainly to the fact that the outer casing of the structure was built of baked brick instead of the usual sun-dried mud brick. Its base measure-ments were 195 × 140 ft. and it consisted of three platforms, one above the other, rising to about 85 ft., with the temple on the topmost platform. At the front, three long impressive stairways meet at the terrace, on the first stage from which a single stairway leads on up to the second and third platforms and the crowning temple. The ziggurat stood within a great court (360 × 260 ft.) with thick walls (*c*. 13 ft. thick) and impressive entrances, with a smaller court beyond (225 × 165 ft.), which had even thicker walls and more monumental entrances. The ziggurat at Uruk was similar in size (*c*. 175 ft. square at base) and stood within the same sort of complex of an inner and an outer court.

The second development in temple building, the broad cella, took place
in those built on level ground. The ideal Sumero-Akkadian temple was now
built on an axial plan, with entrance, forecourt, broad vestibule or ante-cella
and broad cella with a niche or recess for the throne, all on a single axis.
This direct, open approach to the head of the temple is in marked contrast
to the circuitous approach involved in such earlier temples as Tell Asmar
and Tell Agrab. The Ningal temple complex at Ur is a good example of the
new style of temple. It is contained within a huge, almost square, enclosing
wall (c. 235 ft. square), some 15 ft. thick, with towered entrances in the north
and south walls. The temple proper is in the southern half of the complex
and consists of an entrance hall, a courtyard, a vestibule and a broad cella
with a recessed throne in the back wall, all on a single axis c. 130 ft. long. The
temple of Enki in the same city is similarly built, consisting of a gatehouse,
forecourt, antechamber and cella on an axis about 100 ft. long. The Shu-Sin
temple at Tell Asmar has the same axial plan without the antechamber.

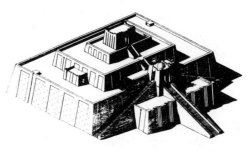

70, 71. The existing remains and a reconstruction drawing of the ziggurat at Ur
built by Ur-Nammu, king of the city during
the third dynasty, when Ur was the capital
of Sumeria. Sumero-Akkadian period,
c. 2200–1990 BC.

The palace of Ur-Nammu and Shulgi at Ur was very much in the Akkadian
tradition as seen at Tell Brak and Ashur. Although much smaller (c. 165 ft.
square), and with a thinner perimeter wall (c. 6 ft.), it is built on the same
lines, with a single entrance giving access to a series of courts, one of them
quite clearly the principal court, each with a series of rooms opening off it.

The most unusual monuments of the Sumero-Akkadian period are the
Royal Tombs of the third dynasty at Ur, close to the pit graves of the first
dynasty mentioned earlier (p. 89). Such structures are an unusual episode
in Mesopotamian archaeology where, unlike Egypt, there is no previous, or
subsequent, tradition of monumental funerary architecture. The tombs consist of underground vaulted burial chambers with steps leading down to them
and a superstructure built above them, after they were bricked up, in the
form of a dwelling-house—just as in Egypt the mastaba tomb was based on
the house of the living. The Royal complex at Ur involved three house super-
structures forming a single mass. The largest, central house (c. 105 × 85 ft.)
had walls 8 ft. thick and consisted, as did the other two, of a central courtyard
with rooms opening off on all four sides. The houses attached to it on either
side followed the same principle but were on a smaller scale. There was

provision for offerings to be made to the deceased in the rooms immediately above the tombs.

The sculpture of the period is well illustrated by the numerous statues discovered at the city of Lagash (modern Telloh), particularly statues of its ruler Gudea, a contemporary of the third dynasty at Ur. The larger figures were mostly of diorite, a very hard stone, and most figures, large or small, conform to the earlier pattern exemplified by the 'worshipper' figures (above p. 89), with a static rather than a dynamic pose, and with hands clasped across the chest [72].

In its turn, the third dynasty of Ur was overthrown by invading tribes from the mountains and the desert and a period of some confusion ensued. The beginnings of a return to more settled conditions were marked by the establishment of the first dynasty of Canaanite Kings at Babylon, c. 1990 BC. Under the sixth king of the dynasty, Hammurabi (c. 1792–50 BC), Babylon became the centre of an empire covering virtually the whole of Mesopotamia. This persisted, although growing weaker after Hammurabi's death, until 1595 BC when the capital, Babylon, was sacked by the Hittites.

THE BABYLONIAN PERIOD

One of the best surviving examples of Babylonian temple architecture, actually from the reign of Hammurabi, is the Ishtar-Kititum temple at Ishchali, which stands within a rectangular temple complex (320 × 220 ft.) with impressive towered gateways on the eastern and southern sides. A large forecourt (140 × 100 ft.), surrounded by rooms, at a lower level, leads via a staircase to one side of the temple forecourt. This has its own impressive towered gateway and gatehouse from the exterior, and at the opposite end gives access to an ante-cella and broad cella with a rear niche. All of these features are on the same axis and the plan is a direct continuation of the Sumero-Akkadian tradition. There is a similar axial, broad cella temple at Tell Harmal. The Ashur temple complex at Ashur is of the same general dimensions as the Ishchali complex (c. 340 × 175 ft.) and is similar in plan, but because only foundation walls have been discovered, neither the position nor the shape of the cella is known.

The palace at Mari has been attributed to the ruler Zimrilim, a contemporary of Hammurabi, and therefore to the Babylonian period, but it seems likely that much of the structure, and possibly the whole of the ground plan, goes back to the Sumero-Akkadian period. It cannot be regarded, therefore, as exclusively typical of the Babylonian period, although no doubt considerable additions were made to the original structure at this time. The palace area was roughly 400 ft. square and consisted of a series of connected courtyards with surrounding rooms. The largest courtyard (no. 131) was about 145 × 100 ft., with a smaller court and a towered gatehouse to the north. To the west was another large court, no. 106 (c. 90 × 80 ft.). Many of the small courts with their surrounding rooms conformed to the pattern of the typical Sumerian courtyard house.

In the field of sculpture only two famous pieces will be mentioned here. One is the stele in diorite containing the law code of Hammurabi, written in cuneiform, below the relief sculpture showing Hammurabi himself, standing before the seated figure of the Lord of Light and Righteousness to whom the code is dedicated [73]. The other, a piece of sculpture-in-the-round, is a nearly life-size figure of a water goddess with a horned crown and a long,

72. Sumerian statuette of a woman, 11¾ in. high, from Lagash, c. 2500 BC. Like the statuette of a man from Tell Asmar [68] this was a worshipper figure, in this case female, placed in the temple she wished to honour.

73. Top of the diorite stele inscribed in the cuneiform script with the law code of Hammurabi, from Susa. Hammurabi (*c.* 1792–50 BC), sixth king of the first dynasty, was one of the greatest rulers of Babylon, famous, among many other things, for his code of law. On this stele he stands before the seated figure of the Lord of Light and Righteousness, to whom the code is dedicated.

74. Reconstructed façade of the temple of Innin at Uruk, Kassite period (*c.* 1595–1157 BC). Among other architectural innovations, the Kassites were responsible for the introduction of relief sculpture as part of the decoration of buildings. This frieze, about 10 ft. high, consisted alternately of a mountain god and a river goddess, each set in a niche, the whole composition being formed of baked clay bricks. (In the background, through the arch, can be seen the whole of Hammurabi's stele–73.)

flounced dress, holding a vase, found in the palace at Mari. Water presumably was made to flow out of the vase since a channel for it is drilled in the thickness of the statue. In the same palace there is good evidence of elaborate wall-painting, not only in the Babylonian period but also in the preceding Sumero-Akkadian period.

Babylon was destroyed in a raid by the Hittite king Mursilis in 1595 BC. Subsequently the city was taken over by the Kassites, one of the ever-threatening mountain tribes, who set up their own Kassite dynasty which ruled Babylon for the next four centuries, until *c.* 1157 BC.

THE KASSITE PERIOD

In spite of falling within the general Mesopotamian tradition, the architecture of this period embraces several important developments which are quite clearly a Kassite and not a Sumerian, Akkadian, or Babylonian contribution. One such development is exemplified in the temple of the goddess Innin at Uruk. It was a free-standing building (itself an unusual feature), with projecting bastions at the corners and an unusual ground plan which lacked the normal courtyard between the entrance and the cella. The most unusual part, however, was the external elevation, where the lower part, to a height of about 10 ft., consisted of a frieze of baked clay bricks moulded, in alternate niches in the wall, in the form of a mountain god and a river goddess. This use of architectural sculpture is something new in Mesopotamia and is an important Kassite contribution which was to be further developed in later periods [74].

One of the great patrons of Kassite building was King Kurigalzu I (from *c.* 1400 BC on). At Ur he pulled down and completely rebuilt the ziggurat complex, built an entirely new temple of unusual plan for the wife of the Moon God (the Ningal temple), and another temple with an impressive barrel-vaulted doorway. Kurigalzu was probably responsible also for the buildings at Dur-Kurigalzu near Babylon, where there are remains of a ziggurat, a temple, a palace, and two towers, the precise functions of which are unknown.

The most notable pieces of Kassite sculpture are the *kudurrus*, in the form of either a stele (a flat, upright slab) or an obelisk or pillar (i.e. round or rectangular in section) [75]. The primary purpose of these stones was to make

75. Limestone *kudurru*, from Susa. Height: 21¼ in.

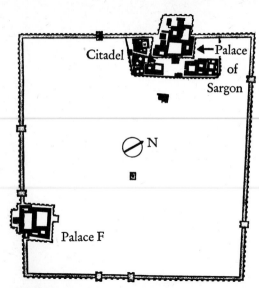

76. Plan of the city of Dur Sharrukin (modern Khorsabad), founded by Sargon II (722–705 BC).

a proclamation in the form of a cuneiform inscription, so that the sculptured portion is, in fact, of secondary importance. The proclamation usually concerned the granting to a particular person—an official or a priest—of a piece of land, or the remission of certain taxes, sometimes associated with the imposition of certain specific duties. The subjects of the sculptures were usually of a religious or mythological nature.

The Kassite dynasty of Babylon was brought to an end c. 1157 BC by the growing power of the Assyrians. Thereafter Babylon was something of a backwater for about 500 years, until the neo-Babylonian period (626–539 BC). The centre of power and interest now shifted decisively from the land of Sumer and Akkad to northern Mesopotamia and the land of the Assyrians.

THE ASSYRIANS

The Assyrian story, however, begins long before the overthrow of the Kassites. All through the second millenium the people of the city state of Ashur were striving to achieve and then retain their independence, with at first mixed success. Although at one stage the princes of Ashur seem to have been sufficiently independent to have their own trading posts in Anatolia, they were for long periods under the political and cultural domination of either Babylon to the south or the kingdom of the Mitanni to the north. Assyria finally achieved independence shortly after 1400 BC, politically on more or less equal terms with the Hittites and the Egyptians. This early Assyrian period lasted about two centuries, until c. 1200 BC, and will not be considered here. Thereafter the whole east Mediterranean/Near-eastern world was affected by the massive folk movements. Associated with these was the migration of the Aramaeans, another group of Semitic nomads, who spread eastwards from the Syrian desert, absorbing everything in their path, with the notable exception of the Assyrians. Discipline and organization enabled the Assyrians to survive, both then and during the next three centuries (c. 1200–900 BC). Little architecture from this period exists, but it was almost certainly the stern, not to say fierce, martial qualities developed then which laid the foundations of the Assyrian Empire which lasted from c. 900 BC to 612 BC, when a re-invigorated Babylon overthrew it and initiated the neo-Babylonian period. It is this period of the Assyrian Empire which will be considered here.

Architecturally, the most important works were the great palaces erected by the Assyrian kings which conformed to a fairly regular plan. This involved two main sections, an outer and an inner court, each with surrounding buildings, separated by the throne room which was clearly, from its size, the most important room of the whole complex. The North-west Palace at Nimrud, built by Ashurnasirpal II (883–59 BC), was one of the earliest examples of the type. The throne room was nearly 150 ft. long and 30 ft. wide, with a platform or podium for the royal throne at one end. There were two entrances from the outer court, via intermediate rooms (presumably some sort of vestibules), and one from the inner court, via a large (100×25 ft.) adjoining room. This group of rooms separated the private, informal part of the palace (inner court area) from the more public (outer court) section, forming a third section where ambassadors, for example, could meet the king in formal, ceremonial surroundings. The arrangement in the palace at Arslan Tash, built, or re-built, by Tiglathpileser III in the eighth century, is on the same lines. So also is the palace of Shalmaneser III in the south-

V. Opposite: crushed skull of a female attendant wearing a headdress and jewellery, as found in situ in the great death-pit at Ur.

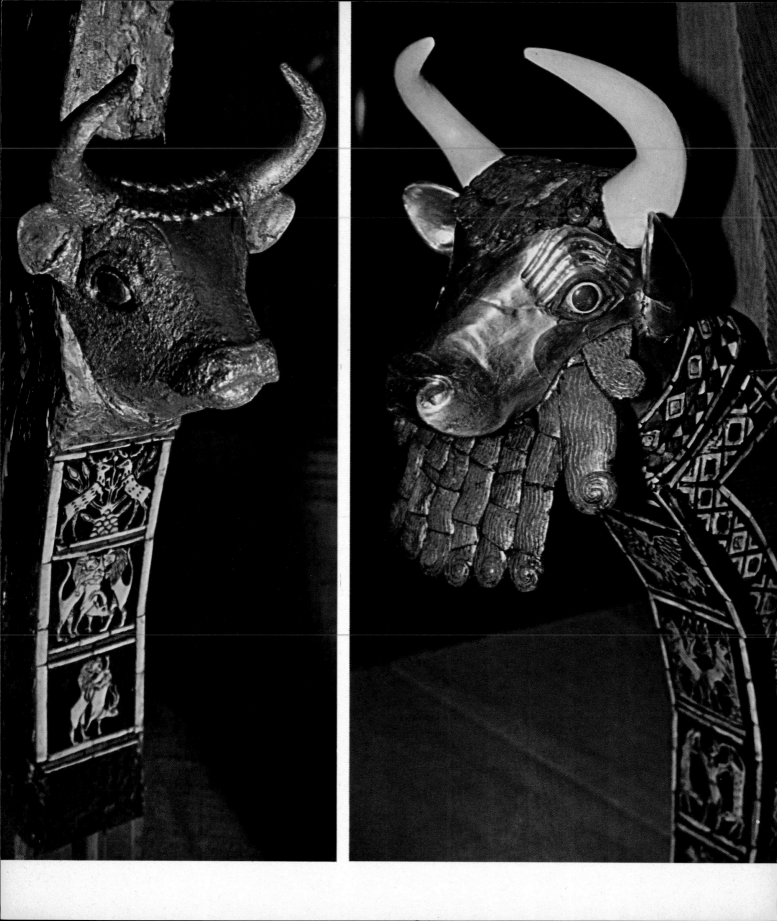

eastern area of Nimrud, the so-called Fort Shalmaneser, which contained not only the royal quarters but also great store rooms for weapons and booty, as well as quarters for officers, horses and chariots.

One of the greatest of Assyrian monuments is the city of Dur Sharrukin (modern Khorsabad), founded by Sargon II (722–705 BC) [76]. The outer wall, nearly square in plan, was almost four miles long, with seven monumental gateways. It contained two palaces, Palace F and Sargon's Palace, both of which straddled the city wall, mostly inside, but with a substantial portion projecting beyond. On the city side, Sargon's Palace was further defended by the citadel wall with two impressive gatehouses. Internally, both palaces have long impressive throne rooms (c. 150 × 30 ft.) as in earlier palaces. They also each have a very distinctive group of three large parallel rooms, linked by a fourth room across one end, closely associated with the throne room. The function of these rooms is not known, but it is worth noting that such a group appeared also in Fort Shalmaneser, at Nimrud, nearly a century and a half earlier, beyond the throne room on one side of the inner courtyard, so that quite clearly there was a strong tradition as far as the layout of the palace was concerned. The citadel area was occupied by large civic and religious buildings, the most important of which was the Temple of the god Nabu, son of the great god Marduk. This illustrates the typical Assyrian temple plan of a wide ante-cella with a long narrow cella beyond, quite clearly a combination of elements from earlier periods.

Two other palaces built by Sennacherib (704–681 BC) and Ashurbanipal (668–26 BC) at Nineveh were quite different in plan from anything that had gone before and the precise functions of the various rooms have not yet been worked out. There is certainly nothing like the large, distinctive throne room of earlier palaces.

In the field of sculpture, the most notable Assyrian achievements were the mythical composite beasts (made up of lions, bulls, birds, and human beings), placed at entrances, and the sculptured panels, in low relief, used to decorate rooms. The composite beasts, *lamassu*, were designed as guardians of the gates and entrances against the entry of evil spirits and are a characteristic feature of Assyrian architecture. They are indeed structural as well as decorative devices. The front part of the beast projects forward beyond the wall on either side of the entrance and this part is carved in the round. The remainder forms the inside surface of the entrance, carrying the brick structure above, and is carved in high relief on the visible face [77].

Internal, low relief sculpture is splendidly represented by a series of panels from the North-west Palace of Ashurnasirpal II (883–59 BC) at Nimrud. A hunting scene is shown in three panels, each c. 7 ft. long and 3 ft. high [78–80]. The king appears in all three, twice hunting from the moving chariot and in the last scene pouring libations over the dead beasts. In two more panels of similar dimensions he is shown receiving prisoners from the hand of his army chief. A group of four panels records a battle scene between Assyrians, in chariots and on foot, and an enemy, some of whom are within a fortress or city wall. Under Sargon II a certain effect of depth and realism was achieved by the inclusion of such things as trees, of different sizes (the smaller suggesting distance?), with figures in front of them. In reliefs from Sargon's Palace at Khorsabad, the scene includes hunters with bows and arrows, trees, birds (flying, falling and captive), and a dead rabbit and a dead deer being carried away by one of the hunters. Towards the end of the Assyrian

VI, VII. Opposite: a silver bull's head on a newly reconstructed lyre (left), and a gold bull's head on a harp with a lapis lazuli beard and inlays below (right), both found in the great death-pit at Ur (cf. Ill. 33).

77. Colossal winged and human-headed bull, with attendant human winged figure (14 ft. 8 in. × 14 ft. 6 in.), from a doorway into the palace of Sargon II, king of Assyria. These figures were believed to guard the entrance against evil influence.

78–80. Panels of alabaster relief sculpture from the walls of the North-west Palace of Ashurnasirpal II (883–59 BC) at Nimrud. Prior to this period interior decoration of the royal palaces had been in the form of wall-painting rather than relief sculpture. The panels are about 7 ft. long and 3 ft. high and they are intended to be seen as a group, depicting a sequence of events, all of which involve the king. He is seen first of all (above) hunting bulls from a chariot, then (below) hunting lions with a bow and arrow, and finally (opposite) in the last ritual act of the hunt, pouring a libation over one of the dead lions.

Empire, the splendid reliefs from the North Palace of Ashurbanipal (668–26 BC) at Nineveh include the two famous reliefs of a dying lion and a dying lioness, each pierced by arrows and spears, and the meticulously detailed scene of the Sacred Marriage in the vineyard.

Ashurbanipal was the last great Assyrian king. Babylon, which had been a relative backwater from the end of the Kassite period (*c.* 1157 BC), under a series of weak dynasties, enjoyed a resurgence of power under its eleventh and last dynasty (626–539 BC), and this neo-Babylonian period forms the last phase of Mesopotamian culture. The succeeding Persian period will be mentioned only briefly.

THE NEO–BABYLONIAN PERIOD

By 612 BC the Assyrians had been defeated and Babylon once again became the centre of a great empire from the Persian Gulf to the Mediterranean. Only Babylon itself, where an enormous amount of rebuilding took place, will be considered here. In fact, virtually all of the visible remains of Babylon are of the neo-Babylonian period. The Babylon of Hammurabi and other kings lies buried deep beneath the existing ruins. The neo-Babylonian city covered some 500 acres and had an estimated population of 100,000. In many ways neo-Babylonian architecture is a quite deliberate return to earlier forms, and differs noticeably from Assyrian practice. The small Ninmah temple, for example, had a broad cella (and broad ante-cella) of the type first encountered in the Sumero-Akkadian period some 1500 years earlier, although the axial alignment with the gatehouse was not strictly adhered to. In size and layout it closely resembled the Enki temple at Ur (above p. 91). The great Marduk shrine with its ziggurat (the original Tower of Babel) built by Nebuchadnezzar was also a return, on a much bigger scale, to earlier practice, with buildings grouped around courts, and the whole complex dominated by the temple on top of the ziggurat standing within its own enclosure—the same sort of layout as seen in the ziggurat complex at Ur.

In the secular field, the palace of Nebuchadnezzar in the southern citadel of Babylon was a result of regular additions to an original nucleus. This nucleus, around the west court, was in essence simply an enlarged version of the traditional Sumerian courtyard house, with the important rooms on the south side. The main court which was added next was quite clearly not simply a courtyard house but designed to add a magnificent throne room (c. 160 × 50 ft.) with three entrances to the complex. Between them, the main court and the successively-added middle and east courts provided three monumental gateways between the exterior and the throne room, and although each court had rooms to north and south, factors other than the traditional Sumerian plan operated here, notably the intention of providing an impressive approach via successive gateways and courtyards. The annexe court, on the opposite side of the west court from the other three, is different in character and much closer to the traditional type. It looks very much as if, in its final form, the main court and the two courts to the east were the formal ceremonial part of the palace, while the west court and annexe courts provided the private quarters.

Perhaps the best known of all neo-Babylonian monuments is the famous Ishtar Gate in the powerful city walls [81, 82]. The most striking feature of the entrance was its colour and decoration. It was covered with blue, glazed tiles with coloured animal figures (bulls, dragons, lions, etc.) in relief, a technique that was heralded a thousand years earlier by the Kassite practice of moulded figures in baked clay bricks on temple façades (above p. 94).

In its turn Babylon fell to the Persians under Cyrus in 539 BC and thereafter Mesopotamia was part of the Persian Empire, which in turn fell to Alexander the Great some two centuries later in 331 BC.

81, 82. The Ishtar Gate at Babylon, built by Nebuchadnezzar II, neo-Babylonian period (612–539 BC). Above: a model of the whole entrance complex; opposite: a reconstruction of one section of the gate.

ANATOLIA

Anatolia, the region, more or less, of modern Turkey, stretches from the Aegean in the west to Armenia in the east and has always been a cultural bridge between Europe and the Near-eastern world. Its outstanding occupants in antiquity were the Hittites, on whom attention will be mostly concentrated in this section. Because of the nature of the country, urban civilization and political power developed later in Anatolia than in Mesopotamia, and it was not until early in the second millenium that written history began there with the establishment of Assyrian trading depots, and their associated records and correspondence, at places such as Kanesh and Hattusas. However, even before 2000 BC, there was evidence of social and political development beyond the agricultural settlement stage. In the north-west corner of Anatolia the first and second cities (or citadels) of Troy (I and II) were built between *c.* 3000 and 2300 BC. Troy II—originally thought by Schliemann to be the Troy of the Homeric poems—was a fortress, and a relatively small one at that (*c.* 300 ft. in diameter), rather than a city, but it does represent a concentration of power and wealth (as evidenced by the so-called Treasure of Priam [83], for example) of the type which, in Mesopotamia, had produced cities and city states. The Troy of the Homeric poems is now known to be the much larger Troy VI and Troy VIIa, covering the years *c.* 1800–1260 BC. Troy III, IV and V were relatively unimportant periods covering the years 2300–1800 BC. Two other Anatolian sites tell the same story as Troy II during the third millenium: great wealth in the form of the treasures from the royal tombs at Alaca Hüyük [84, 86], and powerful defences in the form of the fortress of Kültepe (Kanesh). It is perhaps significant that at the latter site the Assyrians established one of their principal trading settlements, some time between 1950 and 1700 BC. Hittite names first begin to appear in the Assyrian records around 1700 BC and this provides the starting point for Hittite archaeology.

The Hittites spoke an Indo-European language and must have arrived in Anatolia early in the second millenium as a result of the great folk movements around 2000 BC—the same movement which, about the same time, brought the Mycenaeans into Greece, with their branch of the Indo-European language group. Their arrival was opportune in the sense that, although urban life was already in existence, it had not yet developed on any large scale, nor was there as yet any great concentration of political power to be overthrown. Probably the Hittites were relatively few in number, but they were very able and aggressive and became (apparently very quickly) the ruling class. By *c.* 1750 BC Hittite power was consolidated in a ruling dynasty which lasted for about three centuries (until *c.* 1460 BC). This period is known as the Old Kingdom. A new dynasty ushered in the Hittite Empire (1460 to *c.* 1200 BC), which eventually fell to the Phrygians. This was the end of the Hittite Empire as such in its homeland in central Anatolia, but Hittite culture survived for another five centuries or so in North Syria (which had been part of the Empire) in a group of neo-Hittite or Syro-Hittite city states which retained their independence, more or less, until shortly before 700 BC, when they were finally annexed into the Assyrian Empire. The Hittites thus span, in three periods, over a thousand years, from *c.* 1750 to 700 BC.

Of the three periods, the last, neo-Hittite, period has perhaps left the most numerous remains and it is the people of this period who are referred to as

83. Sophia Schliemann wearing the golden ornaments found in the second stratum at Troy: the 'Treasure of Priam'.

84. Opposite: one of the sphinxes forming one side of the gateway at Alaca Hüyük in Anatolia.

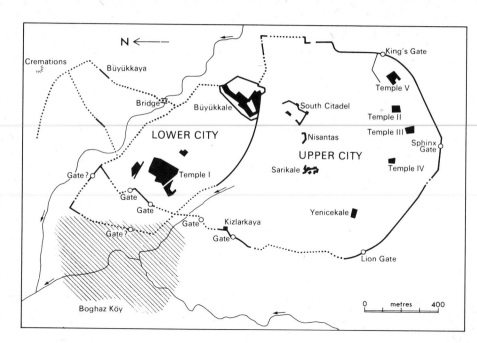

Büyükkaya
Cremations
Bridge
Büyükkale
LOWER CITY
Gate?
Gate
Gate
Temple I
Gate
Gate?
Gate
Kizlarkaya
Gate
Boghaz Köy

N ←

King's Gate
Temple V
South Citadel
Temple II
Temple III
Sphinx Gate
Nisantas
UPPER CITY
Sarikale
Temple IV
Yenicekale
Lion Gate

0   metres   400

85. Left: plan of Hattusas (modern Boghaz Köy), in north central Turkey, the capital city of the Hittites during the Empire period (*c.* 1460–1200 BC).

86. Opposite: ritual figure on the top of a staff, from Alaca Hüyük, Anatolia. ▶

Hittites in the Bible. The Old Kingdom, when Hittite power was still being consolidated, is not so well represented archaeologically, and it is not until the Empire that there is a fairly clear picture of Hittite material culture, shown most spectacularly at the Hittite capital Hattusas (modern Boghaz Köy) in north central Turkey, the Hittite homeland within the bend of the Halys river. The original Hittite capital appears to have been a city called Kussara (which has not yet been located), with Hattusas being one of a number of cities subdued by the early Hittites. However, by Empire times, and probably earlier as well, Hattusas was quite clearly the capital, the reason for its choice as such being possibly its excellent location both for defence and trade. The site is situated on a sloping tongue of land between the rocky gorges of two rivers which join in the north, providing good natural defences on two sides of the triangular area thus isolated. It also stood near the junction of two ancient trade routes, in a position where trade could be controlled and exploited [87].

In its final form Boghaz Köy was roughly pear-shaped in plan, nearly one and a quarter miles from north to south and almost three-quarters of a mile wide, its outermost walls, nearly four miles long, enclosing an area of about 300 acres [85]. However, the earlier city was very much smaller than this and embraced only the northern area above the modern village. It was some three-quarters of a mile long and about a quarter of a mile wide, and was sub-divided by internal walls into four separate areas, the smallest one at the south-eastern end, on a high, flat-topped area of rock called Büyükkale, forming a citadel with very strong defences. This was the form of the city when it became the Hittite capital *c.* 1500 BC. The great outer wall to the south, which more than trebled the city area, was probably added in the Empire by the great king Suppiluliumas. One temple (I) has been uncovered in the earlier city and four (II–V) in the enlarged city.

Perhaps the most impressive aspect of the whole city is its system of defences, particularly those to the south built (probably) by Suppiluliumas.

The base was formed by a great bank of earth which ironed out the unevenness of the terrain and provided a consistent foundation for the wall proper. The sloping outer face of this bank was faced with stones forming what is known as a *glacis*. On the crest of the bank the main defensive wall was built, 15–20 ft. thick, consisting of inner and outer skins, with cross walls dividing it into rectangular compartments filled with stone rubble. The original height is a matter of conjecture but the main wall was almost certainly 30 ft. or more. At intervals of about 75 ft. along the wall there were rectangular projecting towers, *c.* 30 × 25 ft., built in the same manner with a lower filling of stone rubble. In addition to the main wall there was, in the more vulnerable sections, an outer, apron wall between 30 and 50 ft. in front of the main wall, with its own system of rectangular towers at regular intervals. Beneath this double rampart at the southern end of the city was a stone-lined tunnel through the foundation bank which presumably acted as a postern, allowing defenders to pass beneath the walls and appear suddenly beyond, among or behind an attacking force.

The outstanding features of the city defences were undoubtedly the monumental gateways, particularly those in the southern defences, the King's or Warrior's Gate and the Lion Gate [88]. Each gate consists of two great rectangular towers (*c.* 45 × 30 ft.) which link the main wall and the apron. These towers must have been at least 50 ft. high. They stood 20 ft. apart and this roadway width was further reduced to about 11 ft. at the inner and outer archways where the actual, two-leaved, gates would have been situated. Internally the towers are divided into six compartments filled, like the wall compartments, with stone rubble. The approach to the gates from the outside was by means of a ramp, rising more or less parallel with the wall and then turning inwards at a sharp angle to pass between the twin towers. Two other gates, the upper and lower west gates, are built on exactly the same lines. A fifth, the Spinx Gate, is somewhat different. Two long stone stairways lead upwards from the exterior slope to two separate gate towers, some 400 ft. apart, in the apron wall. From there, access is via the parapet between it and the main wall and then through a gateway in a single rectangular tower midway between the two gate towers.

Each of the five temples uncovered at Boghaz Köy consisted of a rectangular courtyard with rooms grouped on all four sides. Access was via a gatehouse or vestibule leading into the courtyard, usually at the opposite end to the cella, although in some cases the entrance was on one side. One, two and sometimes three sides of the courtyard were in the form of open colonnades. Access to the cult room or cella was usually indirect, via a series of vestibules and ante-cellas, involving two or three changes of direction. Superficially these Hittite temples are not dissimilar to some of the Mesopotamian temples described already, but they differ in one important respect in having external windows which reached almost to floor level and must have admitted a great deal of light. Temple I, the temple in the early city, was surrounded by an enormous battery of storage magazines, many times the area of the temple itself.

After the collapse of the Hittite Empire, a form of Hittite culture continued in the neo-Hittite or Syro-Hittite period in a series of sites in the Anatolian/Syrian border region, such as Karatepe, Sinjerli, Sakcegözü, Malatya, Atchana and Carchemish. The political form appears to have been that of city states with no single overall source of power as there had been

87. Vessel in the shape of a two-headed duck, from Boghaz Köy.

in the Empire period. Two of the best known sites are Carchemish and Sinjerli. At Carchemish the outer city wall, over two miles long, enclosed an area of some 200 acres, divided into an outer city, an inner city, and a citadel. The walls, of mud brick with stone foundations, lack the regular towers seen at Boghaz Köy but, as there, special attention was paid to the gates, which were flanked by strong towers. The two most impressive entrances are the South and West Gates of the inner city. The South Gate stands in a double recess between two rectangular towers, each over 30 ft. wide. The entrance passage runs through three portals in line, flanked by two pairs of rectangular chambers, presumably guard chambers and other offices connected with control of access to the city. The West Gate projects forward beyond the line of the main wall. The outer portal is again recessed between two towers, somewhat smaller than at the South Gate, and between it and the second portal is a pair of side chambers. Two more portals further back enclose another pair of side chambers. From front to back the entrance measures some 150 ft.

At Sinjerli, the outer city wall was circular in plan and nearly half a mile in diameter, enclosing ninety acres [89]. Within, near the centre, was an oval-shaped citadel of some ten acres, sub-divided by fortified walls into four smaller areas. The outer, circular wall was double and was pierced by three gates, each of which was in fact a double gate. The most impressive

88. The Lion Gate in the southern defences of Boghaz Köy, added to the existing city by King Suppiluliumas during the Empire period (c. 1460–1200 BC).

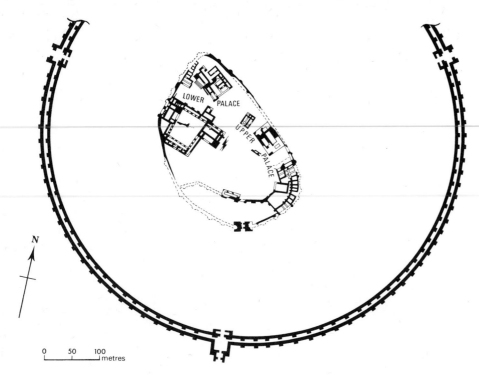

89. Plan of Sinjerli, a city of the neo-Hittite or Syro-Hittite period (*c.* 1200–700 BC). The double outer wall formed a complete circle (not shown in its entirety here) and enclosed some 90 acres. The inner citadel was 10 acres in area.

N

0   50   100
|___|___|___| metres

was the South Gate which projected forward some 100 ft. in front of the outer wall. It consisted of outer and inner pairs of rectangular towers linked by flanking walls to form an open court between inner and outer portals. Two further portals were located between the third, and largest, pair of towers on the inner wall, each *c.* 35 × 20 ft., and standing nearly 30 ft. apart. This entrance was more or less in line with the only gate in the outer wall of the citadel, and this again was a double gate of a sort because the citadel wall in the entrance area was doubled. A noticeable feature of the citadel defences were the semi-circular towers, as opposed to the more common rectangular towers. Within the citadel were the remains of a so-called Upper Palace to the north-east and a Lower Palace to the north-west. Both of these incorporated suites of rooms of a particular type known as the *hilani* or *bit-hilani*, and these are a regular feature of Syro-Hittite architecture. The *bit-hilani* consists of an open-fronted portico, with one, two or three columns, approached in many cases by a flight of steps. This portico gives access to a throne room, the long axis of which is parallel to the portico. A small room at one end of the portico houses a staircase to the upper floors and beyond the throne room there are usually several other small rooms, presumably acting as private quarters. A single palace could incorporate a number of such units around a courtyard, linked together by colonnades.

This last flowering of Hittite culture in north Syria came to an end shortly before 700 BC, when the precarious independence of the cities involved was ended by Assyrian annexation.

PALESTINE
Because of the Biblical background Palestine has always occupied a special place in Near-eastern archaeology and this is reflected in the vast amount of excavation that has been carried out in this relatively small part of the

region. Its geographical position, in the middle of a triangle formed by Anatolia to the north, Egypt to the south-west and Mesopotamia to the east, has made it something of a cultural crossroads, and its history is punctuated by the arrival of new peoples from different directions, initiating new archaeological periods.

The Halaf culture (above p. 85), which came to an end *c.* 4500 BC, did not extend as far as Palestine. Although the position is still not entirely clear, the gap between the Pottery Neolithic B period (above, p. 84) and the proto-urban period (beginning *c.* 3300 BC) is occupied in part at least by the Ghassulian culture, from the type site at Teleilat Ghassul. The site, in fact, consisted of three separate, although obviously closely related, villages of small, closely-set houses with rectangular or trapezoidal rooms, built of mud brick on stone foundations. Fragments of wall plaster show that internal walls were not only plastered but also painted. There is no evidence of a defensive wall around the settlements. Ghassulian pottery and other equipment has now been found in a number of other sites in Palestine. The pottery in particular, which is quite different from any that preceded it in Palestine, shows that the Ghassulian people came into Palestine probably before 4000 BC, from some area which has not yet been identified but which may well be to the east or north-east.

About 3300 BC there was a fresh migration of people into Palestine who very quickly settled down on sites which eventually developed into the cities and city states of the succeeding Early Bronze Age. This period (*c.* 3300–2900 BC) is therefore known as the proto-urban period. Although there is little in the way of architecture, there is clear evidence of occupation in this period at sites such as Jericho, Megiddo, Beth-shan and Tell el Far'ah, which in the succeeding period became substantial urban centres. At the other sites, in spite of proto-urban occupation, there is no subsequent Bronze Age phase and they were presumably abandoned before any substantial development took place.

As in Egypt and Mesopotamia, urban life began in Palestine in or shortly after 3000 BC. Here the comparison ends, for subsequently the pace of progress in the first two areas was much more rapid and included, for example, the development of writing, which was not to appear in Palestine for another 1500 years. It included also great political development, beyond the city state which, however, remained the pattern in Palestine until *c.* 1000 BC. Palestine lacks the often spectacular architecture of Egypt and Mesopotamia, and its cities might perhaps be better described as large towns, more concerned with serving the needs of the immediate neighbourhood than with international trade or international relations.

In the Palestinian period of urban development (the Early Bronze Age, *c.* 2900–2300 BC), the earliest towns appear to have been undefended settlements. But strong surrounding walls became a regular feature at an early stage due, no doubt, to rivalry between the towns, and between the settled agricultural peoples, closely linked to the towns, and the nomadic peoples of the desert, ever ready to prey on richer communities. Jericho was defended by a town wall which shows clear evidence of constant repair and maintenance throughout the Early Bronze Age period [90]. The area enclosed was quite small (*c.* 650 × 230 ft.) and this, in a sense, is symptomatic of the difference between Palestine and Mesopotamia where the roughly contemporary city of Uruk had a city wall six miles in circumference. The early

90. The succession of Early Bronze Age city walls as seen in site M, Jericho. The various layers of stone represent successive foundations, with the walls formed of mud-brick on top.

wall at Jericho, standing on the crest of the 50 ft. high mound or tell which had accumulated during the pre-Bronze Age period, was relatively thin, *c.* 3½ ft. across, and was built of mud bricks (*c.* 14 × 10 × 2 in.) set in mud mortar and standing on a stone foundation. Its original height is a matter for speculation but at such a thickness it is unlikely to have exceeded 15 ft. and probably 10–12 ft. would be nearer the truth. It is impossible to give a complete history of the wall throughout the Early Bronze Age because more often than not erosion, collapse or destruction and the evidence of subsequent rebuilding was confined to one section, with adjacent sections relatively undisturbed. However, it is possible to follow some of the wall's development in one section: Trench I, the great slice cut across the tell in the excavations there by Miss K. M. Kenyon in the 1950s. The earliest wall (*c.* 3½ ft. wide) can be seen with its foundation stones dug into the earlier, Neolithic levels, preserved to a height of *c.* 3 ft. By a series of steps this was eventually replaced by a tripartite wall (each part still *c.* 3½ ft. thick) which can be seen in section above, and is therefore later than the simple wall. This new wall had the additional protection of an outer ditch, *c.* 25 ft. wide and 10 ft. deep, dug into the side of the tell some 36 ft. down the slope from the foot of the wall. Above the tripartite wall are the foundations of another, later Early Bronze Age wall, which judging by its foundations was about 11 ft. thick and probably in the region of 20 ft. high. It too was accompanied by an outer ditch (*c.* 35 ft. wide and 15 ft. deep) dug into the side of the tell. At a later stage again, but still within the Early Bronze Age, a new town wall (*c.* 8 ft. thick) was built some 22 ft. beyond the wall just described, and this too was repaired and rebuilt on a number of occasions, and like it was accompanied by an outer ditch. In all there were no less than seventeen successive structural phases in the defences on the west side of Jericho during the six hundred years of the Early Bronze Age.

At Tell Far'ah there was a well-developed Early Bronze Age town before any defences were constructed. These consisted, on the north, of a stone rampart, 27 ft. thick, standing at the head of an external slope or glacis of beaten earth, and on the west, of a mud-brick wall of similar dimensions, pierced by a gateway with two flanking towers. At Khirbet Kerak, the Early Bronze Age town wall was about 25 ft. thick while at Ai there were eventually three closely-set stone walls, the inner one being the earliest. At Arad the stone wall was *c.* 8 ft. thick with projecting semi-circular bastions or towers.

The best evidence for burial is from Jericho. There the normal Early Bronze Age tomb was a subterranean rock-cut chamber entered by a vertical shaft. This could contain the remains of as many as a hundred bodies, together with pottery and a few objects of personal adornment such as beads. Very often a body is represented only by the skull, the remaining bones having been thrown out when the chamber became too full.

The pottery from the tombs supplements that from the sites, and is mostly in the form of sherds (i.e. broken pieces), which are abundant in the Early Bronze Age period. The main forms are open bowls, dishes, handled jugs and juglets, the latter being only a few inches high [91]. Technically much of the pottery is of high quality, due to the use of the right kind of kiln, with combustion chamber and oven separate, so that firing is even over the whole vessel. The most common colour was red, produced by the application of a red slip which was then burnished by hand.

The Palestinian Early Bronze Age ended dramatically at Jericho with a great conflagration and there was a similar abrupt end everywhere else in the country. The cause appears to have been a massive invasion by nomadic peoples who, temporarily at least, brought an end to city life. Their arrival initiated a period, which will not be dealt with here, between the Early Bronze Age and the Middle Bronze Age, known for convenience as the E.B.–M.B. period, lasting from *c.* 2300 BC until shortly before 1900 BC.

Once again a new period, the Middle Bronze Age, is ushered in by the arrival of new people, with new types of pottery, new burial customs and new fortification techniques for the towns and cities, which once more became the focus of normal life. Perhaps the most dramatic change was in fortification and this is well exemplified at Jericho. In the early part of the period there was a mud-brick wall some 7 ft. thick, similar to the Early Bronze Age type. Shortly afterwards, however, at Jericho and at many other sites, an entirely new and much more elaborate defence technique appeared. At Jericho the new-style wall was rebuilt twice during the course of the Middle Bronze Age and from the remains of the three, successive ramparts it is possible to build up a complete picture [92]. The outermost feature was a stone retaining wall, 15–20 ft. high, which formed the foot of a great, triangular mound of earth. Above and behind this wall the surface of the mound sloped up steeply to the crest and was covered with a layer of smooth

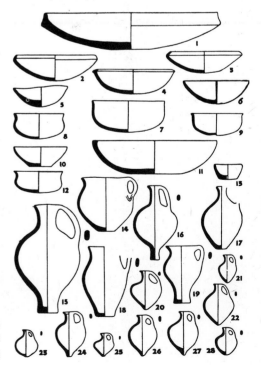

91. Pottery of the Early Bronze Age III period from Tomb F4 at Jericho. Pottery found in tombs is normally intact, as here; pottery found stratified in the tell is inevitably, in almost every case, in fragments (sherds).

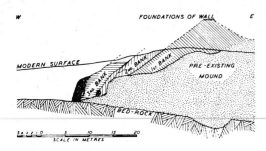

92. Reconstructed section of the great Middle Bronze Age rampart at Jericho, showing its three structural phases, all on more or less the same lines and all demonstrating the new development in fortification technique.

VIII. Opposite: the Great Sphinx in front of the pyramid of Chephren at Giza.

plaster, so that ascent would have been very difficult. At the crest was the wall proper, behind which the mound sloped down to the interior of the city. At Jericho the whole system was at least 90 ft. wide and 60 ft. high. With minor variations, similar defences have been uncovered at Tell Duweir, Tell Jeriseh, Tell Ajjul, Tell Fara, Hazor, and several other sites. One possible explanation of the technique is that it made attack by battering ram virtually impossible, since it would be difficult to get anywhere near the wall proper, even without the encumbrance of such a heavy burden.

Judging by the remains at Jericho and Tell Beit Mirsim, living conditions were very crowded, with houses and shops cheek by jowl, opening on to narrow streets 6–7 ft. wide. However, there is evidence of more spacious accommodation at Tell Beit Mirsim where one house, with more than one storey, had a rectangular courtyard in front (*c.* 36 × 18 ft.), and a range of rooms opening from its back.

Middle Bronze Age burials are very informative, particularly at Jericho. They were communal, probably family, graves consisting of a narrow vertical shaft (blocked after each burial), *c.* 10–12 ft. deep, from the side of which opened a circular, domed burial chamber, *c.* 10 ft. in diameter. The rich grave goods, considered necessary for the after-life, included pottery containing liquid, drinking vessels, the remains of joints of meat, wooden platters, rush mats and a range of wooden furniture including tables, beds, and stools. These are all, presumably, typical of the domestic equipment in normal use in Middle Bronze Age Jericho and Palestine.

Shortly after 1600 BC the Middle Bronze Age was brought to an end by disturbances originating in Egypt. These destroyed both Jericho and Tell Beit Mirsim and they were not reoccupied until the second half of the Late Bronze Age, although there is no break in occupation at many other sites. This second period (*c.* 1400–1200 BC), when the Israelites settled in Palestine, was one of great upheavals and the archaeological evidence, although plentiful, is too complex to follow here.

The disturbances in the east Mediterranean world around 1200 BC, which brought down both the Hittites and the Mycenaeans, had their effects further south as well—in Palestine and in Egypt. The invading tribes were finally defeated by Ramesses III in about 1196 BC, and subsequently some of them settled on the coasts of Syria and Palestine. Among the tribes were the Pulaste or Philistines, who were later to expand inland to dominate considerable areas of Palestine. The names of many other tribes suggest that they may have originated in mainland Greece, Asia Minor, Crete or even further west, Sardinia or Sicily for example, so that many different influences were involved in the new period from *c.* 1200 BC on. The break-up of the Hittite world also meant that the knowledge of iron-working spread fairly rapidly and, although bronze was still used for many things, iron now began to appear, so that 1200 BC, in round figures, marks the beginning of the Palestinian Iron Age. Around 1100 BC the Philistines began to expand from the rich coastal plain into the hill country occupied by the Israelites, and the period of conflict which ensued is described in the Bible.

This very brief account of Palestinian archaeology ends with the establishment of the kingdom of Israel *c.* 1000 BC. There is still a great deal of archaeology in the following thousand years, but the story of Palestine is now written history as much as archaeology and will not be pursued here.

Egypt, Africa, India, China

The long sequence of events outlined in the last chapter, from 10,000 BC on, did not take place in isolation from the surrounding areas. The Near East lies at the very heart of the Old World, at the western end of its own vast continent of Asia, and immediately adjacent to two other continents, Africa to the south-west and Europe to the north-west. All three continents were profoundly affected, although in different ways and to differing degrees. The effects on Europe will be considered in Chapter 7. Here, attention will be focused on Africa, with particular reference to Egypt, and on Asia, with particular reference to India and China.

AFRICA: EGYPT

The Nile valley, the setting for the spectacular civilization of ancient Egypt, lies in the north-eastern corner of Africa, between the Near East and the remainder of the continent. Egypt has always occupied a special place in the imagination, not least by reason of its spectacular monuments which will form much of the subject matter of this section. In the fifth century BC, the Greek writer and traveller Herodotus described Egypt as the gift of the Nile, and this close identity of the country and the river is an essential aspect of Egyptology. In spite of its political frontiers, both ancient and modern, the country, i.e. the place where virtually the whole population lives, is effectively the Nile valley, a strip of fertile land a few miles wide (apart from the Delta) but a thousand miles long (as far as the 2nd Cataract) [93]. It was (and still is) the annual inundation of this valley by the river, bringing with it rich, fertile silt from the heart of Africa, which assured Egypt's prosperity in ancient times, and it was on the basis of this prosperity that the rich and complex civilization of Egypt developed.

The long history of Egypt is divided into thirty-one dynasties, following Manetho, an Egyptian priest who wrote a *History of Egypt* (in Greek) around 250 BC. For greater convenience these dynasties are grouped into a smaller number of periods as follows (dates in round figures):

Dynasties I–II	Early Dynastic or Archaic	3100–2700 BC
Dynasties III–VI	OLD KINGDOM	2700–2200 BC
Dynasties VII–X	First Intermediate Period	2200–2100 BC
Dynasties XI–XII	MIDDLE KINGDOM	2100–1800 BC
Dynasties XIII–XVII	Second Intermediate Period	1800–1600 BC
Dynasties XVIII–XX	NEW KINGDOM	1600–1100 BC
Dynasties XXI–XXV	Late New Kingdom	1100– 650 BC
Dynasty XXVI	Saite Period	650– 525 BC
Dynasties XXVII–XXXI	Late Period	525– 332 BC

IX. Opposite: back of the throne of Tutankhamun, showing the king and his wife, Queen Ankhesenamun. Tutankhamun is sitting on an upholstered lion's-leg throne and the queen stands in front of him, wearing a crown of feathers and a long pleated robe. Above them, the sun casts down its life-giving rays, ending in hands.

The last date, 332 BC, marks the conquest of Egypt by Alexander the Great and the end of the native Egyptian dynasties. The three great periods of Egyptian civilization are the Old, Middle and New Kingdoms and these, containing as they do the bulk of the famous monuments, will receive the greatest attention in this section. The period before dynasty I (from *c.* 4500 BC on) is known as the pre-dynastic period and this will be considered first, albeit briefly.

THE PRE-DYNASTIC PERIOD

On the evidence of Carbon-14 dating, farming developed in Egypt some time between 5200 and 4000 BC. The communities involved fall into two groups—one in Lower Egypt and one in Upper Egypt—and it is not very clear how the two groups are related to each other. In Lower Egypt the three main pre-dynastic sites are Merimde, El Omari, and the Fayum. In Upper Egypt, about which much more is known, there is a well-established sequence of four periods leading up to dynasty I: Tasian, Badarian, Nagada I (Amratian), and Nagada II (Gerzean). Amratian and Gerzean are simply alternative names for the Nagada I and II periods respectively. The Tasian and Badarian people who, like the Lower Egyptian people, practised mixed farming lived mainly on spurs overlooking the valley bottom. It was only in the following Nagada I period that people moved down and settled in the fertile valley itself. In the Nagada II period there is evidence of increasing contact with the rest of the Near East in the form of painted pottery and copper metalwork, axes, daggers and knives being the principal forms. By late Nagada II times the separate villages and communities had developed into two groups or kingdoms, one in the Delta region, from Memphis, near Cairo, northwards (Lower Egypt), and one in the rest of the Nile valley, from Memphis southwards (Upper Egypt). It was the unification of these two kingdoms under one ruler by the first king of dynasty I (Menes) that marks the beginning of Egyptian history. This event is commemorated by Pharoah's titles, Lord of the Two Lands, King of Upper and Lower Egypt, which formed a permanent part of the royal titulary down to the end of dynastic times, nearly 3000 years later.

ARCHAIC AND OLD KINGDOM (Dynasties I–VI)

The Old Kingdom is noted above all else for the pyramids, possibly the most spectacular monuments ever erected by Man. The Giza group (dynasty IV), which are probably the best known, are only three of about eighty such monuments built in the Nile valley. The pyramid seems to have developed out of the mastaba, a type of tomb in use from dynasty I onwards (hence the inclusion of the Archaic period here), and the nature and development of mastaba tombs from dynasties I to VI will be described first.

Mastabas

The word mastaba is Arabic for bench and was applied to these tombs because their remains resembled, on a large scale, the simple bench outside present-day Egyptian houses. In pre-dynastic times the dead were buried in a simple pit in the ground covered by a mound of sand for greater protection. Sand is, however, unsatisfactory as a permanent covering and by dynasty I king and nobles were buried beneath substantial mastabas of mud brick. These were rectangular in plan and divided internally into as many as thirty cells or chambers for the storage of all the domestic and other

93. Opposite: map of Egypt from the Nile Delta to the 2nd Cataract.

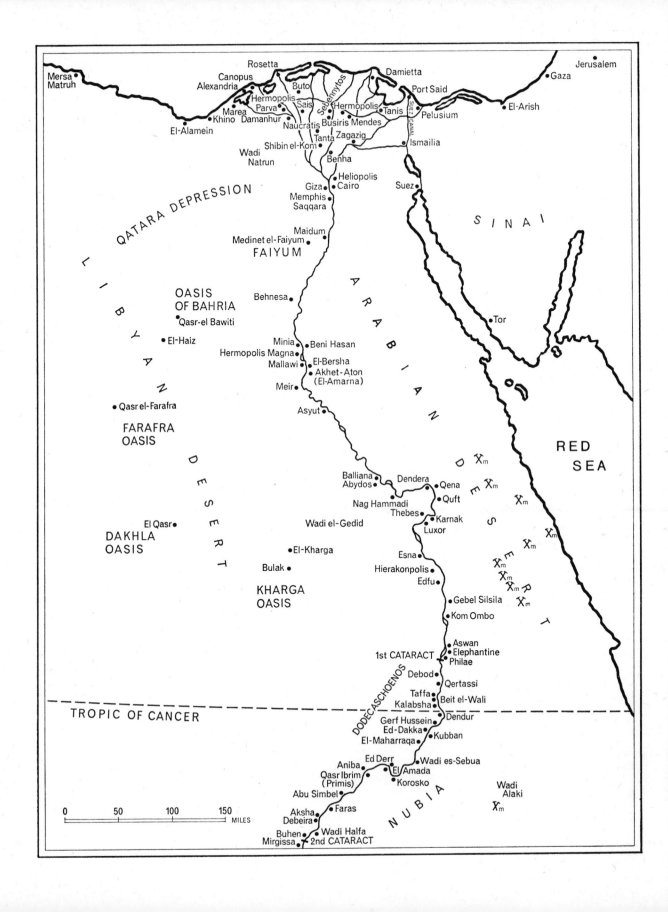

Mersa
Matruh

Rosetta
Canopus
Alexandria
Hermopolis
Marea   Parva
Khino   Damanhur
El-Alamein

Buto
Sais
Naucratis
Tanta
Shibin el-Kom

Damietta
Port Said
Sebennytos
Hermopolis   Tanis
Busiris Mendes
Zagazig
Benha

Gaza
Jerusalem
El-Arish

Pelusium
Ismailia

QATARA DEPRESSION

Wadi
Natrun

Heliopolis
Giza • Cairo
Memphis
Saqqara

Suez

S I N A I

Maidum
Medinet el-Faiyum
FAIYUM

L
I
B
Y
A
N

OASIS
OF BAHRIA
•Qasr-el Bawiti

• El-Haiz

Behnesa

Minia
Hermopolis Magna
Mallawi
Meir

Beni Hasan
El-Bersha
Akhet-Aton
(El-Amarna)

A
R
A
B
I
A
N

Tor

RED
SEA

•Qasr el-Farafra

D
E
S
E
R
T

FARAFRA
OASIS

Asyut

Balliana
Abydos
Nag Hammadi

Dendera
Qena
Quft
Thebes

El Qasr•
Wadi el-Gedid

DAKHLA
OASIS

•El-Kharga

Bulak •

KHARGA
OASIS

Karnak
Luxor

Esna

Hierakonpolis
Edfu

Gebel Silsila

Kom Ombo

Aswan
1st CATARACT •Elephantine
Philae

D
E
S
E
R
T

Debod
Qertassi
Taffa
Kalabsha Beit el-Wali

TROPIC OF CANCER

Gerf Hussein Dendur
Ed-Dakka
El-Maharraqa Kubban

D
O
D
E
C
A
S
C
H
O
E
N
O
S

Aniba
Qasr Ibrim
(Primis)
Abu Simbel

Ed Derr
El Amada
Korosko

Wadi es-Sebua

Wadi
Alaki

Aksha
Debeira
Buhen
Mirgissa

Faras

Wadi Halfa
2nd CATARACT

N
U
B
I
A

0   50   100   150
|____|____|____|
            MILES

equipment which the dead man would need in the after-life [94]. Almost certainly the mastaba was a simplified representation of the contemporary houses, with such things as doors and corridors omitted because the spirit of the dead man was presumed to be able to move freely from room to room through the walls. The external walls of the early mastaba consisted of elaborately ribbed alternating projections and recesses, although from dynasty II onwards plain walls were more common, sloping inwards towards the top. No roofs are preserved but a flat or convex form seems highly probable. Incorporated in some early mastabas are mounds of sand and these quite clearly preserve the idea of the simple pre-dynastic burial. In more elaborate versions, and for greater stability, the mound is retained by stepped walls of mud brick. Beneath the mastaba superstructure was the burial pit or chamber, sometimes sub-divided, dug into the ground, and protected, in theory at least, by the elaborate structure above. During dynasties II and III, for greater security, the mastaba superstructure became a solid mass of rubble faced with brick; the system of chambers was transferred below, dug into the solid rock and reached by a vertical shaft and a flight of steps, both filled with rubble and sealed after the burial and then covered with the solid mass of the mastaba. Stone was first used for royal mastabas in dynasty III and for the nobility from dynasty IV on. All these precautions, however, failed to defeat the tomb robber. In dynasties V and VI the mastaba superstructure was occupied by columned halls and chambers, again recalling the houses of the living, elaborately decorated in relief sculpture with scenes from the owner's life.

Pyramids

Although mastabas continued as tombs for the nobility, in dynasty III the decisive step was taken which transformed the royal tomb into pyramid form. King Zoser was buried at Saqqara in what, in its final form, was a step pyramid with six stages, the work of his architect Imhotep. However, investigation has shown that it attained this form as a result of a whole series of changes of plan, and that, in fact, it started life as a mastaba, although one of unusual plan [95, 96]. The nucleus and first stage of the structure is a square mastaba 25 ft. high and 205 ft. along each side. In stage two about 14 ft. was added to each side (233 ft. square). Stage three was a 28 ft. addition on the east side only, making the plan oblong (261 × 233 ft.). In stage four a fundamental change took place. The mastaba was extended by $9\frac{1}{2}$ ft. on each side and this became the first step of a step pyramid some 140 ft. high— the first pyramid, even if still in step form. In fact, almost immediately, very substantial additions were made on the north and west sides (making it c. 410 × 360 ft.) and the structure was eventually completed as a six-step pyramid 195 ft. high. This impressive structure stood within an elaborate enclosure c. 1800 ft. long and 900 ft. wide, containing a series of stone buildings and courtyards and surrounded by a massive limestone wall with alternating recesses and projections. The main element in the complicated substructure of the step pyramid was a rectangular shaft, 23 ft. square, sunk to a depth of 92 ft. with the tomb chamber at the bottom, and a complex series of other passages connected with it. The step pyramid of Zoser is one of the great pieces of original architecture in the world. There was no earlier example on which it was or could be based and it must be attributed to the creative genius of Imhotep.

The step pyramid was the first of the long series of pyramids built during the Old and Middle Kingdoms, at first in step form and later in true pyramid form. Only a few of the main developments can be considered here. A later king of dynasty III, Sekhemkhet, started but never completed a seven-step pyramid, also at Saqqara, some 395 ft. square and intended to be about 230 ft. high. Another dynasty III king, probably Khaba, also started but did not complete a step pyramid of six or seven steps, 276 ft. square.

Early in dynasty IV the change was made from the step to the true pyramid. The name of Senefru, the first king of the dynasty, is associated with no less than three pyramids: two at Dashur and one at Meidum. It seems quite clear that he built two pyramids, possibly demonstrating his joint rule of Upper and Lower Egypt, but whether the third is, in fact, his has yet to be proved. The Meidum pyramid appears to have started as a seven-step pyramid, although there may be earlier stages as well [97]. It was then heightened by 45 ft. and an additional step added. The final alteration was the filling-in of the steps and the covering of the whole structure with a smooth facing of limestone, transforming it into a true pyramid. The two pyramids at Dashur appear to have been conceived from the beginning as true pyramids, although only one was completed as such. The so-called Bent Pyramid (c. 620 ft. square) inclines inwards at a shallower angle about half-way up and is possibly the result of hasty, and economical, completion. The second pyramid at Dashur is, in fact, the first to be both started and completed as a geometrically true pyramid. It is notable for the relatively shallow angle of its sides, very similar to the upper portion of the Bent Pyramid.

The achievement of the true pyramid was followed, in dynasties IV, V and VI, by a whole series of magnificent pyramids, including those at Giza which are, in the words of I. E. S. Edwards, 'possibly the most celebrated group of monuments in the world' [98]. The pyramids of Cheops, Chephren, and Mycerinus at Giza represent the main works of dynasty IV. The Great Pyramid of Cheops, which marks the peak of pyramid building, was 755 ft. square and rose originally to a height of 481 ft. Its base covered over 13 acres and it has been estimated to contain some 2,300,000 separate blocks of stone, weighing from $2\frac{1}{2}$ to 15 tons each. The pyramid of Chephren was only slightly smaller. All three pyramids, and the Sphinx, formed part of a great necropolis or cemetery consisting of dozens of mastabas—the burial places of nobles who wished to be near the royal tombs. The pyramids of dynasties V and VI were much smaller than those of Cheops and Chephren but, like them, conformed to what may be regarded as a regular plan. The pyramid is, in fact, only one element in a whole complex of associated buildings. These consist of the valley temple, the causeway, the funerary temple, the pyramid enclosure and the small subsidiary pyramids to house close relatives such as the wives and daughters of the king.

THE MIDDLE KINGDOM (Dynasties XI and XII)

After the end of dynasty VI, during the First Intermediate period, there was a period of anarchy for nearly a century in Egypt when central control broke down and most of the monuments just described were ravaged and destroyed by tomb robbers. Only in the second half of dynasty XI was there a return to more settled conditions under three kings all named Mentuhotep. The first of these, Nebhepetre-Mentuhotep, built an unusual funerary temple at Deir el-Bahri incorporating a small pyramid and a rock-cut

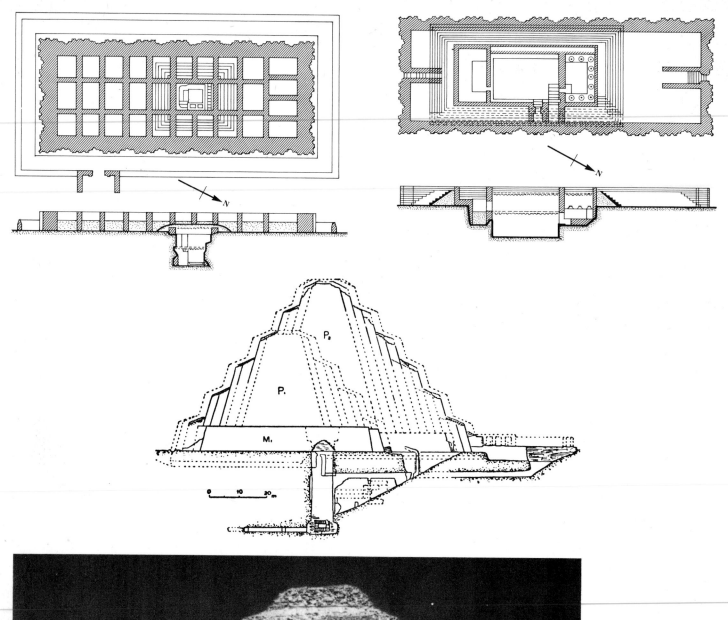

94–98. During dynasties I and II the standard form of burial for both king and noble was the mastaba tomb. In dynasty III King Zoser and his architect Imhotep developed the royal mastaba into the step pyramid, and this in turn led to the pyramid as we know it. The nobles continued to use mastabas throughout the remainder of the Old Kingdom (to the end of dynasty VI) and, on a lesser scale, still later. Many of the early mastabas (in dynasty I for example) incorporate a mound of sand at their centre (opposite, top left), in some cases retained by a stepped wall of mud brick (opposite, top right), and this would appear to be a recognition of an earlier (pre-dynastic) tradition of a simple covering mound of sand.

The transition from the mastaba to the step pyramid can be clearly seen on the longitudinal section of the step pyramid of Zoser at Saqqara (opposite, centre); key: M, the original, square mastaba; P1, the four-step pyramid developed from it; P2, the final six-step pyramid, a view of which is shown below the section.

The pyramid at Meidum illustrates the change, early in dynasty IV, from the step to the true pyramid (right). It probably began as a seven-step pyramid, but was then heightened by 45 ft. and another step added. The original steps were then filled in and the entire structure was covered with a smooth facing of limestone, transforming it into a true pyramid. This gave rise to, among others, the magnificent dynasty IV pyramids of Cheops, Chephren and Mycerinus at Giza (below).

burial chamber situated beneath the cliff against which the temple was placed. This again was quite unlike anything that had gone before and must be regarded as an original architectural concept. The principal kings of dynasty XII, one of the greatest in Egyptian history, were Amenemhat I, II and III and Sesostris I, II and III, all of whom built pyramids on more or less conventional lines. One of the best preserved is that of Sesostris I, second king of the dynasty, at Lisht. The pyramid itself, 352 ft. square and 200 ft. high, stood within a double enclosure with most of the subsidiary pyramids between the inner and outer walls. The later kings of dynasty XII used brick instead of stone for the inner core of their pyramids. A few pyramids were built during the Second Intermediate period but the form of burial was abandoned at the beginning of dynasty XVIII and the New Kingdom.

Apart from royal burials in pyramids, the burial practice for Middle Kingdom nobles and officials included both mastabas and rock-cut tombs. The main use of the mastaba tomb was in dynasties I–VI, but even in Middle Kingdom times some court officials were still buried in them near the royal pyramids, as in the Old Kingdom. However, use was increasingly made of rock-cut tombs. This practice had begun in the latter part of the Old Kingdom but only in the Middle and New Kingdoms was it used on a large scale. Use was made of the cliff faces found in many places close to the Nile. Instead of a mastaba superstructure containing a pillared hall and chambers, the whole complex was dug out of the solid rock, with a shaft or passage leading down to the actual burial. As in mastabas, the walls were decorated with scenes and inscriptions illustrating the occupant's life, either carved in relief or painted. Externally there was often an elaborate architectural façade. In some cases there were external buildings as well, such as valley temples, following pyramid practice.

In the field of military architecture, there is striking evidence from dynasty XII in Nubia. The rich mineral resources of Nubia had been of interest to the Egyptian kings from the beginning of dynastic times and by dynasty XII Nubia was a colony of Egypt, controlled by a string of powerful fortresses, many of them built or enlarged by Sesostris III (fifth king, dynasty XII). Among others, about a dozen fortresses were built along the Nile in Upper Nubia, from the region of the 2nd Cataract to Semna. Like most non-religious structures in ancient Egypt, they were built of mud brick and not stone. The most northerly is the fortress at Buhen which is rectangular in plan (*c.* 480 × 290 ft. internally). The main defensive wall was 16 ft. thick and 33 ft. high, with closely-set rectangular bastions and large rectangular towers at the corners. Below the wall was a terrace defended by a parapet with semi-circular bastions which projected into a rock-cut ditch some 31 ft. wide and 20 ft. deep. At the main entrance the flanking towers project forward across the ditch and beyond, enclosing a narrow entrance passage some 70 ft. long. The same general characteristics appear in most of the other fortresses. At Mirgissa there is no ditch but the same effect is achieved by double walls 70 ft. apart. Within the forts the buildings (houses, temples, and public buildings) are laid out to a regular plan along straight streets, as at Urunarti, Shafalk, and Askut.

THE NEW KINGDOM (Dynasties XVIII–XX)

Between the Middle and New Kingdoms are the five dynasties (XIII–XVII) of the Second Intermediate period (1786–1567 BC), some of which may, in

fact, be contemporary with each other, one dynasty ruling in Lower Egypt and one in Upper Egypt. Two of these dynasties are those of the Hyksos: Asiatic settlers in the Delta who gradually took political control and extended their influence, if not their direct rule, over much of Egypt. The end of Hyksos domination and the Second Intermediate period came with the growing power of the dynasty XVII princes of Thebes in Upper Egypt, who claimed authority over the whole of the country. Eventually they were successful, and the Hyksos were defeated *c.* 1567 BC by Amosis, founder of dynasty XVIII and the New Kingdom.

In dynasty XVIII royal burial in pyramids was finally abandoned. The pyramid superstructure was too clear an indication of a rich burial and too much of an attraction for tomb robbers. In the New Kingdom the opposite approach was adopted, that of concealing the burial so that there was no surface indication that it existed. The site chosen for the royal tombs was a remote valley in the western hills behind Thebes, and there the kings of dynasties XVIII, XIX and XX were buried in rock-cut tombs cut deep into the heart of the mountain [99]. There were no subsidiary buildings immediately associated with these tombs, as in the case of the pyramids, since this would have betrayed the location of the burial. The funerary temples were built in the Nile valley itself, on the other side of the inter-

99. Tombs in the Valley of the Kings in the western Theban mountains. Over sixty such tombs are known, although only seventeen are open to visitors. In them were buried virtually all the Pharaohs of the eighteenth, nineteenth and twentieth dynasties (1552–1085 BC), beginning with the tomb of Tuthmosis I (1506–1494 BC).

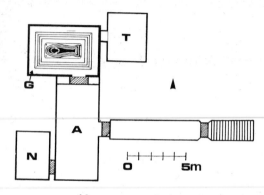

100, 101. Above: ground plan of the tomb of King Tutankhamun in the Valley of the Kings. Key: A, antechamber; G, burial chamber with the four shrines and the sarcophagus; T, treasury; N, annexe of the antechamber. Opposite: Lord Carnarvon and Howard Carter at the entrance of the burial chamber.

vening mountain, on the edge of the cultivation zone. Over sixty rock-cut tombs are known in the Valley of the Kings, the earliest being that of Tuthmosis I, third king of dynasty XVIII. No two are identical but most of them incorporate the same general range of features. From the entrance a series of alternating staircases and descending passages lead deep into the mountain. In some corridors a deep shaft occupies the full width to make access difficult for robbers and also to drain off any surface water running down into the tomb. There are also, in some cases, side chambers opening off the corridors. At the end of this system of corridors and staircases there is the suite of rooms, usually including at least one pillared hall, which formed the tomb proper. The tomb of Ramesses III (second king, dynasty XX) was tunnelled some 300 ft. into the rock and included, among a number of chambers, two pillared halls. The innermost one, with eight pillars, measured 60 × 36 ft. and contained the sarcophagus, and there were smaller associated chambers, three beyond and one at each corner. The tomb of Queen Hatshepsut (fifth ruler, dynasty XVIII), by far the longest of all the rock-cut tombs, is cut 693 ft. into the mountain, descending in that distance no less than 315 ft. Many of the corridor and chamber walls in these rock-cut tombs, are decorated with relief sculpture and texts illustrating the king's journey through the underworld and were intended to help him on his way.

In spite of these elaborate precautions, the plundering of royal tombs continued and none of the funerary equipment of the many great kings of dynasties XVIII, XIX and XX has been found. What did escape the tomb robbers, except for some very minor interference, was the tomb of Tutankhamun, twelfth king of dynasty XVIII [100]. Tutankhamun reigned for only nine years and was still very young when he died. His tomb was very small as compared with most others in the Valley of the Kings and he was not, in fact, historically a very important king. His importance to us lies in the fact that his grave and all his burial equipment were found virtually intact. The richness of this, the burial of a minor king, makes one wonder how rich would have been the burial of one of the great kings of the New Kingdom, such as Tuthmosis III (sixth king, dynasty XVIII) or Ramesses III (second king, dynasty XX). The tomb consists of a stairway leading down to a corridor which in turn leads to the largest room in the layout, the antechamber (c. 26 × 11 ft.). This contained much of the very rich equipment, such as the famous Golden Throne, which the king was deemed to need for the after-life. Opening off one end of the antechamber was the actual burial chamber, only 22 × 13 ft., and this contained the most spectacular of all Tutankhamun's funerary equipment. The burial chamber was virtually filled with the outermost of four wooden shrines (17 × 11 ft.), one inside the other, each one covered with gilded stucco, leaving a space less then 2 ft. wide between it and the four walls of the room. The innermost shrine contained the stone sarcophagus and this in turn contained three mummy-shaped coffins, one inside the other. The outer and middle coffins were of gilded wood, but the main one, containing Tutankhamun's mummy, was of solid gold. In addition, the head and shoulders of the mummy were covered with a mask, also of solid gold. The story of the discovery of this tomb by Howard Carter in 1922 has been told many times. It was the result of many years of painstaking and unrewarding work in the Valley of the Kings which was almost at the point of being abandoned when the discovery was made [101].

The rock-cut tombs in the Valley of the Kings were designed only for the

body of the king and the offerings made at the time of burial. The funerary temple to perpetuate the king's memory was, in order not to reveal the tomb's whereabouts, situated elsewhere. The funerary temples of the New Kingdom rulers were, in fact, on the other side of the mountain from the Valley of the Kings, in the neighbourhood of the modern town of Luxor, where together with the monuments on the east bank of the river, at Karnak, they form the greatest concentration of monuments in the Nile valley. Two of the most elaborate funerary temples are those of Ramesses II (third king, dynasty XIX) and Ramesses III (second king, dynasty XX), both built on very much the same lines. In fact, their funerary temples are only part of a complex of buildings within a great enclosure wall which includes also a royal palace, houses for the priests and other officials and, above all, great batteries of magazines or storage chambers. The temple of Ramesses III is the best preserved. Perhaps its most striking aspect is the fortress-like range of defences surrounding it. The inner group (temple, palace and magazines) is surrounded by a 14 ft. wall, with another wall beyond, and beyond this again is the main enclosure wall, 59 ft. high, with entrances flanked by towers 70 ft. high. Perhaps the most unusual of the funerary temples is that of Queen Hatshepsut, whose tomb was mentioned above. She chose a site against the cliffs at Deir el-Bahri, next to the equally unusual funerary temple of the dynasty XII king Mentuhotep, and built a temple on not dissimilar lines, but without the pyramid. The funerary temples of Ramesses II and III and of Hatshepsut are only three, although perhaps the most spectacular, of a huge range of monuments associated with the Valley of the Kings which stretches for some three miles in the neighbourhood of modern Luxor—ancient Thebes, capital of Egypt during New Kingdom times.

Thebes is also, inevitably perhaps, the site of the greatest temple complex in Egypt, at Karnak, just north of Luxor on the east bank of the Nile. The temple as a whole is dedicated to the god Amon-Re, but it incorporates also the cult of Mut, Amon's wife, and of Khons, son of Amon and Mut, and in fact consists of at least a dozen temple buildings, in three separate but linked enclosures. The main temple has a very complex structural history covering nearly two thousand years of additions and alterations from Middle Kingdom to Roman times, although the bulk of the existing remains are of New Kingdom date, including the famous Hypostyle Hall. This hall (330×170 ft.) contains 134 columns, the twelve largest of which are 64 ft. high and 33 ft. in circumference, rising above the remaining columns to allow the admission of light by means of a clerestory.

Rock-cut tombs have been mentioned already. In addition to his funerary temple at Thebes (the Ramesseum), Ramesses II also built the two famous rock-cut temples at Abu Simbel, now removed from their original site and re-located at a higher level out of reach of the waters of the Aswan High Dam [102]. The larger temple has two colossal statues of Ramesses II, 65 ft. high, on each side of the entrance, carved out of the cliff face. Behind these is a suite of rock-cut chambers, including a hypostyle hall, two smaller halls, six long narrow storage chambers and, c. 150 ft. from the entrance, the sanctuary itself with statues of the king and the three gods to whom the temple is also dedicated: Amon-Re, Re-Herakhty and Ptah. The smaller temple, dedicated to Ramesses' wife, Nefertari, and the goddess Hathor, has six rock-carved figures in front, but these are only c. 33 ft. high.

One of the most unusual episodes in Egyptian history took place during

102. Opposite: the four colossal seated statues of Ramesses II (third king of dynasty XIX) in front of his rock-cut temple at Abu Simbel. This and another similar, adjacent temple have now been removed from their original sites and re-located at a higher level, but in a similar setting, out of reach of the waters of the Aswan High Dam.

the reign of Akhenaten (tenth king, dynasty XVIII, 1379–1362 BC). He adopted the cult of the sun-disk, Aten, and forbade the worship of the traditional Egyptian gods. To further this cult he removed his capital from Thebes to a newly built city called Akhetaten in Middle Egypt (modern El-Amarna). There, extensive excavations have revealed palaces, temples, and private houses built on a lavish scale, although the whole enterprise was short-lived and after Akhenaten's death the capital returned to Thebes. The great Aten temple was unlike the traditional Egyptian temple in that it was largely an open-air affair, with altar and offering tables in a series of linked courtyards.

THE PTOLEMAIC PERIOD (332–30 BC)

After dynasty XX and the end of the New Kingdom the late dynastic period (dynasties XXI–XXXI) occupies the years 1085–332 BC, and will not be dealt with here, although it contains one period, the Saite (dynasty XXVI, 664–525 BC), when there was a return to Egypt's former splendour under six kings: Psammetichus I, Necho II, Psammetichus II, Apries, Amasis and Psammetichus III. Alexander's conquest in 332 BC brought the Egyptian dynastic period to an end and, after his death, power eventually fell into the hands of the Greek governor Ptolemy Lagus who, in 305 BC, declared himself king under the name of Ptolemy Soter. The Ptolemaic period embraced twelve rulers named Ptolemy (I–XII) and Cleopatra, whose death in 30 BC brought the Greek dynasty to an end. The most notable visible achievements of the Ptolemaic period are the temples at Edfu, Kom Ombo, Dendera, Esna, and Philae. The temple of Horus at Edfu is one of the best preserved of all Egyptian temples, with much of the roof still intact [103]. Its most noticeable feature is the huge pylon, which gives access to the forecourt and then, via two pillared halls, to the sanctuary, surrounded by a series of chapels. The smaller temple at Kom Ombo was generally similar, although it had to make provision for two sanctuaries (Suchos and Haroëris), and this is evident in the plan, starting with the double entrance. The temple of Hathor at Dendera was started late in the Ptolemaic period and was in fact completed in Roman times by the Emperors Augustus and Tiberius; like the Edfu temple it is in an excellent state of preservation. It has no pylon and no colonnaded forecourt but is otherwise built on the same lines as the other two temples. The temple of Khnum at Esna has an external colonnade in the manner of a Greek temple but otherwise follows a normal Egyptian arrangement. The Great Temple of Isis on the island of Philae, near Aswan, is the centre of a complex of buildings, many of them erected by the Roman Emperors.

DOMESTIC ARCHITECTURE

In contrast to the wide range of stone-built and rock-cut burial and religious monuments, not much is known about Egyptian domestic architecture, including royal palaces, mainly because it was built for the most part of perishable mud brick. However, we do have remains of a number of workers' villages and, at a higher social level, of houses or villas occupied by officials at the city of Akhenaten, together with evidence from tomb-paintings and house models found in tombs. One thing which emerges from all this is that it is necessary to distinguish between town houses and country houses. The tomb-paintings show quite clearly that the town houses of the Middle and

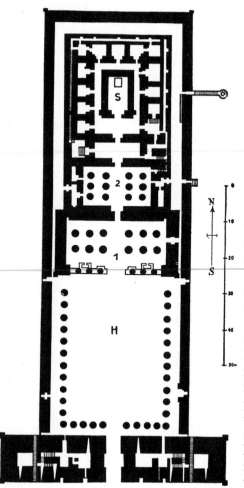

103. Plan of the temple of Horus at Edfu. Key: H, court; 1, pronaos; 2, hypostyle hall; S, sanctuary.

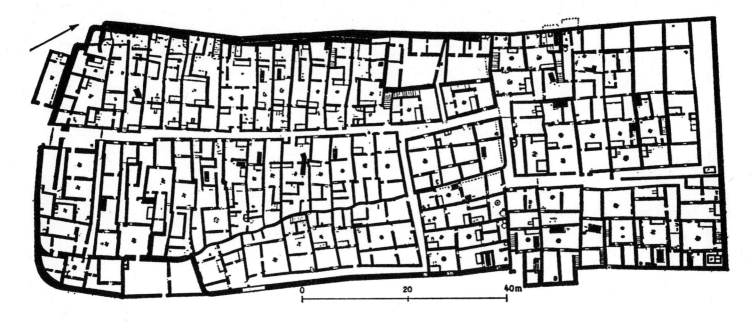

0   20   40m

New Kingdom periods were of two or three storeys, with kitchens and servants quarters on the ground floor, living rooms and bedrooms on the upper floors and bins for the storage of grain on the roof. Such a town house is quite clearly that of a well-to-do or important person. A similar house, but this time with all the accommodation on one level, is represented by the Amarna type at the city of Akhenaten (dynasty XVIII). In this, the rooms are grouped around a large, square central hall with two or four columns, and this rises above the others to let in light. On one side of the hall are the porch, vestibule, and entrance loggia, and opening from the hall are self-contained suites of rooms for the family and for visitors. The house stood within a walled garden which contained the kitchen, servants quarters, stables, and granaries, as well as, in some cases, an ornamental pool and a private chapel or shrine.

A much humbler standard of living is represented by the three workers' villages at Kahun (Middle Kingdom), Amarna and Deir el-Medineh (both New Kingdom), although two of them also contained larger houses, presumably for officials. Kahun, built in connection with the construction of the pyramid of Sesostris II (fourth king, dynasty XII), contained a governor's mansion, ten or twelve very large houses and hundreds of very small houses, back-to-back on parallel streets. The Amarna village contained only one large house and the remaining houses (about seventy, on five streets) were built to a fairly uniform plan of four rooms (outer hall, living room, kitchen and bedroom, with stairs leading up to the roof). Each house covered just over 500 square ft. ($31 \times 16\frac{1}{2}$ ft.). Both Kahun and Amarna were obviously carefully planned with straight streets and a rectangular enclosing wall. Deir el-Medineh, on the other hand, was much more irregular in plan and was built to house men working on the royal tombs in the Valley of the Kings [104]. However, the house plan was similar to that in Amarna.

The clay models of houses (soul-houses) placed in tombs give some further information about domestic architecture. They vary in type but the most elaborate consist of a rectangular, walled courtyard with the house set at

104. Plan of Deir el-Medineh, western Thebes.

the back. The front of the house consists of a columned portico with a row of rooms behind or, more elaborately, with a columned entrance hall behind and rooms opening off this on three sides. The upper rooms, reached by an outside staircase, may also have a portico, or else their front wall is flush with the portico below. The courtyard would suggest that houses of this type were built in the country rather than in the towns.

EGYPTIAN WRITING

Nothing is more closely associated with ancient Egypt than the way, or one of the ways, in which the Egyptian language was written down. Hieroglyphic, although the most striking way of writing the language, was by no means the only form in which Egyptian was expressed. As can well be imagined, for business purposes something which could be written rather more quickly than the very decorative hieroglyphic was required, and the hieratic form of writing was used in parallel with the hieroglyphic form throughout dynastic times. In the later stages of Egyptian history two other forms were used, Demotic and Coptic.

Hieroglyphic is much more than simple picture writing although presumably it had its origins therein. Basically, hieroglyphic signs are of two types: ideograms or sense signs which convey their meaning pictorially; and phonograms, or sound signs which, like the letters of our alphabet, have an agreed sound value. Most Egyptian words written in hieroglyphic consist of a combination of the two. For example, the word for boat, *dpt* (vowels were not written in ancient Egyptian), consists of the sound signs for *d* (⬭), *p* (☐) and *t* (⌂) followed by a picture of a boat (the determinative), which has no sound value but which helps to make clear or determine the meaning of the word: ⬭☐⌂⛵. This example will show that, in spite of its pictorial appearance, hieroglyphic writing involved correct spelling just as much as any other form of writing. Equally it involved the correct use of a sophisticated system of grammar which was as far removed from simple picture writing as any other language of the ancient world.

Hieratic is, in effect, a simplified, cursive form of the more precise hieroglyphic shapes, resulting from the use of a reed pen on papyrus for business purposes, where speed was more important than a decorative appearance. The results are easier to illustrate than describe. In spite of its overall appearance, the derivation from the hieroglyphic forms is still reasonably clear. The same is not true of the third form of writing, Demotic, which developed around 700 BC. This was a very abbreviated and rapid form of hieratic and much more difficult to relate to the original hieroglyphic forms. Under the Ptolemies, Greek became the official language although Egyptian survived in the bulk of the population to become Coptic, that is, Egyptian written in the Greek alphabet, which is still used today in the liturgies of the Coptic church.

AFRICA: GENERAL

The special experience of Egypt, conditioned by the Nile valley and by close proximity to the Near East, was not repeated in the rest of Africa, where a very different pattern of events took place. Broadly speaking, Africa participated fully with Europe and Asia in the development of Lower and Middle Palaeolithic culture as described in Chapter 3. In the Upper Palaeolithic stage, however, Africa as a whole differed markedly from the rest of the Old

World. South of the Sahara, progress virtually stopped at the Middle Palaeolithic stage, until this was superseded by a Neolithic culture which spread south only very gradually and very late in comparison with events in the Mediterranean world. There is nothing in the southern half of Africa which corresponds to the well-established Upper Palaeolithic sequence of Europe. Even in the northern half of the continent (i.e. the Sahara and Northwest Africa) there is still a very marked difference of experience as compared with Europe.

Up to about 40,000 BC (i.e. the beginning of the Upper Palaeolithic in Europe and western Asia) Africa was more or less in step with the rest of the Palaeolithic world. Thereafter much of the period occupied by the five-period sequence of Europe (Châtelperronian to Magdalenian) was taken up in North Africa by the Aterian culture, named after the site of Bir-el-Ater in Tunisia, and by Levalloisian/Mousterian survivals. The most notable features of the Aterian are the tanged points, some small enough to be arrowheads, others large enough to be spearheads, which are found widely over North-west Africa and the Sahara. The Aterian seems to have developed out of the Mousterian culture so that it is basically of Middle Palaeolithic type. Tanged points closely resembling the Aterian are found in the Solutrean period in Spain (20,000–15,000 BC) and this probably indicates the approximate period of use in Africa. The broad pattern of events in North Africa, then, would appear to have involved, from 40,000 BC on, a survival of the Middle Palaeolithic Mousterian culture (instead of the new, Upper Palaeolithic cultures as in Europe and the Near East), with the development out of it, c. 25–20,000 BC, of an Aterian culture, with both Mousterian and Aterian surviving as late as 12,000 or 10,000 BC. In the period following the Mousterian/Aterian cultures, North-west Africa and the Sahara need to be considered separately.

NORTH-WEST AFRICA

In North-west Africa the change to stone and flint tools based on the blade technique (i.e. the technique of the Upper Palaeolithic elsewhere) took place as late as 12–10,000 BC. The two cultures involved are the Oranian and the Capsian, although their exact relationship has for many years been a matter of dispute. However, the advent of Carbon-14 dates in recent years suggests that the Oranian is the earlier, beginning at the date indicated above, c. 12–10,000 BC. It occurs in Morocco and the coastal regions of Algeria and Tunisia. Its outstanding tool is the backed blade (above p. 69). Between 7000 and 6000 BC there was a further change which saw the introduction of microlithic tools as the main ingredient in the Capsian culture, although backed blades continued in use. The Capsian is found mainly in the inland areas of Tunisia and eastern Algeria, i.e. where the Oranian did not occur, and it has been suggested that there existed also in this region a Lower Capsian, contemporary with the Oranian elsewhere. This is a problem still to be resolved. The Capsian (or Upper Capsian if a Lower stage is distinguished) thus occupies the same sort of position as the Mesolithic of Europe and western Asia, succeeding Upper Palaeolithic-type blade industries on the one hand and immediately preceding, and affecting, the following Neolithic cultures on the other. Indeed, the name of the North-west African Neolithic, the Neolithic of Capsian Tradition, adequately indicates the relationship between the two cultures.

The arrival of the Neolithic in North-west Africa is part of the broader pattern of Neolithic expansion from the Near East which from *c.* 6000–5500 BC on affected virtually the whole Mediterranean world and much of central and western Europe as well. The distribution pattern of Carbon-14 determinations indicates the establishment of a Neolithic economy in the western Mediterranean (i.e. Spain and North-west Africa) in the period 4000–2800 BC. In spite of the new features (pottery, polished stone tools, domestic animals and cultivated plants) the bulk of the Neolithic equipment is in the Capsian style, suggesting that the Capsian people still formed the bulk of the population, hence the name, Neolithic of Capsian Tradition. Presumably it was the arrival of new ideas, brought in by a few people rather than the influx of a vast new population, which initiated the Neolithic period in North-west Africa. The source of these new ideas is almost certainly the east Mediterranean area where already by 5000 BC a Neolithic economy had reached south-eastern Europe. The route by which they arrived in North-west Africa is indicated by pottery decorated with impressions of cardium shells. Such pottery is found in virtually all the coastal regions of the western Mediterranean and indicates very clearly arrival by sea.

Very little is known about habitation sites in North-west Africa. Caves and rock shelters were certainly popular but because evidence in them is more easily preserved than in open-air sites, especially in the existing climate, it is difficult to estimate just what proportion of the total they represent. Neolithic equipment, in addition to the range of traditional Capsian microlithic and other tools, included polished stone axes and adzes, stone rings (for digging sticks?), grooved stones (for straightening arrow shafts), querns and occasional stone bowls or mortars [105]. Bonework was common and included awls, needles, knives, spatulas, and burnishing tools. Ostrich egg shells were used both as containers and as the raw material for the manufacture of beads, which were made also from natural pebbles and from seashells. Neolithic pottery is rarely found complete so that much more is known about decoration than shape. As far as can be ascertained from surviving remains, round or conical bases seem to have been more common than flat bases. Decoration was mostly by simple impression with a pointed tool or a finger-tip, although more complex patterns were produced by a comb-like implement either impressed into or drawn across the soft clay.

There is, of course, no Bronze Age period in Africa outside Egypt so that the African Neolithic persisted until the advent of an iron-using economy. In North-west Africa this was brought in first by the Phoenicians, who founded the city of Carthage *c.* 814 BC, so that the North-west African Neolithic can be said to have lasted for about 3000 years, from shortly after 4000 BC to a little after 1000 BC. From Carthage, at the north-eastern corner of the region, knowledge of iron tools gradually spread over the whole of North-west Africa, bringing the Neolithic to an end. By the time this process was complete the whole west Mediterranean area was emerging into the light of written history, beyond which point the story of North-west Africa will not be pursued here.

THE SAHARA

Events in the Sahara followed an even simpler course than those in North-west Africa. The Capsian and Oranian industries found there occur only rarely in the desert, and then only in late forms. Apart from these, the main

105. Opposite: Neolithic flintwork from North-west Africa, including backed blades (1, 2, 5), notched blades (3, 4), scrapers (6, 7), simple blades (11, 12), and a range of microlithic tools (24–38).

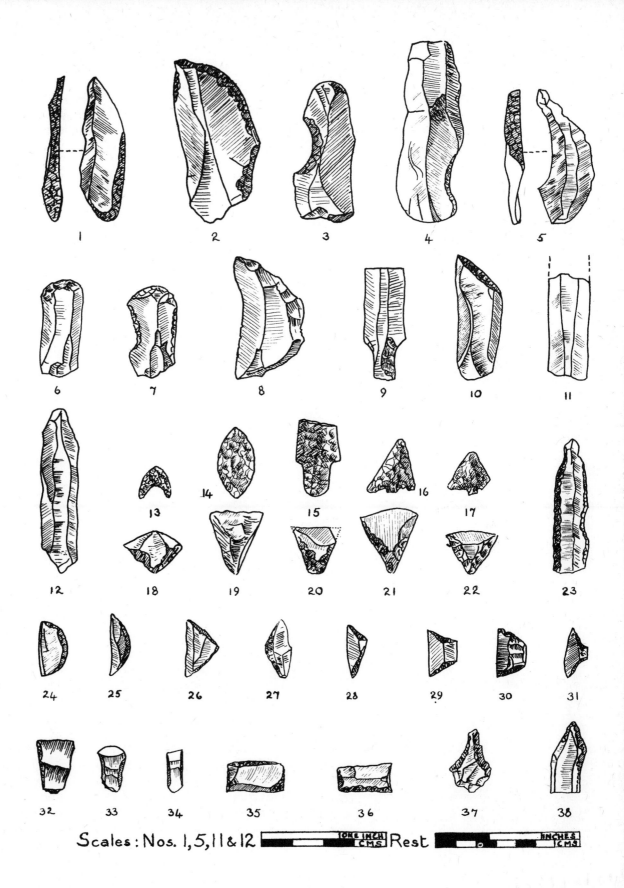

Scales: Nos. 1,5,11 & 12 [ONE INCH CMS] Rest [INCHES CMS]

pre-Neolithic Saharan industries are the Mousterian and the Aterian, already encountered in North-west Africa, which may have persisted even beyond the dates mentioned there, *c.* 12–10,000 BC. Just how they were related to the Saharan Neolithic is difficult to say. Because of the severe erosion caused by the desert climate, virtually all sites have been reduced to surface assemblages and all stratigraphy has been destroyed, making it extremely difficult to establish any chronological relationships. The fact that assemblages exist at all suggests that the climate was different, since no Neolithic culture could have been established in present-day Saharan conditions. Further confirmation of this is found in the rock-drawings (to be considered later) which depict animals that could not survive in a desert environment.

In the period under discussion Europe was in the grip of the last (Würm) glaciation, bringing with it Siberian-like tundra conditions over most of what is now temperate Europe. The general effect of the southward advance of the ice-sheet over northern Europe was to push all the climatic zones further south than they are today. In particular, some at least of the relatively mild, rain-bearing westerly winds which produce the present-day European climate must have been diverted sufficiently far south to affect the Sahara, giving it enough rainfall to make life possible in what has since become a dry wilderness. Quite clearly, if the glacial advance had this effect on the Sahara, then equally the end of the glacial period, from *c.* 10,000 BC on, would also profoundly affect conditions there. As the ice retreated, so the rain-bearing westerly winds withdrew further to the north until eventually they assumed their present position across Europe, leaving the Sahara a prey to increasing desiccation, ultimately to become what we think of today as the Sahara— a vast, uninhabited part of the world's surface.

It was against this climatic background that the later prehistory of the Sahara evolved. From *c.* 40,000 BC on, the Sahara, wetter than now, supported the surviving Mousterian culture and its derivative, the Aterian, much as in North-west Africa. The North-west African Capsian and Oranian cultures, however, did not penetrate the Sahara to any great extent, so that presumably the Aterian survived even longer there (beyond 12,000 BC) than in the North-west. It survived, however, in a deteriorating climate, and if it had not been replaced it would have eventually died out, and that would have been the last episode of Saharan prehistory. However, the climatic deterioration was gradual, spread over several thousand years, and was still not sufficiently far advanced to prevent the establishment of a Saharan Neolithic culture.

With agriculture and stock-breeding well established both to the east (Egypt) and to the north (North-west Africa and Cyrenaica), it would be difficult to suggest any other source for the origins of the Saharan Neolithic than one or other of these areas, in the period from *c.* 4000 BC on. Apart from pottery and polished stone axes, the outstanding feature of the Saharan Neolithic were the arrowheads, indicating a strong hunting element in the economy. Although many of the arrowheads were skilfully flaked on both faces and were similar to Egyptian types, many others were of much simpler manufacture, resembling Aterian types and suggesting a survival of Aterian traditions in the area. In the northern half of the desert, most sites are associated with the sand-dune areas or *ergs*, and this is understandable when it is realized that the *ergs* overlie (and indeed are a result of) the elaborate but now fossilized Saharan river system. In the southern half, polished stone axes and other polished stone equipment occur in much greater quantity,

106. Opposite: rock-painting of a herdsman and cattle, from Tin Tazarift, Tassili, in the central Sahara, indicating the existence, at some time in the past, of less severe climatic conditions than exist there today.

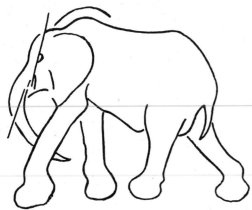

107. Rock-drawing of an elephant, from the Fezzan in the central Sahara. The drawing was carried out by making a grooved line in the dark surface of the rock and exposing the lighter rock beneath. The climatic conditions in which elephants can exist are now to be found only to the south, many hundreds of miles from such rock-drawings.

suggesting a greater emphasis on agriculture and a settled, sedentary way of life.

The most striking illustration of the difference between the prehistoric and present-day Sahara is provided by the rock-drawings which are found mainly in the northern half of the desert [106, 107]. These depict such species as the giraffe, elephant, rhinoceros, hippopotamus, and crocodile, as well as domestic animals such as cattle, all carried out in the same range of styles. It has been suggested that the drawings of the wild animals belong to a pre-Neolithic (presumably Aterian) phase, but the fact that they are carried out in the same technique and the same styles (naturalistic to schematic) as the domestic species indicates that all belong to the Neolithic period. More than anything else, the wild animals which appear in the rock-drawings show how different the Sahara must have been 4000–6000 years ago. The environment in which they exist now, savannah with open forest or woodland, suggests the sort of conditions which must have prevailed in the Sahara in the Neolithic period.

The gradual climatic deterioration to present-day desert conditions eventually brought about the abandonment of the Sahara, with the displaced population moving both north and south, at some time within the last 2000 years BC. The movement brought Neolithic culture into sub-Saharan Africa but at the same time the onset of desert conditions virtually sealed off the southern half of the continent from developments in the Mediterranean world. In the circumstances, a Saharan Iron Age cannot be looked for. By the time the use of iron could have begun to spread from North-west Africa, the trend of all movements would have been out of, not into, the desert, if indeed by that time it had not already been completely evacuated.

The present-day Sahara is flanked to the south by a great east–west band of savannah from the Atlantic coast to the upper reaches of the Nile and beyond. Neolithic culture in the western part of this band is almost certainly derived from the Sahara and ultimately North-west Africa. South of the savannah is the tropical forest zone and this may have been a barrier to any further spread. In any case the western sector is soon terminated to the south by the coast, so that it is in a sense something of a dead end as far as the spread of culture is concerned. Africa is, however, open to penetration from another source. The savannah zone provides ultimately a link with Egyptian civilization, via the Nile, and the Neolithic culture in the western sector may have been derived from there as much as from the Sahara. Certainly, in the southern Sahara there are close resemblances between the Neolithic in the Khartoum area and sites far to the west, suggesting strong east–west contact. However, the greatest significance of the upper Nile region is that of bringing Neolithic (and later, Iron Age) culture into east and eventually southern Africa. The east African route by-passed the tropical forest zone and consequently allowed most of eastern and southern Africa to be affected by developments in the Mediterranean world, albeit in some cases at a very late date.

INDIA

Indian archaeology is dominated by the Indus civilization, centred on the Indus river valley in the north-west, and by its two major sites, Mohenjo Daro and Harappa. Before dealing with the Indus civilization, however, something must be said about the preceding cultures in the same general area. There can be little doubt that the knowledge of agriculture and stock-breeding reached the Indian sub-continent from the north-west, ultimately from the ancient centres of the Tigris/Euphrates valley, some time during the fourth millenium BC. Virtually all the early sites are found in the Baluch hills in the region of Quetta, at the end of a natural route from the Balan Pass. These early settlers in India were already using copper and were making their pottery on the wheel. By the middle of the third millenium BC a pattern of agricultural village cultures was widespread in the area to the west of the Indus valley. Variations on the same basic pattern are indicated most clearly by the pottery, which also indicates some of the links of the cultures involved. Thus the decoration on Zhob and Togau pottery (friezes of humped oxen with elongated legs) may be compared with similar decoration on pottery from Tepe Hissar and Tepe Sialk in Iran, a thousand miles to the west. Similarly the tethered bulls on the black-painted Kulli pottery are in the same style as bulls from Susa and Sumeria in the early dynastic period. Other Baluchistan styles include Quetta ware, from the region immediately around Quetta, and Nal and Amri wares, found in the triangular area south-wards from Quetta to the coast, west of the Indus river.

While there is no doubt that these agricultural village communities are earlier as a whole than the Indus valley or Harappan civilization, they occupy an entirely separate area, and as yet no clear relationship has been established between the two. The origins of the Indus valley civilization have yet to be found. Presumably they lie in the valley itself, buried deep beneath the more spectacular remains of the Classic period of Indus civilization.

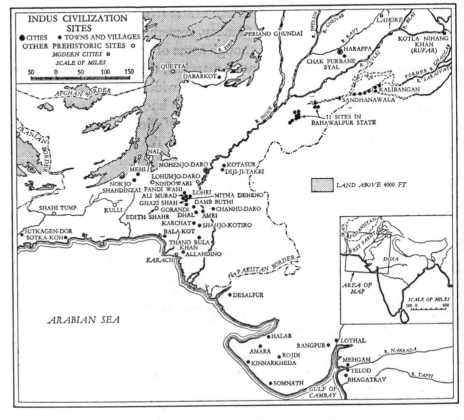

108. Distribution map of the Indus civilization.

THE HARAPPA CIVILIZATION

There is clear evidence of the Harappa or Indus civilization from over seventy sites along the Indus valley and its tributaries and along the coast in both directions for some 350 miles [108]. This is an enormous area, 1000 miles from Rupar in the north-east to Sutkagen-dor in the west and 800 miles to the sites around the Gulf of Cambay in the south. The sites include villages, towns, and cities, notably Mohenjo Daro and Harappa. Before describing some of the principal sites of the culture, one or two more general points can be made. Without getting involved in details of chronology it can be stated that, in round figures, the Harappa civilization flourished from *c.* 2500–1700 BC. Its downfall has in the past been attributed to the Aryan invasions but these were almost certainly a couple of centuries too late (*c.* 1500–1400 BC) and other reasons have to be sought. There may have been a climatic change or an uplift in the level of the Indus valley, causing widespread flooding. A change in the balance of nature, caused by the extensive use of timber for firing bricks, may have had adverse effects on food production. Some or all of these factors may have been involved, but as yet the final solution has still to be found.

The outstanding sites of the Indus civilization are undoubtedly the two great cities of Mohenjo Daro and Harappa, possibly twin capitals, some 350 miles apart. They show evidence of careful planning and layout and bear a remarkable resemblance to each other, as far as can be ascertained from excavation and the existing remains [109]. Each city appears to have had a

109. Comparative layouts of Mohenjo Daro and Harappa, the two principal cities of the Indus civilization in north-west India. Although some 350 miles apart they display notable similarities in plan. In particular, they have strongly defended citadels of similar size and shape on the western sides of the city.

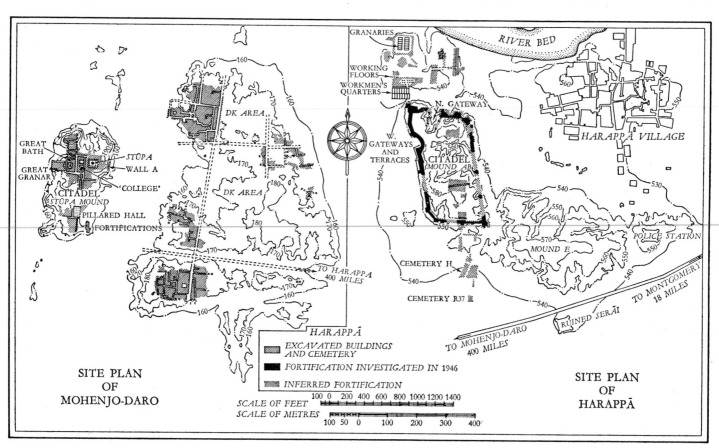

136

110. The Great Bath in the citadel at Mohenjo Daro. Although the precise functions of the bath (39 × 23 × 8 ft. deep) are not known, it was almost certainly used for ritual purposes rather than for relaxation.

circumference of about three miles. In each case there is a noticeably higher mound on the western side of the site, with its own defences, forming a citadel dominating the rest of the city. The citadels are rectangular in plan, *c.* 1400 × 700 ft., and are both, perhaps by chance, orientated north and south. The rest of each city appears to have been laid out in accordance with a grid pattern.

At Harappa, the best-known sector of the city is the citadel on the western side. This is a parallelogram in plan, defined by massive defensive walls some 45 ft. thick at the base, but tapering towards the top, built of mud brick, but with an outer facing, 4–7 ft. thick, of baked bricks. At intervals along the wall were rectangular bastions or towers which appear to have risen above the height of the wall. The principal entrance seems to have been on the north side where the ramparts turn inwards, parallel to each other. Not much is known about the internal buildings, although it is quite certain from the remains that the area was densely occupied. The whole of the citadel rested on a massive platform of mud and mud brick 20–25 ft. high above the surrounding area.

The pattern in the citadel at Mohenjo Daro is the reverse of that just described: the internal buildings are well preserved, while only small parts of the defensive system are known. It, too, is built on an artificial platform of mud and mud brick 20–40 ft. high above the surrounding plain. The principal buildings revealed by excavation are the Bath, the Granary and the Assembly Hall, as they are known. Perhaps the most famous and most remarkable of the three is the Great Bath or Tank, 39 ft. long, 23 ft. wide

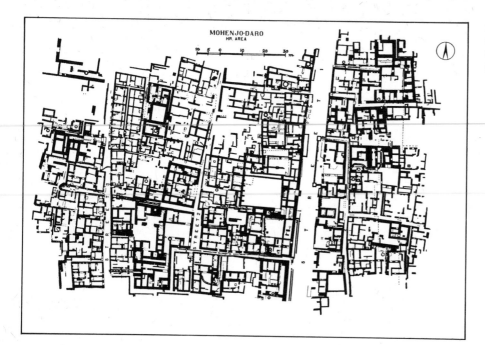

MOHENJO-DARO
HR. AREA

and 8 ft. deep, with flights of steps descending into it at the north and south ends. The Bath was made watertight by gypsum mortar and bitumen [110]. Surrounding the courtyard in which the Bath stood was a corridor beyond which were ranges of rooms on all four sides. Immediately to the west of the Bath were the foundations of what was almost certainly a Granary. These consisted of a series of solid rectangular brick pillars *c.* 5 ft. high, separated by narrow spaces to allow for the circulation of air. On these piers was built a rectangular Granary originally 150 ft. long and 75 ft. wide. North and east of the Bath and Granary are a series of buildings, the precise functions of which are not known. In the southern half of the citadel the principal named building is the Assembly Hall. This is a room about 90 ft. square, divided into five aisles by four rows of pillars, five pillars in each row. Assembly seems the most likely function for such a room.

Apart from some well-defined remains immediately north of the citadel (a block of granaries, a block of humble dwellings and some working floors), not much is known about the Lower City at Harappa, certainly not enough to draw the plan, even in outline. At Mohenjo Daro, on the other hand, the layout of the main streets, and of some of the minor streets, is fairly clear [111]. As far as can be ascertained, the city consisted of three main north–south arteries and two main east–west arteries, dividing it into twelve main blocks or insulae, each about 1200 ft. from north to south and 800 ft. from east to west. The middle block on the west side formed the citadel and the remaining eleven blocks the Lower City. If the number of blocks, and their dimensions, are correct, then the original city would have been square in plan with each side approximately one mile long. The main streets or arteries were 30 ft. wide while the smaller streets or lanes which sub-divided the insulae were 5–10 ft. wide [112]. Most of the houses opened on to these lesser roads, rather than the major roads. The basic pattern of the houses was that of a central open courtyard surrounded by ranges of rooms in the manner of Mesopotamian houses. Some houses of this pattern were on a noticeably larger scale than others, with very much thicker walls, and may be interpreted as palaces or some sort of public buildings. One of the most notable features of the city was the elaborate system of brick drains, which were of very advanced construction for the period.

Following the collapse of the Harappa civilization (for reasons which as yet we do not know), the next major event in Indian history was the invasion of Aryan-speaking peoples, probably in or after 1500 BC. Unlike the relatively sophisticated Harappan people, the Aryans were semi-barbaric stock breeders and farmers, living in villages rather than cities and towns, and making use of copper and bronze. There is little doubt that the Aryans entered India from the north-west, from the direction of Iran and the ancient Near East. This period also saw an extension eastwards, beyond the Indus area and into the Ganges basin and the eastern part of northern India, of copper-using communities of the same general type, based on stock-raising and cereal-growing. In parts of southern and eastern India, and in places very close to or overlapping the copper-using communities, are the remains of 'Neolithic' cultures characterized by polished stone axes and hand-made pottery. The earliest of these simple peasant communities date from shortly after 2000 BC, but they appear to have persisted for a considerable period alongside the more advanced copper-using, Aryan-speaking people. Knowledge of iron-working

112. View of a narrow lane in area HR of Mohenjo Daro, the main area shown on the plan (opposite).

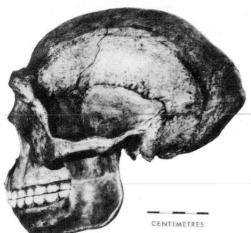

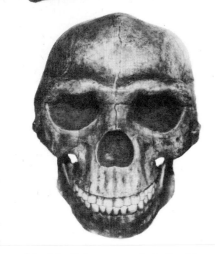

CENTIMETRES

113. Model of the restored skull of Peking Man, from a cave deposit at Chou-k'ou-tien, China.

must have come into northern India at the latest by 516 BC, when the Persian king Darius conquered the area and included it in the Persian Empire, and it may well have come in a century or two earlier, again ultimately from Iran and the Near East.

Persian domination was succeeded by Alexander's conquest some two centuries later. To a great extent his intervention in Indian affairs drew the many petty Indian rulers together in opposition, and his death in 323 BC marked the beginning of a period of unity under Chandragupta Maurya. For practical purposes this is the beginning of written history in India and, although by no means the end of the archaeological picture, is as far as it will be pursued here.

CHINA

The earliest periods of Chinese prehistory, the Palaeolithic and Mesolithic, will be dealt with only briefly here. The most famous Lower Palaeolithic site in China, and one of the best known in the world, is Chou-k'ou-tien, the site where Peking Man was discovered in 1921 [113]. Two other major sites of the period are Lan-t'ien and K'o-ho [116]. The stone tools used were mainly of the chopper variety. In the succeeding Middle Palaeolithic period there was a considerable advance in flint technology and the human remains were of Neanderthaloid type. In the Upper Palaeolithic period *Homo sapiens* appeared and the stone equipment was based on a blade technique. In the Chinese Mesolithic, as in the European, life was based on a hunting/fishing economy and much of the stonework was of microlithic type.

The post-Mesolithic periods of Chinese archaeology will be dealt with under four main chronological headings: the Yang-shao culture; the Lung-shan culture; the Shang civilization; and the Chou civilization. This brings the story down to 221 BC, the end of the feudal period in China and, in 207 BC, to the beginning of the Han Dynasty and a unified Chinese Empire which will not be considered here.

The Yang-shao culture, the Neolithic of China, first developed on the middle reaches of the Hwang-ho river in the northern part of the country. The Yang-shao peasants occupied loess soils and presumably therefore were able to cope with forest clearance. In keeping with this picture is the fact that their main domestic animal was the pig, ideally adapted to grubbing in a woodland environment, and the fact that their houses involved substantial amounts of timber. The main crop grown was millet and in the earlier periods the ground was probably cleared by the slash-and-burn technique, which implies only temporary occupation. However, in the fully-developed Neolithic stage there is abundant evidence of permanent occupation and more advanced methods of cultivation. The stone equipment included heavy, polished stone axes (for tree felling?) and lighter polished stone adzes, possible for the dressing and shaping of timber. Certainly the dressing of timber uprights is suggested by the house remains from some of the Yang-shao settlements.

One of the most carefully investigated villages is Pan-p'o-ts'un, which in each of its two main periods of occupation appears to have contained about one hundred separate dwellings, either round, rectangular, or square [114]. These were built of wattle-and-daub on a substantial timber framework. The floors, in some cases sunk below ground level, were plastered. The dwelling area was surrounded by a ditch about 18 ft. wide and 12 ft. deep.

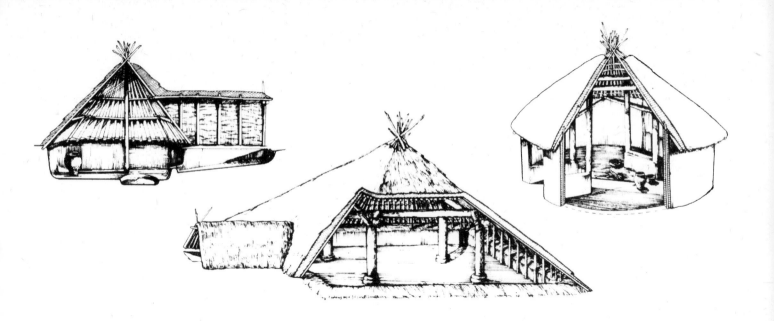

114, 115. Above: reconstructed house types at Pan-p'o-ts'un, a village of the Yang-shao culture, the first period of the Chinese Neolithic. Below: reconstruction of a house of the much later Shang period (1850–1100 BC) at Hsiao-t'un, Anyang.

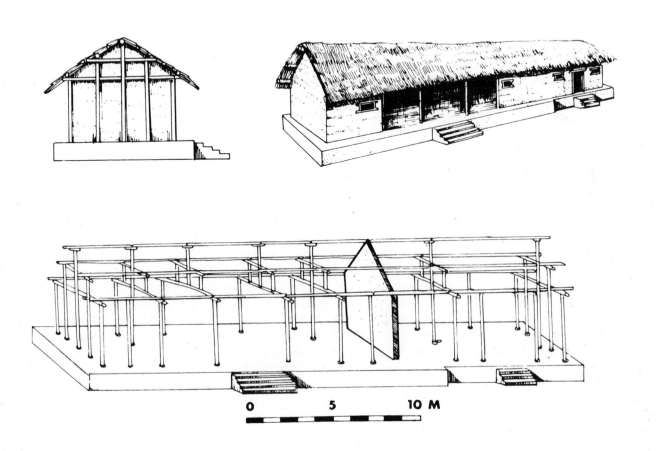

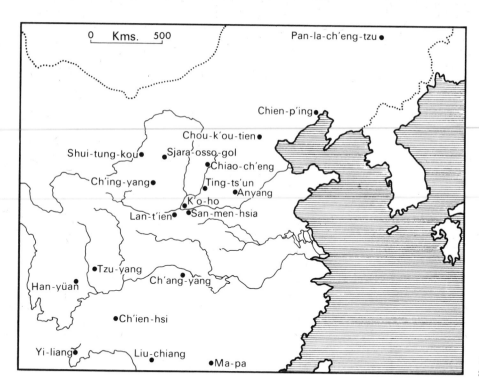

116. Left: distribution of Palaeolithic cultures and fossil Man in China.

117. Opposite: painted pottery of the Yang-shao culture. ▶

Beyond it to the north was the village cemetery, with more than 130 adult burials, and to the east was the kiln area where pottery was manufactured. This division of the village area into dwellings, cemetery, and kilns was the standard pattern of Yang-shao villages.

Yang-shao pottery includes plain, incised, or impressed wares and a wide variety of painted pottery [117]. The latter is normally brick-red or yellow-brown in colour and is painted with red or black pigment. In some cases a white slip or coating was applied before painting. On the whole painting in black was rather more common than painting in red. Designs included fish, animal, and plant patterns as well as geometrical shapes such as spirals, wavy lines, zigzags, circles, semi-circles, triangles and lozenges. The range of shapes was fairly limited and included open bowls, narrow-mouthed globular jars, and onion-shaped vessels with narrow necks and loop handles at the widest points. The non-painted pottery was usually of sandy paste with incised and cord-impressed decoration. Shapes included open bowls, globular pots with narrow mouths, and hemispherical vessels with three legs.

A second, more advanced Neolithic is represented by the Lung-shan culture, which developed in the eastern part of the Hwang-ho basin, possibly from the same source as, but later than, the Yang-shao culture and benefiting to some extent from its experience. The two existed side-by-side and between them accounted for virtually the whole of the Hwang-ho basin. The Lung-shan peasants practised a more intensive agriculture than the Yang-shao. There was greater clearance of the forest for farming purposes and the domestic animals included cattle, sheep and horses. There is more evidence of settled communities in long-term occupation, making substantial defences a necessary adjunct. During the Lung-shan phase there was a great expansion of the area in which agriculture was practised, the main additions being the

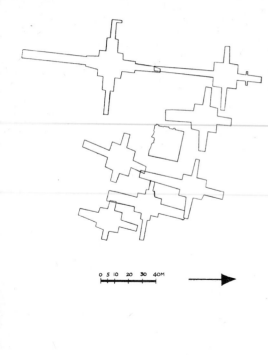

0 5 10 20 30 40M →

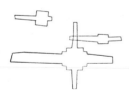

118. Plan of the royal tombs in the Hsi-pei-kang cemetery, Anyang.

great Yangtse basin to the south of the Hwang-ho and the whole coastal region, eventually as far as South-east Asia. In return, as it were, rice, which in its wild form is at home in South-east Asia, was brought into the range of Chinese agricultural produce.

With the succeeding Shang civilization Chinese history begins, defined by written records, as opposed to the preceding prehistoric Yang-shao and Lung-shan Neolithic cultures. The Shang civilization (c. 1850–1100 BC) also witnessed the development of bronze metallurgy, so that altogether it represented a considerable advance on the Lung-shan culture. In spite of this, however, it appears to have developed out of the latter, the marked difference being due to an acceleration in development rather than a complete change of population. Although Shang remains are found in most parts of China, the major sites are found on the middle reaches of the Hwang-ho and in the area to the north and north-east. One of the most important Shang sites is (modern) Cheng-chou (possibly the ancient capital Ao), which demonstrates the striking difference between the Shang civilization and the Lung-shan period. Cheng-chou was a city, defended by a substantial wall enclosing an area of over a square mile. The wall still survives to a height of 30 ft. and is over 100 ft. thick at the base. It was built of successive layers of compressed earth, each layer four or five inches thick. Because it is overlaid by the modern city, not much excavation has been possible in the interior of the site, but there are many other ancillary sites in the same area, indicating that the city was an important centre in Shang times.

In the case of Anyang there is no doubt that it was the capital city, Yin, during the last 270-odd years of the Shang civilization, c. 1370–1100 BC. Like Cheng-chou it was surrounded by a series of lesser sites, setting it off as an important centre [115]. Its importance is further indicated by the presence of what is usually interpreted as a royal cemetery, consisting of eleven elaborate subterranean graves, these coinciding in number with the eleven kings who are known to have ruled from Anyang [118]. Each grave consists of a great rectangular pit with sloping sides, approached by descending ramps on one or two, or, more commonly, four sides, producing a cruciform plan. The pits are up to 60 ft. square and 40 ft. deep, and the longer ramps start up to 170 ft. back from the edge; usually one ramp is considerably longer than the other three. The main burial was placed in a wooden chamber in the centre of the pit, accompanied by sacrificial burials in other parts of the pit. The main, presumably royal, burial was furnished with a rich range of material equipment, much of it among the best examples of Shang art, and included pottery, bronzes, and articles of stone, jade, shell, and bone.

One of the most brilliant achievements of the Shang civilization was in bronze-casting. Bronze was used mainly for the manufacture of ceremonial, military, and hunting equipment, i.e., for a very limited section of the population. The bulk of the everyday tools and weapons used by the population as a whole was still mainly of stone, wood, etc. Among the most complicated of Shang products are the bronze vessels, often three-legged, with intricate cast decoration. These necessitated a fairly complex multi-piece mould. The process involved the modelling of a replica in clay of the desired vessel with all its decoration. This is baked hard and then soft clay is applied to the outside in a series of separate sections to receive the imprint of the model. These are then removed and the model is broken away from the core. The mould sections are re-assembled around the core and the space between,

formerly occupied by the model, is filled with molten bronze which assumes the shape of the desired vessel [121].

Shang agriculture embraced wheat, millet, and rice, two crops of the latter being harvested each year, possibly with the aid of irrigation. Hemp and silk were also produced. Domestic animals included pigs, dogs, cattle, sheep, horses, and chickens. Hunting, pursued possibly more for pleasure than necessity, is indicated by the remains of tiger, leopard, bear, rhinoceros, deer, hare, etc.

The recognizable pattern of traditional Chinese civilization was firmly established in the Chou period (c. 1100–221 BC), which succeeded the Shang civilization. One of the most notable features of the Chou civilization was the rise and development of many substantial cities, their areas in most cases clearly defined by surviving city walls. These show that the cities were carefully laid out, often to a rectangular plan with straight sides, and were sometimes sub-divided by internal walls. The ancient city of Chiang, for example, formed a rectangular enclosure over 1½ miles long and nearly a mile wide, defined by a massive wall with an external ditch. Abutting the inside of the north wall was a small enclosure, with a similar wall, about half a mile square. Other cities were even larger, with more sub-divisions. An-yi, for example, was sub-divided into three areas, with the outermost nearly 3 miles long and between 1½ and 2 miles wide [119]. As in the preceding Shang period the walls were in every case built of *pisé*, or rammed earth.

Although the cities, by their size and number, give some idea of the physical growth of China during the Chou period, many of them are still incompletely explored and much of the more detailed archaeological evidence of the Chou civilization comes, as in so many other civilizations, from graves and their contents. A typical Chou grave (probably for the well-to-do rather than the bulk of the population) was a rectangular pit approached by one or more ramps, in much the same way as the royal Shang graves, although generally on a rather smaller scale. The lower parts of the pit were sometimes stepped in, leaving a ledge or shelf all round, and occasionally niches were dug in the side walls. Walls and floors were often plastered and the former were sometimes painted. A wooden-plank chamber was built in the bottom of the pit and in this the body was placed in a wooden coffin. After the grave goods (pottery, bronzes, weapons, food, etc.) had been placed in the chamber or on the surrounding ledge, the pit was filled, often with rammed earth, and a covering mound was built over the grave. An alternative, and later, form of grave consisted of a vertical shaft with a burial chamber opening from one side at the bottom.

In the metallurgical field, iron began to appear towards the end of the Chou period, but for the greater part of it bronze was the dominant metal. Again, for mundane purposes, stone, flint, and wood were still widely used, with bronze reserved for finer products, most notably the elaborately shaped and intricately decorated bronze vessels which are such an outstanding achievement of the Chou civilization [120]. The main categories of bronze products are as follows, although it should be noted that within each category there is a considerable range of types: cooking and dining vessels; drinking vessels; water utensils; musical instruments; weapons; horse and chariot fittings; mirrors and belt hooks.

This brief account of Chinese archaeology can be concluded with the introduction of iron-working, probably during the sixth century BC, although

XI. Jade funeral suit of the Princess Tou Wan, found in 1968 in her tomb at Man-ch'eng, Hopei, China. Western Han dynasty: 202 BC–AD 221.

119. Plan of the city of An-yi, state of Wei, near Hsia Hsien, Shansi.

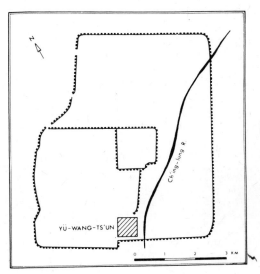

YÜ-WANG-TS'UN

Ch'ing-lung R.

0   1   2   3 KM

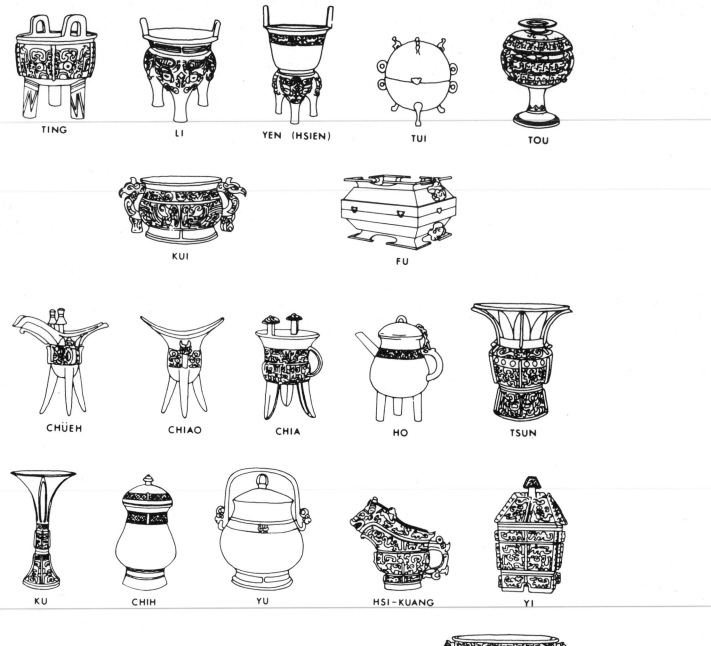

TING LI YEN (HSIEN) TUI TOU

KUI FU

CHÜEH CHIAO CHIA HO TSUN

KU CHIH YU HSI-KUANG YI

P'AN

CHIEN

NIAO-TSUN HU LEI YI YÜ

120, 121. Left: major types of Shang and Chou bronze vessels. Opposite: a bronze wine ewer, *Kuang*, Shang period, late twelfth century BC. Height: 12⅜ in.

it was not until about 450 BC that iron implements began to appear in any quantity. The most notable feature of Chinese iron metallurgy was the appearance not only of wrought iron, as in the Near East and prehistoric Europe, but also at the same time of cast iron, which was not to appear in Europe until relatively recent times. Unlike bronze, iron was used on a large scale for the production of everyday equipment, principally agricultural implements, including spades, sickles, hoes, axes, and adzes. Iron ploughs are also recorded from the same period. This new equipment undoubtedly represents a significant economic change, arising out of its greater efficiency as compared with stone tools, and no doubt the greater agricultural production played a considerable part in the growth of population and the development of cities.

6
American Archaeology

In terms of Old World prehistory the arrival of Man on the American continent is a relatively recent event, contemporary only with the latter part of the Upper Palaeolithic period of Europe and Asia, which began *c.* 40,000 BC. The route by which the earliest settlers arrived is not in doubt (via the Bering Straits, between north-east Siberia and Alaska), although there is some dispute as to when the route was first used. The prevailing climatic conditions narrow the dispute down to a simple choice of dates during the final phase of the Glacial era in North America. Between *c.* 35,000 BC and 15,000 BC, according to geologists, any movement to the south from such a crossing would have been blocked by a continuous ice sheet. After 15,000 BC, the early cultures of the American continent, characterized by projectile points, are fairly well documented and will be considered briefly below. The dispute arises over the possibility of arrivals earlier than 35,000 BC, possibly as early as 40,000 BC. The evidence, such as it is, consists of assemblages of crude stone implements, forming, it is claimed, a Pre-Projectile Point stage, although crudeness of manufacture is not necessarily proof of an early date. However, some of these assemblages are associated with evidence of burning which has produced Carbon-14 dates of as early as 38,000 or 40,000 BC, although there is no proof that the burning represents a man-made hearth. The fires may be simply accidental. Moreover, in some cases implements of much later date, and better manufacture, have been found with or near such assemblages, suggesting that the two levels of technology could have existed side-by-side. This is not to say that the cruder technique could not be a survival of an earlier tradition, brought in before the formation of the ice barrier *c.* 35,000 BC, and until more conclusive evidence is available the question of a Pre-Projectile Point stage on the American continent must be left open.

Because of the great size of the American continent, this chapter will be divided into three geographical sections: Canada and the U.S.A.; Mexico and Central America; and South America. These will be preceded by a short section dealing with early Man (from *c.* 15,000 BC on), which is the foundation on which the three geographical sections rest.

THE PALAEO-INDIAN STAGE

The first clearcut, well-documented phase in America, both North and South, is known as the Palaeo-Indian Stage which, according to the available Carbon-14 dates, began around 15,000 BC. An alternative name, the Big-game Hunting Tradition, indicates the economic basis on which these early inhabitants of America existed. Much of the evidence comes from what are known as kill sites, places where the animals (mammoth, bison) were killed and

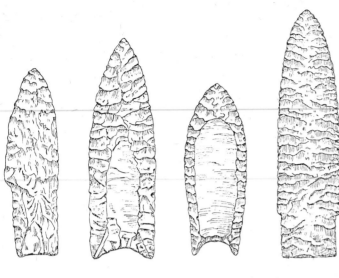

122. Typical projectile points of the Palaeo-Indian and Desert Traditions: from left to right, Sandia Cave type, Clovis type, Folsom type, Portales type and Gypsum Cave type. Carbon-14 determinations indicate the same chronological order, Sandia Cave giving a date as early as 18,000 BC, although there is some doubt about its accuracy.

butchered on the spot, separate joints rather than whole carcasses being carried away to camp sites. Found among the bone remains at these and other sites are the very characteristic stone and flint lance- or spearheads with which the game was killed. A number of different types can be distinguished, among them the Cascade point, a leaf-shaped form, found from Alaska to Argentina, which could well be related to a similar leaf-shaped form in the Siberian Upper Palaeolithic. Other forms, which seem to be native American developments, are the Sandia point (a shouldered type which could equally be a knife) and the Clovis and Folsom fluted points which are found widely in the South-west, the Plains, and the eastern woodlands of North America [122]. It is interesting to note that there is not much difference in dates between North and South America, suggesting that once the Palaeo-Indians arrived they spread very rapidly throughout the whole of the American continent.

The end of the Glacial epoch caused a shift to the north in the climatic zones and an end (although spread over a considerable period) of the Big-game Hunting Tradition, which seems to have survived in the central Plains area down to at least 4000 BC. In the areas to the east (woodlands) and west (Rockies), however, it is replaced as early as 7000 or 8000 BC by the Archaic and Desert cultures respectively.

THE DESERT CULTURE

This seems to have originated in the Great Basin area of the Rockies where the Big-game Hunting Tradition was never strong and to have gradually spread at its expense, as the climate became more arid, over much of the surrounding area, including the South-west, the main area in North America to be described here. Although big game was still hunted where available, the Desert culture people had to rely mostly on much smaller prey and on the gathering of wild seeds, berries, vegetables, etc. The abundant big game of the preceding period was gone. Among the material equipment was a range of food-grinding implements, a much wider range of stone and bone tools, as well as basketry, all of these indicating a different mode of life from the Big-game Hunting period. In spite of its antiquity, starting c. 9000–10,000 years ago, the Desert Tradition survived among certain groups of North American Indians (e.g. the Paiute) into recent times. In the South-western

United States the Desert Tradition is particularly important because the classic Pueblo culture eventually developed from it.

THE ARCHAIC TRADITION

In the woodlands and valleys of eastern North America, the end of the Glacial epoch saw a marked change in climate and vegetation (as in the Mesolithic phase in northern Europe), and indeed the mode of life which developed there, the Archaic Tradition, was not dissimilar to the way of life in early post-Glacial Europe. Subsistence was based on the hunting of small woodland game, on fishing, and on the collection of wild fruits and vegetables. The equipment included flint arrowheads and food-grinding implements. In the later stages of the Tradition (*c.* 5000 BC on), much of the stone material was of the polished types, including a range of polished stone wood-working tools—axes, adzes, gouges, etc.—some of them grooved, reflecting the woodland environment. There was also a well-developed bone-working tradition in both implements and personal adornments. As with the Desert culture, some Archaic Tradition groups in Canada and the Gulf coast of Texas survived until recent times [123, 124].

123, 124. Above: a banner-stone, a weight used for balancing a spear-thrower; below: three beaten copper spearheads. All from Eastern U.S.A., Archaic Tradition, *c.* AD 500.

In the American continent as a whole, both North and South, the Desert and Archaic cultures (or cultures of the same general type, varying only according to area) between them provide the base from which most, if not all, of the subsequent cultures developed. As indicated above, some areas or groups never progressed beyond one or other of these two stages, while the remainder progressed to varying degrees, some only marginally, others spectacularly to the point of urban living and sophisticated stone architecture. Some of these developments will be examined in the three following geographical sections.

CANADA AND THE U.S.A.

By approximately the beginning of times AD America north of the Mexican border had developed a number of different regional cultures which varied according to the climate, terrain, natural resources, etc., of the different areas. In the eastern, woodlands area there was a relatively large number of separate archaeological cultures (about ten), but in the western part of the region the pattern is much simpler. To the west of the woodlands area the broad band of the Plains area, with its own distinct culture, stretched from Canada to Texas. Beyond this again much the greatest archaeological region is the South-west, with a few smaller groups to the west and north in California, the Plateau area and on the north-west Canadian coast. In the far north are various Eskimo groups in Alaska and the Hudson's Bay/Greenland area.

Only one region, the South-west, will be dealt with in any detail here, but before beginning this one or two other cultures can be mentioned briefly. In the eastern woodlands area as a whole, earthworks, particularly round burial mounds, are very common and there are also various kinds of earthwork enclosures, including some with inturned entrances which, if encountered in Europe, would be termed hillforts. In three of the areas bordering the Gulf of Mexico (The Caddo, Lower Mississippi and Florida areas [125]) there are remains of rectangular, flat-topped mounds with sloping sides, often of considerable size (40–80 ft. high), with ramps leading to the summit and crowned (originally) with timber temples or shrines. The resemblance to the

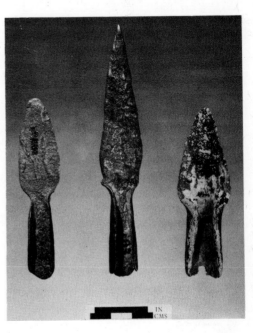

great stone temples of Mexico is quite obvious, indicating either derivation from there or a religious tradition common to both areas and finding expression in temples elevated by means of great man-made supporting mounds. In the three areas involved, these earthen mounds are relatively late in the prehistoric sequence, *c.* 1300 AD onwards. Such mounds are not found in the other archaeological regions to the north.

To the west, in the Plains area, the picture is much simpler and the area involved much larger than any one of the separate eastern woodlands groups. In the previous section it was pointed out that the Big-game Hunting Tradition survived in the Plains area longer than anywhere else, down to at least 4000 BC. In fact, although there was some fluctuation in the pattern, hunting remained a basic part of Plains Indian life until very recent times, even when, from *c.* AD 900 onwards, Indians from the woodlands area moved into the Plains and brought the practice of agriculture and more settled village life, as opposed to the nomadic or semi-nomadic pattern of the original Plains hunters. The acquisition of the horse in the Early Historic period (AD 1600–1800) caused the reversion of many hunting/farming communities to an entirely hunting economy, since the buffalo could now be pursued with ease. With the horse, too, the Plains Indian becomes recognizable as the Indian of popular legend and the western film, although it should be clear from what has been said already that the Plains represent only one aspect of North American Indian life.

A radically different one is represented by the North-west coastal region, centred mainly on British Columbia, where a culture depending almost entirely on fishing and hunting, with no agriculture, seems to have survived virtually unchanged from an early period into comparatively recent times, thus making it difficult to distinguish early archaeological periods. The North-west coast Indians relied heavily on the sea for their food supply, using large dugout canoes, together with nets, hooks, harpoons and spears. Because of this, their villages were normally strung out along the water's edge. The houses were large, rectangular structures made of split planks, fastened to a substantial timber framework, and were often sub-divided for use by a number of families, possibly related to each other. These few facts are sufficient to demonstrate that North-west coast Indian life was a far cry from the North American Indian life of popular imagination, riding the Plains and attacking wagon trains.

THE SOUTH-WEST
The South-west is one of the classic areas of North American archaeology and consists of south-west Colorado, a great part of southern and eastern Utah, the western half of New Mexico, the greater part of Arizona, and parts of the adjacent areas of Nevada to the west and Mexico to the south. This is, in fact, the area defined by the great Pueblo culture of the years 700–1700 AD, although the whole area was not occupied throughout this period. The term Pueblo is the Spanish word for 'village'. When the early Spanish explorers first encountered the Indians in the 1540s in the Rio Grande valley they were living in substantial villages, one of the hallmarks of the Pueblo civilization, and from this they called them Pueblo Indians.

The beginnings of the South-western story are in the Desert culture. In the South-west the Desert culture is known under the name of the Cochise culture, and is divided into four phases: Sulphur Springs, Cazador, Chiricahua

125. Opposite: a deer-head mask in carved wood, originally painted, with large leather-hinged ears, AD 1400–1700. This was found at Key Marco on the Gulf Coast of Florida, where the wood had been preserved by continuous immersion in water.

and San Pedro, covering the years from *c.* 7000 BC down to about 300 BC or later, according to area. As it emerges from the Cochise culture stage in the late centuries BC and the early centuries AD, three different regional traditions or ways of life can be distinguished in the South-west. A thousand years later (*c.* 1100 AD) one of them, the Anasazi Tradition, was to absorb the others, but in the meantime the three developed on generally similar but separate lines. The Anasazi Tradition occupies the largest area, in the northern half of New Mexico, north-eastern Arizona and the southern portions of Colorado and Utah. The Mogollon Tradition occupies much of the area in the southern half of New Mexico and south-eastern and central Arizona. South-western and western Arizona forms the Hohokam territory. The transition from the Desert Tradition economy to a sedentary, agricultural economy can be followed in all three regions, but is perhaps best documented in the Mogollon region where it is earlier than anywhere else in the South-west and where pottery appears earliest.

The Mogollon Tradition

The influences which transformed the late Cochise (Desert) culture into the Mogollon Tradition of settled villages and an agricultural economy almost certainly came from Mexico, the northern territories of which are immediately to the south of the Mogollan area. The earliest finds of maize in the South-west are from Bat Cave (New Mexico), dated by Carbon-14 to *c.* 3000–2000 BC, and these appear to have been followed by squash (pumpkin), gourds, and (*c.* 1000 BC) by the red kidney bean, and the trio of maize, beans and squash eventually established itself as the basis of all South-western agriculture. However, settled village life in the Mogollon area is first known *c.* 300 BC at Cave Creek in south-east Arizona, where pit dwellings similar to those of the later Mogollon periods were found, suggesting the beginnings of settled village life. By *c.* 100 BC pottery appeared for the first time and this marks the change from the transitional period to the full, sedentary, agricultural Mogollon culture.

The Mogollon Tradition is divided into five periods: 1, 100 BC–AD 400; 2, AD 400–600; 3, AD 600–900; 4, AD 900–1000; and 5, AD 1000–1100. In Period 5 the changeover to above-ground architecture began, and by *c.* AD 1100 the Mogollon Tradition had been assimilated to the Pueblo or Anasazi Tradition and faded out as a separate entity. During Periods 1–4, Mogollon villages consisted of up to twenty separate pit-dwellings, about 15 ft. in diameter and sunk 2–5 ft. into the ground. The roof, of timber capped with earth and stones, was either conical or flat with internal support sometimes provided by upright posts. In the late Mogollon periods (3 and 4) there was a tendency for the pit to become almost rectangular in plan, with rounded corners. There were also longer pits with a central row of posts and a gabled roof. In nearly every case entrance was by means of a sloping ramp at one side. Food was stored in bell-shaped pits outside the house and in niches in the walls and pits in the floor of the houses. The houses were also used for burials, the bodies being placed either in the pit-dwelling itself, which was then sealed up, or under the floor so that occupation could continue.

Mogollon material equipment included stone querns and rubbing stones, pestles and mortars, axes, stone dishes, stone (and baked clay) pipes, arrowheads, bone awls, needles and pins, beads, bracelets and pendants of shell and stone, basketry, sandals, fur and feather blankets, and cotton clothing. A great deal of such material accompanied Mogollon burials, which tended to grow richer as time went on. As in so many parts of America, the achievement in the pottery field was outstanding. The early red and brown plain wares (Mogollon 1) were followed by painted pottery with red-on-brown designs (Mogollon 2). In Mogollon 3, white-slipped ware and red-on-white appeared and in Mogollon 4 and 5 the culmination was reached in the now-famous Mimbres black-on-white which appears mostly on the inner surface of open bowls about 10 in. in diameter. The commonest design is a human or an animal figure within an often intricate but meticulously executed geometric border. The black-on-white technique (but not the design) is part of a much wider pottery tradition in the South-west which will be encountered again in the Anasazi Tradition.

The same transition from the Cochise culture to a South-western sedentary agricultural tradition took place, although at somewhat later dates, in the Hohokam and Anasazi Traditions. For reasons of space only the latter will be considered here. Eventually, like the Mogollon, the Hohokam Tradition became assimilated to the Anasazi Tradition *c.* 1100 AD, and from then on the three traditions are merged into a single story.

The Anasazi Tradition

The word 'Anasazi' is derived from a Navajo Indian word meaning 'old peoples', those who formerly inhabited the houses and villages (the *pueblos*) which are now in ruins. The area of the Anasazi Tradition (the northern half of the South-west) is the homeland of Pueblo culture and this Tradition is now interpreted as embracing the culture of the region from the end of Desert Tradition times down to recent times. The earlier part of the period is known as the Basket-maker period, and is followed, *c.* AD 700, by the full Pueblo culture which, within about 400 years, embraced the greater part of the South-west, including the areas of the two other major Traditions, the Mogollon and Hohokam. The Basket-maker period is divided into two phases: Basket-maker (*c.* AD 1–500) and Modified Basket-maker (*c.* AD 500–700). The earlier period is, in fact, a transitional phase between the Desert Tradition and the sedentary agricultural tradition, indicating that at this period the Anasazi Tradition was less advanced than the Mogollon, where settled village life was already in existence by 300 BC.

Most Basket-maker sites are concentrated in what is known as the four-corners region, the area where the corners of the states of Colorado, Utah, New Mexico, and Arizona meet, and if northern Arizona and New Mexico are the homeland of the Anasazi Tradition, this is the heartland, and remained so for most of the period. It is also known as the San Juan region after the San Juan river which flows through the middle of it to drain into the Colorado river to the west. In the early Basket-maker period livelihood still depended mainly on hunting, trapping, snaring, and collecting, although a primitive form of agriculture (maize and pumpkin) was carried on. The equipment for these purposes included wooden digging sticks, clubs, spears, spear-throwers, and nets, but as yet no bow and arrow. Houses were still somewhat flimsy, probably because permanent long-term village life had not yet begun. No pottery was known, but, as the culture name implies, basketry was developed to a high degree and performed many of the functions of pottery.

In the Modified Basket-maker period (AD 500–700) settled life in permanent villages began and the bow and arrow and pottery appeared for the first time in the Anasazi Tradition. Beans were now added to the range of crops, which were cultivated more intensively than before; agricultural produce was form-

126. Coiled basket, Modified Basket-maker period, AD 500–700, from Canyon del Muerto, Arizona. The Modified Basket-maker period forms the transition from the Basket-maker period proper to the first phase of the full Pueblo period (Pueblo I, AD 700–900).

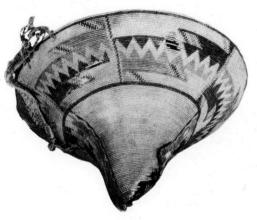

ing the more important part of the food supply, although hunting, trapping and food-gathering were still carried on to give variety and balance to the diet. Basketry and bonework were both highly developed [126], but perhaps two other aspects of the culture, pottery and architecture, were most significant for the succeeding Pueblo period; both were possibly due to contact with the then more advanced Mogollon Tradition to the south. Apart from plain grey cooking pots and some imported wares from other regions, the main Modified Basket-maker pottery (Lino black-on-grey and La Plata black-on-white) is a prelude to the great, long-enduring tradition of Pueblo black-on-white pottery. The pots, often simple hemispherical bowls, were either white or grey, with a simple geometric design in black or dark brown, almost certainly based on basketry patterns. In architecture, the Modified Basket-maker people seem to have adopted the Mogollon pit dwelling, forming villages of from ten to twenty houses. These appear to be the prototype of the Pueblo kiva, which will be discussed later. But the same people also began above-ground building, simple rectangular rooms of *jacal* construction (upright poles plastered with mud), forming a continuous structure, either straight or curved. Frequently the pit-dwellings and above-ground structures formed part of the same site; in such cases the pit-dwelling provided the living accommodation while the above-ground rooms were mainly for storage, although as time went on they began to be used as dwellings as well. Like the pit-dwelling, the above-ground blocks of contiguous rectangular rooms foreshadow what is perhaps the outstanding aspect of Pueblo civilization, and the one which in fact gave it its name, its architecture, of great multi-storey apartment blocks.

The Pueblo Civilization

The Pueblo period, from AD 700 to the present day, is sub-divided into periods in accordance with two different systems, as follows:

Pueblo I: 700–900
Pueblo II: 900–1100 } Developmental Pueblo.
Pueblo III: 1100–1300   Great Pueblo.
Pueblo IV: 1300–1700   Regressive Pueblo.
Pueblo V: 1700– present Historic Pueblo.

Pueblo I and II will be treated together here, albeit briefly, as Developmental or Early Pueblo. The two most important periods are 1100–1300 and 1300–1700 and for these Pueblo III and Pueblo IV are more convenient terms than Great and Regressive, the latter, in any case, being a somewhat misleading term for a period which, although different from Pueblo III, was in many ways no less important.

Developmental Pueblo (I and II). The Developmental stage (700–1100) marks the greatest geographical extent of Pueblo culture in any one period. The subsequent Great Pueblo (III) development took place in a more restricted, although still very large, area, with the outlying regions, mostly Utah and eastern New Mexico, remaining in the Developmental stage [127]. Agricultural economy and settled village life were now firmly established and this is a period of great experiment and discovery, particularly in building and in pottery, hence the justly descriptive term Developmental Pueblo. By the second half of the period, houses were entirely above-ground constructions and the pit-dwelling had become the kiva (from a Hopi Indian word meaning 'old house'), which will be considered under Pueblo III.

127. Distribution of population during the various periods of Pueblo history: Early Period (Pueblo I and II, AD 700–1100); Great Period (Pueblo III, AD 1100–1300); Late Prehistoric Period (Pueblo IV, AD 1300–1500); Period of the Conquest (*c.* AD 1600).

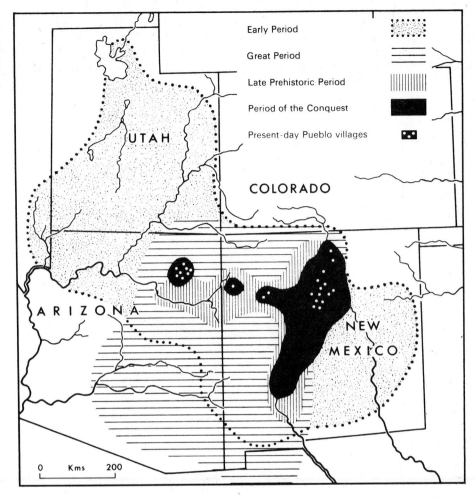

Dwellings were either single-room structures or, more commonly, multi-room, one-storey buildings built in a curve or a straight line. Construction was much more solid and massive than previously and a wider range of materials was used: wattle and daub, stone with adobe or mud mortar, or adobe alone, puddled and shaped up into walls by hand. These developments were the foundation on which the great Pueblo Tradition of architecture was built in Pueblo III and Pueblo IV.

Pueblo III. In Period III (*c.* 1100–1300) the central part of the Developmental Pueblo area advanced to the peak of Pueblo civilization, leaving areas to the north-west (much of Utah and north-west Arizona) and to the south-east (eastern New Mexico) as peripheral regions, which never progressed beyond the Developmental stage. The classic area for Pueblo III is the four-corners or San Juan region centred on such major sites as Chaco Canyon (New Mexico), Mesa Verde (Colorado) and Kayenta (Arizona), although Pueblo III civilization as a whole covered a much wider area, broadly the western half of New Mexico and the eastern half of Arizona, as far to the south as the Mexican border. In Pueblo III architecture reached its peak and is particularly well represented in the three areas mentioned above. Pueblo settlements were built in two main forms, cliff dwellings and villages on level ground. In both cases there are a number of features to be observed

128. Pueblo Bonito (Beautiful Pueblo) is one of a group of nineteen major pueblos, all within a distance of a few miles, in Chaco Canyon, New Mexico. Generally regarded as the peak of Pueblo architecture, it is D-shaped in plan and there is clear evidence from the surviving remains that it was originally seven stories high. It belongs to the Pueblo III period (AD 1100–1300).

129. Opposite: Cliff Palace, Mesa Verde National Park, Colorado, certainly the most famous and one of the most spectacular examples of the Pueblo practice of building houses and even whole settlements in recesses formed by the erosion of soft layers of rock between harder layers in the cliff faces of canyon walls.

peculiar to Pueblo building. A Pueblo settlement does not consist of separate houses, but of a contiguous mass of rooms, all normally of the same size, with no corridors, communication being directly from room to room. The ground plan gives only a part of the picture since such structures were multi-storey, up to seven storeys being proved in one case. From this it will be clear that many rooms would be in the heart of the building, several rooms removed from the outside, and these were used, among other things, for storage and sometimes for burial, the room thereafter being sealed off. Externally the superimposed storeys often formed a stepped structure, although vertical walls rising to the full height of the building are also known. Pueblos on level ground are best represented at Chaco Canyon, and cliff dwellings at Mesa Verde and Kayenta.

Chaco Canyon consists of the remains of nineteen major pueblos as well as several smaller structures. Many of them are E-shaped in plan, although in some the central projection is missing; they are between 200 and 400 ft. long, with as many as 150 rooms at ground-floor level. In a number of cases the plan was completed (making it D-shaped) by a single curving row of rooms closing the space in front of the main structure and forming a plaza. The rooms facing on to the plaza were almost certainly stepped back as they rose. The outer walls were vertical. In addition to the rectangular rooms, circular kivas were incorporated in the structure or less frequently were built as free-standing structures in the plaza. Without question, the most impressive of all the Chaco Canyon pueblos is Pueblo Bonito (Beautiful Pueblo). Like many others it was D-shaped in plan, but in this case the main block of rooms formed the curved portion while the straight side was a single row of rooms [128]. It was over 500 ft. long and 300 ft. wide, with about 150 rooms and 20 kivas at ground-floor level. A portion of the curving back wall is preserved to a considerable height and in it can be seen evidence of no less than seven storeys, over fifty feet high.

130. The Great Kiva at Aztec, New Mexico. Aztec (not its original name) is a great rectangular pueblo of the Pueblo III period, of the same type as Pueblo Bonito [128]. Like all pueblos it has associated with it many circular, subterranean ceremonial chambers known as kivas. A feature of the Pueblo III period is the development of the Great Kiva, a much larger version, partly subterranean and partly above ground. The Great Kiva at Aztec has been carefully reconstructed to show its original appearance.

The other two San Juan sites, Mesa Verde and Kayenta, are noted chiefly for their cliff dwellings, although surface pueblos were built there as well. Before describing the sites, something must be said about the cliff setting in which they occur. The ideal site is a recess in a canyon wall big enough to house a substantial settlement. Such recesses are the result of erosion. Where there is a relatively soft layer of rock between two harder ones, the effect of heat, wind, and rain is to eat away the soft layer, often to a considerable depth. The recess in which Spruce Tree House (Mesa Verde) is built is 216 ft. long, 35 ft. high and 89 ft. deep from front to back. Such recesses in the sides of canyon walls are not uncommon in the South-west and the Indians made great use of them for their settlements. Probably the most famous of all cliff dwellings is Cliff Palace (Mesa Verde), which contained about ninety-five ground-floor rooms and twenty-three kivas, and rose in places four storeys high [129]. The nearby Spruce Tree House contained eight kivas, about seventy rooms at ground level and about 114 in all. Kietsiel in the Kayenta region was built in a recess *c.* 300 ft. long and 50 ft. deep, containing some 150 ground-floor rooms and half a dozen kivas. Probably the most spectacular of all cliff dwellings is the so-called Montezuma Castle (nothing to do with Montezuma of Mexico), outside the San Juan region, in central Arizona. This is much smaller than those considered so far but it appears from below as if it is literally hanging on to the cliff face.

Intermediate, in a sense, between surface pueblo and cliff dwelling is the so-called talus house, built against a cliff face at the head of the slope or talus of debris which accumulates at the cliff bottom through erosion. Such talus houses often cluster below a major pueblo built on the mesa above or above a pueblo sited in the canyon bottom below.

Kivas have been mentioned as forming an integral part of all pueblos described so far. Very simply a kiva appears to have been a special version of the early pit-house dwelling, retained out of veneration as a place for ceremonial and other purposes. They were circular in plan with the roof

flush with the ground, entered via the central smoke hole by means of a ladder. There was a ventilator shaft on one side and a deflector to prevent a direct draught on the fireplace. A low bench ran round the sides. Such places were very much a male preserve and apart from their ceremonial use they have been described as men's club houses, which may reflect a great deal of their actual use. Kivas of this size (*c.* 10-20 ft. in diameter) were very common. Less numerous but much bigger and more elaborate were the Great Kivas which developed in Pueblo III. These had a considerable above-ground structure in addition to their subterranean part. One of the most impressive of these Great Kivas is at Aztec (again nothing to do with the Aztecs of Mexico, simply the name of the local town), which has been carefully excavated and restored [130].

Apart from architecture, one of the great Pueblo achievements was in pottery. South-western archaeologists distinguish no less than five hundred types of pottery in the area, of which about two hundred are variations of black-on-white, which is *par excellence*, the pottery of the Pueblo Indians. The range of shapes is quite limited, only about half a dozen main forms being used. The huge variation occurs in the decoration, where some two hundred regional styles have been distinguished, such as Chaco b/w, Mesa Verde b/w, Rio Grande b/w, and so on [131]. Apart from black-on-white and a smaller amount of black-on-red, many of the remaining styles are described as polychrome, i.e. more than two colours, and these likewise are distinguished by regional names such as Sikyatki Polychrome or Sholow Polychrome. In addition to all these painted wares there is also a considerable quantity of plain or corrugated culinary ware.

Apart from architecture and pottery, the Pueblo III Indians had an impressive range of material equipment including such things as basketry, matting, cotton cloth, bonework, and a wide variety of stone tools and weapons for the hunting, collecting, and preparation of food.

Pueblo IV. At the end of Pueblo III times (*c.* 1300) there was a drastic reduction in the area occupied by the Pueblo Indians. The four-corners region was abandoned and occupation was restricted to the Rio Grande valley in New Mexico, with a lateral extension westwards into north-east Arizona. The reasons for this are not absolutely certain. There appears to have been a change of climate *c.* 1280–1300 which may have made agriculture difficult over much of the Pueblo III area. Another possible explanation is the arrival in the area of the Navajo and Apache Indians, aggressive nomadic peoples who could have made life very unpleasant for a sedentary village people such as the Pueblo. There may well have been other factors as well of which we are not as yet aware, but the fact remains that from *c.* 1300 on Pueblo civilization was drastically reduced from the wide area covered by Pueblo III.

The main change to be described here was in architecture. Although Pueblo III represents the peak of Pueblo architecture stylistically, there is no question that the largest pueblos were built in Pueblo IV. Greater size, however, was not the only difference. Many of the Rio Grande pueblos were built or developed to a rectangular plan, with more or less equal numbers of rooms on all four sides of the plaza. At Puyé, for example, the apartment block, which was continuous except for one entrance at the corner, was between seven and ten rooms wide and contained nearly five hundred rooms at ground-floor level. Allowing for a stepped arrangement above, there could have been as many as twelve hundred rooms in all and this sort of size is

131. A pot of the Pueblo III period (AD 1100–1300), in the black-on-white style.

XIII. Opposite: one of the enormous stone heads, about 8 ft. high, characteristic of the Olmec civilization.

161

132. Remains of a large Spanish mission at Quarai, New Mexico. An important part of the Conquest pattern was the conversion of the Indians to Christianity, and in the early-seventeenth century the Church established many mission stations to facilitate this work. Some, such as this, were on an imposing scale, larger than many a contemporary parish church in Europe, the size no doubt intended as much to impress the natives as to meet purely religious needs.

typical of the Pueblo IV villages. The rectangular form seems to have been arrived at by a process of growth from a simpler structure, and in some cases L-shaped or three-sided pueblos occur, apparently abandoned before they developed into the fully enclosed, rectangular form. A few more or less circular pueblos are known, at Bandelier National Monument, near Santa Fe, for example, which was up to nine rooms wide, possibly four storeys high, with a single narrow entrance and three kivas in the plaza. Allowing for three upper storeys, the whole structure may have contained over eight hundred rooms. Many of these Rio Grande pueblos must have been still occupied when the Spaniards first arrived in 1541, at which time they recorded the existence of over seventy major sites.

In spite of the Spanish contact, Pueblo civilization continued largely unaffected until *c.* 1700 when the Pueblo V period begins. This is the period of the recent and present-day Pueblo Indians who still occupy some thirty pueblos in the Rio Grande valley and on the Hopi mesas in Arizona. Many of the structures are now single storey but the stepped style can still be seen at Taos, New Mexico, and Oraibi, Arizona, as well as one or two other places.

The later archaeology of the South-west is represented by a fine series of Spanish mission stations [132], many of which, in spite of their size, had a relatively short period of use (*c.* 1630–80), and by early American military posts, in particular, Fort Union, on the Santa Fe trail (1851–91).

MEXICO

Mexico was the setting for two of the great civilizations of ancient America, the Maya and Aztec, but the same sort of reservations have to be made here as in Classical archaeology, where Rome occupies a relatively late position in the story. Thus, in Mexican archaeology, the Aztec civilization belongs only to the last few centuries before the Spanish conquest. The Maya (often called the Greeks of the New World) were still in existence then, although the peak of their civilization had long since passed, and there had been other civilizations such as the Zapotec and the Toltec. The latter, in particular, occupied an intermediate position between the Classic Maya (*c*. AD 300–900) and the Aztecs (from *c*. AD 1200 on), similar in many ways to the position occupied by the Etruscans, culturally and chronologically intermediate between Greece and Rome.

Mexico is a large country, some 2000 miles from north-west to south-east, only part of which was occupied by the higher civilizations to be considered here [133]. The greater part of the country, the north and west, was a sparsely inhabited, semi-arid zone. Only in the south and east, in a great arc from northern Yucatan around the Gulf of Campeche to the area of Mexico City, occur the great urban centres which are the hallmark of the various Mexican civilizations. In simple terms, the western end of the arc is the Aztec region, the eastern end the Maya, but this picture has to be adjusted in accordance with the chronological observations made above about the late date of the Aztec civilization. In order to make clear the position of the main civilizations in both time and space, a brief survey of the major developments in the critical area of Mexico will be given first.

In the very early periods, *c*. 15,000 BC onwards, life in Mexico was no different from that described already for the American continent as a whole. However, the moves towards food production (as opposed to food-gathering) were made earlier in Mexico than in the United States. Recent evidence from the Tehuacan valley has shown that maize was being gathered as early as 5200 BC, although domestic varieties did not appear until 3400 BC. By about 1500 BC, agriculture had developed sufficiently for it to become worthwhile living in settled village communities, and with them came domestic equipment, such as pottery, appropriate to sedentary living. These dates for agricultural village life and pottery may be compared with the dates for similar developments in the South-western area of the United States where they are very much later (*c*. 300 BC). The era of village communities with well-established agriculture is known as the pre-Classic period in Mexico and extends, in round figures, from *c*. 1500 BC to about AD 300. In fact, the last three centuries were a transitional period, from pre-Classic to full Classic, during which the great ceremonial cities of ancient Mexico first began to develop.

One very special (and rather puzzling) aspect of the pre-Classic period was the so-called Olmec civilization which at a very early date, possibly as early as 1000 BC, foreshadowed the great urban development (and much else) of the Classic period. The Olmec civilization seems to have developed in the hot, humid coastal zone to the south of the Gulf of Campeche, in the southern part of Veracruz and in Tabasco. While much of Mexico was still in the agricultural village stage the Olmecs (not their original name, which is unknown), starting, presumably, from the same stage, seem to have very rapidly developed great ceremonial centres, stone architecture, and sculpture —three striking aspects of their culture which were extremely important for the later civilizations of Mexico. Perhaps the most magnificent of all Olmec products were the great stone heads—as much as 10 ft. high with their rather negroid features carved in basalt. At the other end of the scale there were small figurines carved with great skill in jade and other hard stones. The distribution of these figurines, and of pottery, show that Olmec influence spread widely throughout Mexico during the first millenium BC. One of the most important Olmec sites is La Venta, where there is a complex of structures built on a north-south axis, the main feature of which is a flat-topped pyramid structure of clay about 160 ft. square, with other mounds to north and south together with stone heads, altars, stelae, and an enclosure formed by columns. This is quite clearly a ceremonial centre and sets the general pattern for all subsequent ceremonial centres in ancient Mexico, whatever the particular civilization involved. At other Olmec ceremonial centres (Tres Zapotes and Cerro de las Mesas) stone and stucco were used as facing material for the earth mounds. At the most recently excavated Olmec site, San Lorenzo Tenochtitlán, the layout of the fully developed ceremonial centre resembled that of La Venta.

The Olmec civilization seems to have come to an end some centuries before the Christian era, although its influence lingered on in much of the subsequent development. Many of the features of the Classic Mexican civilizations were quite clearly already present in the pre-Classic Olmec period.

The Classic period began c. AD 300. From this date, or shortly after, three contemporary cultures or civilizations emerged in three different parts of Mexico. In the southern part of the Yucatan peninsula there developed the great Maya civilization which endured in its Classic form for some five or six hundred years, until c. AD 900. On the plateau at the western end of the arc there developed a civilization centred on the city of Teotihuacán which endured until c. AD 750. Unlike the Maya (above) and the Zapotecs (below), we do not know the name of the Indians responsible for this very rich, Classic civilization. The third civilization, that of the Zapotecs, flourished in the Oaxaca region, some 250 miles south-east of Teotihuacán, centred on the city of Monte Albán. The Zapotec civilization endured until c. AD 1000, apparently unaffected, or at least much less affected, by the events which brought about the dramatic decline in fortunes of both the Maya and Teotihuacán civilizations.

The next important event in ancient Mexican history is the arrival of the Toltecs and the development of Toltec civilization in the plateau area and in Yucatan. The Toltecs seem to have arrived from somewhere in the northern part of Mexico around AD 900, when the great ceremonial centres of the Teotihuacán civilization were already in ruins. They founded their capital at Tollan (modern Tula). Eventually they came to dominate the whole of the plateau area, their power enduring until AD 1168 when the capital was abandoned, possibly under pressure from further invading tribes. Toltec civilization also had a profound effect on the Maya peoples. As a result of religious conflict in the late tenth century, a body of Toltecs left the plateau area and migrated into northern Yucatan. The southern Maya cities had been abandoned a century or so before, but in the north the arrival of the Toltecs brought about a Maya-Toltec Renaissance, c. AD 1000–1200, seen most clearly in architecture.

It is only at this relatively late stage that the Aztecs enter the picture. They, in fact, called themselves the Tenochca or Mexica—and because they were the controlling power when the Spaniards arrived, the name Mexico was applied to the whole country. For the same reason, they tend to be thought of as the major manifestation of ancient Mexican civilization, but

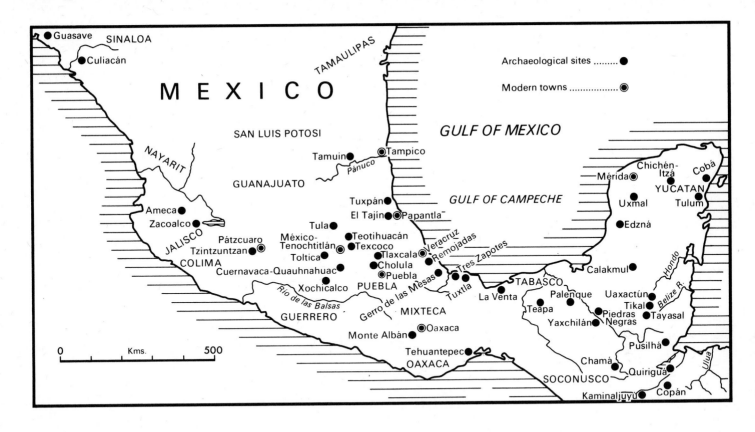

as even this brief survey will have shown, the Classic civilizations had waxed and long since waned before the Aztecs ever appeared in the country. The Aztec arrival probably formed part of the tribal movements which dispersed the Toltec peoples throughout Mexico from 1168 onwards. After many vicissitudes, the Aztecs eventually founded a capital at Tenochtitlán (now buried beneath Mexico City) in 1345. Within less than a century they were one of the dominant powers on the plateau. In 1428 they formed a triple alliance with Texcoco and Tlacopan and began a programme of military expansion which, by the time of the Spanish conquest in 1519, embraced much of present-day Mexico. Although nominally equal partners, the other two members of the alliance were very much overshadowed by the Aztecs and the empire conquered in the name of the alliance was effectively an Aztec dominion.

This concludes the survey of main historical events in Mexico from pre-Classic times to the Spanish Conquest. In the remainder of this section ancient Mexico will be considered under the following headings: Teotihuacán (the city, rather than the whole civilization); the Maya civilization; the Toltecs; and the Aztec civilization.

TEOTIHUACAN

Teotihuacán, which means 'the city of those who have become gods', is quite clearly not the original name of the city. It is a Nahuatl word (the language of the Toltecs and Aztecs), applied to a city which had been long in ruins. The city has in the past been attributed to the Toltecs but it is now known to be much earlier. Better candidates are the Totonacs of the Gulf

133. Map of ancient Mexico.

coast, who had a tradition that their ancestors had built the city. There were certainly close connections between the coast and the plateau when Teotihuacán was in existence, c. AD 200–750.

Teotihuacán is situated twenty-five miles north-east of Mexico City and covers an area of about three square miles. Two of the principal features (in an enormous complex of buildings) are the Pyramid of the Sun and the Pyramid of the Moon, situated on the main axis of the city, the so-called Avenue of the Dead, a name (*Miccaotli*) given to it by the Aztecs [134]. This runs north and south for over a mile and is 150 ft. wide. At the northern end there is a ceremonial plaza over 400 ft. square in front of the Pyramid of the Moon. This structure, which is strictly speaking a stepped pyramid, and flat-topped, is 511 × 400 ft. at base level, with a rectangular dais (c. 160 × 70 ft.) on the south side facing down the Avenue of the Dead. Access to the dais is by means of a steep flight of steps and further flights, on the same axis, lead to the summit (c. 140 ft. high) where the temple was situated. The Pyramid of the Sun, about half a mile to the south on the east side of the Avenue of the Dead, was even larger (760 × 720 ft. at base level), roughly the same size as the Great Pyramid in Egypt, although not nearly so high (216 ft. as compared with 481 ft.). Its arrangement, with a dais and successive flights of steps on the same axis, was similar to the Pyramid of the Moon. The core of the mound was of sun-dried bricks in horizontal layers, with an outer facing of stone and lime plaster.

The so-called Citadel near the southern end of the Avenue was probably a ceremonial centre rather than a defensive site and no doubt included living quarters for the priests. It was square in plan (1250 × 1250 ft.) and consisted basically of a rectangular plaza surrounded by raised terraces on which were situated fourteen small (two-) stepped pyramids with staircases on all four sides. There were many other important buildings, both on the Avenue and elsewhere in Teotihuacán, which cannot be described here. The most recent excavations have produced evidence of more humble structures, the living quarters, which must have been of considerable extent for a city of the size of Teotihuacán. They consist basically of rectangular rooms grouped around courtyards and plazas connected by narrow passages. The structures were single-storey and flat-roofed and had an elaborate system of drains to carry away rain-water. One area excavated consisted of 175 rooms grouped around twenty-one small courtyards, grouped in turn around five larger courtyards or plazas. Beneath the stucco floors of these houses were numerous burials, some of them of children.

THE MAYA CIVILIZATION

Unlike the other civilizations, the Maya occupied a very distinct and separate part of Mexico, from the Yucatan peninsula in the north to the Guatemala highlands in the south (some 600 miles), and from British Honduras in the east to the state of Chiapas in the west (c. 300 miles). This area is sub-divided geographically into three zones: Yucatan, a flat, fairly dry lowland area in the north; a hot, swampy central zone with tropical forest; and the most pleasant region of all, the Guatemala highlands in the south. Surprisingly, the latter was an outlying region in Maya times. The major centres of Maya civilization in the Classic period (AD 300–900) were, in fact, in the least hospitable of all three zones, the hot moist tropical forest area of the centre. The low-lying northern zone was also occupied during the Classic period, but was less

important then. It came into its own only in the post-Classic Maya-Toltec revival (AD 1000–1200), when the Classic Maya cities to the south were in ruins.

Although we refer to them as cities, the great monumental centres of Classic Maya civilization were not cities in the normal sense of the word. They were largely ceremonial and administrative centres, with the bulk of the population living in villages in the surrounding jungle. Like those of ancient Greece, however, each Maya city seems to have been an independent unit, a city state, but forming part of a single (Maya) cultural tradition. Arising out of their main functions, the two principal types of building found in Maya cities are temples, standing on flat-topped pyramids, and palaces (so-called), presumably the accommodation for the priests, administrators, and other officials in charge of the city's affairs. Some of the main cities will be described below but one or two more general points about the Maya civilization will be made first.

In spite of the obvious splendour of their architecture, probably the greatest of all Maya achievements were in the two subjects of astronomy and mathematics. Maya astronomer priests formulated accurate tables of solar and lunar eclipses and recorded the phases of the moon and the movements of the planet Venus. They also evolved a calendar system more accurate than the Julian

134. The city of Teotihuacán, near Mexico City: aerial view showing the Pyramid of the Moon (bottom left), the Avenue of the Dead (bottom left to top right), the Pyramid of the Sun (centre) and the Citadel (top right). These formed the central features of a city some three square miles in area. The name Teotihuacán means 'the city of those who have become gods', given to it when it had been long in ruins. The original name is not known.

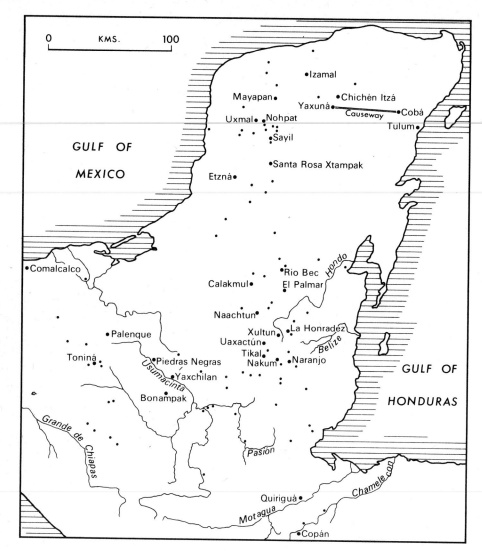

Map content:

KMS. 0 100

GULF OF MEXICO

Izamal
Mayapan
Yaxuná • Chichén Itzá
Causeway • Cobá
Uxmal • Nohpat
Tulum
Sayil
Santa Rosa Xtampak
Etzná

Comalcalco

Rio Bec
Calakmul El Palmar
Hondo
Naachtun
Palenque Xultun La Honradéz
Uaxactún Belize
Toniná Tikal
Piedras Negras Nakum Naranjo
Yaxchilan GULF OF
Usumacinta
Bonampak HONDURAS

Grande de Chiapas
Pasión

Quiriguá Chamelecon
Motagua
Copán

135, 136. Left: archaeological map of the Maya area, showing the four principal sites mentioned in the text: Uxmal and Chichén Itzá in the north and Tikal and Copán in the south. Only the most important sites are named, the locations of the others being indicated by dots. Opposite: Temple I, Tikal, Guatemala, one of five such temples (I–V), all of the same general design, which are the dominant feature of the city centre of Tikal. Maya temples are very steep-sided as compared with those of central Mexico and normally have only one stairway, running in a single sweep from ground level to the summit.

calendar then in use in Europe. Much of this evidence is recorded in stone on decorated stelae, one of which refers to dates four hundred million years ago.

Although they lacked wheeled vehicles, and even draught animals, the Maya were responsible for some excellent roads. These were normally constructed of stone blocks set in cement with a wearing surface of cement or stucco about 30 ft. wide. The longest such road ran for 60 miles and, in a marshy section, was carried on a causeway. Other shorter roads around cities were presumably, in part at least, for ceremonial use. The same engineering skill was brought to bear on the problem of drainage. In the central, wet tropical forest zone rainfall was not only heavier than elsewhere in Mexico but also more sudden and more violent. To counteract this, cities were equipped with underground drainage systems, many of them quite complex.

The Maya Classic period is normally divided into two sub-periods, Early Classic (AD 300–600) and Late Classic (AD 600–900). In the Late Classic period the basic Maya architectural style which had developed before and during the Early Classic became richer and more ornate and regional varia-

tions in style are distinguishable. In the Late period, too, there was a notice-able development of cities in the northern region, in Yucatan, at sites such as Chichén Itzá and Uxmal. However, the major centres of Classic culture are in the central, tropical forest area and these will be considered next.

All the centres of Maya civilization have been divided, by S. G. Morley, an authority on the Maya, into four groups, as follows: Class 1, Metropolises (4); Class 2, Cities (19); Class 3, Large Towns (39); Class 4, Small Towns (54), giving a total of 116 sites in all [135]. This is by no means the final figure. Because of conditions in the central area there must be many sites still to be discovered. Moreover, the classification of certain sites may need to be changed. Dzibilchatun in Yucatan was placed by Morley in Class 4, but as a result of excavations started in 1956 it is now known to be the largest of all Maya sites, covering some twenty square miles.

One of the oldest and most important centres of Maya civilization is Tikal in the tropical forest zone of present-day Guatemala, classed by Morley as one of his four metropolises. Pyramids were being erected there as early as 200 BC. The plan of the central part of the Classic city is known in some detail, and covered an area of about half a square mile; beyond this however, in all directions, are the ruins of plazas and their surrounding buildings, stretching outwards for several miles. The great central plaza and its associated buildings stand on a levelled tongue of land between two ravines (north and south) with other important groups of buildings beyond, linked to the centre by a series of man-made causeways. The outstanding monuments at Tikal are the five great pyramid-temples (I-V) which by their height dominate the city and, incidentally, demonstrate the characteristics of Maya pyramid architecture [136]. Maya pyramids are very steep-sided as compared with those of the Mexican plateau—Temple IV, for example, has an overall height of 229 ft., but is only 193 ft. wide at the base. Instead of rising in separate flights there is usually only a single range of steps rising very steeply on one side of the pyramid. The temple on the top was a massive construction of stone and cement, with thick walls, a triangular, corbelled vault and very small rooms. It was surmounted by a roof comb, an ornamental feature designed to increase the height and impressiveness of the structure. All five main temples in Tikal conform to this pattern. There are many smaller pyramids and numerous remains of the so-called palace type, ranges of rooms around rectangular courtyards and plazas. The last dated stela at Tikal bears the year AD 869 and presumably shortly after that the city, like all others in the central, tropical zone, was abandoned for reasons which are still not very clear.

Copán, in Honduras, was another major Maya centre classed by Morley as a metropolis (Class 1). It included sixteen outlying groups of buildings, one up to seven miles from the centre. In the central group the so-called Acropolis or main complex covered over twelve acres, and as a result of successive additions and rebuildings had grown into a single structural mass, with many earlier periods buried beneath. The Acropolis consisted of a series of temples, pyramids, terraces and plazas or courts, including a ball-court where a ritual ball-game was played, a practice which was widespread in Mexico and in other parts of the Americas [137]. One of the most impressive monuments at Copán is the 'Hieroglyphic Stairway', on the western side of a pyramid at the northern end of the Acropolis. The risers of the sixty-three steps, each 30 ft. wide, are carved with 2500 hieroglyphs. The Maya had an

elaborate system of hieroglyphic writing but, apart from dates, this has not as yet been deciphered. A considerable portion of the eastern side of the Acropolis has been eroded by the Copán River, so that the whole central complex must have been even larger originally. Happily the course of the river has been changed artificially to protect the site from further damage.

Tikal and Copán, together with many other cities and towns, are in the central tropical forest zone which is the homeland of the Maya culture. The two other metropolises distinguished by Morley, Uxmal and Chichén Itzá, are in Yucatan, in the northern zone, together with other cities and towns. These northern centres flourished during the New Empire or Maya-Toltec Renaissance (AD 1000–1200), when the Classic cities had been long in ruins, but they were also in existence for many centuries before, during the Late Classic period (AD 600–900).

Uxmal contains some of the most beautiful of all Maya architecture [138]. One of the outstanding buildings in the central group (c. 3000 × 1500 ft.) is the so-called House of the Governor [139]. This stands on a triple terrace which covers in total five acres of ground. The house proper, on the highest terrace, is

137. The ball-court, Copán, in Honduras. Ball-courts were a common feature of Maya cities, there being no less than five, for example, in the central area of Chichén Itzá. It seems unlikely that they were for purely recreational purposes. The important positions they occupy in the central areas of the cities, among the temples, suggests a ritual and religious significance.

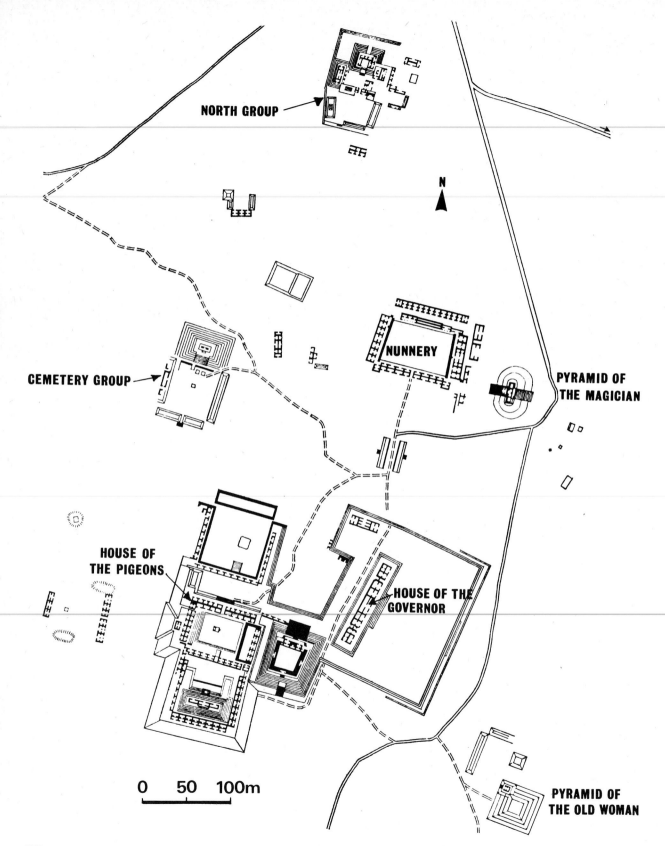

NORTH GROUP

N

CEMETERY GROUP

NUNNERY

PYRAMID OF
THE MAGICIAN

HOUSE OF
THE PIGEONS

HOUSE OF THE
GOVERNOR

0   50   100m

PYRAMID OF
THE OLD WOMAN

320 ft. long, 40 ft. wide and 26 ft. high and contains 24 rooms. Externally, the lower parts of the walls are plain but the upper parts are richly decorated with carved geometric patterns and grotesque masks. Its size and position certainly suggest that this was the most important of the non-religious monuments in the city and it may well have housed its ruler, whatever his title. The Nunnery Quadrangle to the north is equally imposing and may have housed the priests and administrators involved in running the city. It is entered through the middle of the South Range via a corbelled entrance passage, which gives access to the central courtyard. The opposite, North Range is at a higher level and is reached by an imposing stairway over 90 ft. wide. All four ranges of building conform to the same general pattern as the House of the Governor. In between the latter and the Nunnery Quadrangle is a ball-court, and there is another large, terraced complex to the west and smaller groups to the north-west and north.

At Chichén Itzá both Classic Maya and Mexican (i.e. Toltec) architectural styles are clearly distinguishable, the latter belonging to the late period (AD 1000–1200) when the city was at the peak of its development and importance. The main, central group of buildings covers a quarter of a mile square but there are many groups beyond and the whole city covers a much larger area than Uxmal [140]. The outstanding religious monuments at Chichén Itzá are the Temple of the Warriors and the Castillo, both characterized by the use of the feathered-serpent column, introduced to Yucatan by the Toltecs from Mexico [141]. Kukulcan, the Feathered Serpent, was the patron deity of Chichén Itzá and the name Kukulcan is the Maya version of the Toltec god Quetzalcoatl. Another distinguishing feature of the city was the extensive use of colonnades which flank three sides of a great open plaza (some $4\frac{1}{2}$ acres in area) known as the Group of the Thousand Columns. Scattered around the central area of the city were no less than five ball-courts, the largest 545 ft. long and 225 ft. wide externally, with a playing area 480 × 120 ft. One of the most interesting buildings at Chichén Itzá is the Caracol, an astronomical observatory in the form of a round tower about 41 ft. high, standing on a

138, 139. Opposite: plan of the central part of the city of Uxmal showing the so-called House of the Governor and the Nunnery Quadrangle. The latter may have housed the priests and administrators involved in running the city. The House of the Governor, a view of which is shown above, is the largest and most imposing non-religious building in the city and may well have been the residence of its ruler, whatever his title was.

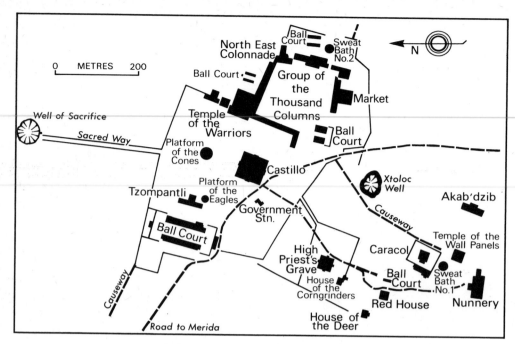

140, 141. Left: plan of the central area of Chichén Itzá, in northern Yucatan. Note the five ball-courts, particularly the very large one (bottom left). Other outstanding features at Chichén Itzá are the Caracol (an astronomical observatory), the Temple of the Warriors, and the great open plaza surrounded by colonnades known as the Group of the Thousand Columns. Opposite: the Castillo, the main temple pyramid of the city, built in the style of central Mexico by the Toltecs in the Late Period (AD 1000–1200). Compare with a typical Maya temple at Tikal [136].

double terrace 31 ft. high. The tower is solid except for the entrances, a spiral staircase, a small observation chamber, and, from the latter, a series of apertures through the thickness of the tower to the outside, fixing certain sighting lines of astronomical importance, for instance those connected with the spring and autumn equinoxes.

Only the four major Maya centres have been mentioned here, but there are many more, somewhat smaller but no less interesting and significant in Maya culture. Palenque [142], Uaxactún, Quiriguá, Cobá, Calakmul, Rio Bec, Yaxchilan, and many others were all classed by Morley as cities, and below these are dozens of sites, classed as large towns and small towns, where there are notable remains of Maya civilization of all periods, from the Early Classic period (AD 300–600) to the Spanish Conquest some thousand years later, when even the great days of the Maya-Toltec Renaissance (AD 1000–1200) were long since past and the surviving Maya cities were exhausting themselves with interminable squabbles and petty, consuming warfare.

THE TOLTECS

The Maya-Toltec Renaissance in Yucatan was a secondary result of the Toltec period in the main part of Mexico which began between AD 800 and 900. The Toltecs appear to have arrived from the north and brought to Mexico for the first time the Nahuatl language spoken (later) by the Aztecs. The Toltecs were a vigorous and lively, but still semi-barbaric, people who quickly absorbed many of the elements of the Classic civilization of Teotihuacán and evolved out of it a distinctive Toltec civilization of their own. This civilization is important in its own right as another facet of ancient Mexican culture, but it is also important in another respect. As has been already pointed out, the Aztec civilization belongs to a very late period in Mexican history and it was, in fact, through the medium of the Toltec civilization that it inherited so much of the accumulated store of ancient Mexican culture. The Classic period (AD 300–900) was long since over when

142. The palace at Palenque. The city was founded *c.* AD 100 and the ruins extend for over five miles in the foothills of Chiapas. The central part of the city consists of the temple of the Inscriptions, the temples of the Cross, the Foliated Cross and the Sun, and the palace. The latter stands on a terrace 300 × 240 ft., and consists of rooms and galleries grouped about four internal courtyards. It is surmounted by a tower and the whole complex may not, in fact, be a palace but an observatory.

XIV. Opposite: the Caracol, Castillo and Temple of the Warriors at Chichén Itzá.

the Aztecs appeared on the scene, but the Toltecs, who had arrived just at the end of the Classic period, were able, as it were, to hand over to them a much more vigorous cultural tradition than would have otherwise been the case. Early in the Toltec period some sort of social or political upheaval led to the migration of a considerable body of Toltecs from the central plateau area into Yucatan where, as already described, they were largely responsible for the Maya-Toltec Renaissance.

The Toltecs established their capital at Tollan (modern Tula), about fifty miles north of Mexico City. Here are clearly exemplified the characteristic features of Toltec architecture seen already in the Maya region in Yucatan: feathered-serpent columns, columns used internally to support roofs, and columns used in great colonnades [143]. Much of the Toltec capital remains to be excavated but the principal buildings known are the ball-court, the Temple of the Morning Star, two palaces and a colonnade. The ball-court (*c.* 190 ft. long) was in the form of a double-ended T, and this henceforward was the standard form throughout Mexico. The Temple of the Morning Star stood on a five-tier pyramid about 30 ft. high and 84 ft. square at the top. Access was via a stairway on the southern side. The temple proper on the summit was 65 × 43 ft. Its wide entrance, on the southern side facing the head of the stairway, was supported by two feathered-serpent columns. Internally the flat roof, resting on wooden beams, was supported by eight columns, each 15 ft. high. To the east and west of the temple pyramid are structures described as palaces. These are rectangular buildings with internal courtyards surrounded by colonnades. To the south of the temple pyramid was a great

L-shaped colonnade of fifty-one columns in three rows; the columns have now disappeared but the marks made by their square bases can still be seen.

THE AZTEC CIVILIZATION

The Aztec civilization represents the last major development in ancient Mexico before the Spanish conquest. The Aztecs (Mexica or Tenochca as they called themselves) entered the Valley of Mexico as a barbarian tribe in the late twelfth or early thirteenth century from the north-west, following the collapse of the Toltec civilization. For a century or so they lived a very unsettled existence, moving or being moved by the various city states in the area, until they finally settled on a group of uninhabited islands on the western side of Lake Texcoco [144]. Here, in 1345, they founded the town (later the city) of Tenochtitlán, the Aztec capital and one of the greatest cities of ancient Mexico, the name of which means Place of the Prickly Pear Cactus. Unfortunately Tenochtitlán was razed to the ground by the Spaniards in 1521 and the capital of New Spain, now Mexico City, was built on the ruins. The growth of the city over the last four and a half centuries has made any investigation of the remains extremely difficult. Fortunately the balance can be redressed to some extent by descriptions written at the time of the conquest (some of them illustrated by drawings), supplemented with what little excavation it has been possible to carry out.

Before dealing with the city of Tenochtitlán something must be said, briefly, about Aztec history and the Aztec civilization in general. As pointed out earlier, the political pattern in ancient Mexico was one of independent city states, perpetually fighting and squabbling with each other over territory, and this was the situation in the early days of Tenochtitlán, in the fourteenth and early fifteenth centuries. For a long time Tenochtitlán and Tlatelolco, another Aztec town, together with many other cities around Lake Texcoco, were under the domination of the city of Azcapotzalco on the western side of the lake. Eventually, in 1428, united action by some of the subject cities enabled them to throw off the yoke of Azcapotzalco, and thus a new phase in Aztec history began. From its humble beginnings in 1345, Tenochtitlán had now developed into the equal, if not the superior, of any other city state in the Valley of Mexico. The major parties involved in the overthrow, Tenochtitlán, Texcoco (on the east side of the lake) and Tlacopan (on the west), now formed themselves into a Triple Alliance which was to be a dominant factor in Mexican history until the conquest. In fact, the Aztec Empire encountered by the Spaniards in 1519 had, strictly speaking, been conquered in the name of the Triple Alliance, although the two other participants very quickly became junior partners and the Empire was in fact Aztec, if not strictly so in name. By the time of the conquest the Empire covered a great, rectangular block of territory in central Mexico, from the Gulf of Campeche in the north to the Pacific in the south (between 250 and 350 miles), and an even greater distance (nearly 400 miles) from east to west. It was, moreover, still in the process of expanding territorially and developing culturally when the Spaniards arrived and, had it not been stopped, would almost certainly have continued to do so for a considerable time to follow. It had, after all, achieved its independence less than a century before and might well have been expected to survive and flourish for a similar period, if not longer, in the future.

XV. Opposite: Machu Picchu, an Inca citadel, built on a high ridge near Cuzco, in the central Andes. This dates from the time of the Inca Empire (AD 1438–1532).

143. Four of the eight columns that supported the flat roof of the Temple of the Morning Star at Tollan (modern Tula) were huge standing figures, 15 ft. high, known as 'Atlantes' (opposite). This temple was built in honour of Quetzalcoatl, and these 'Atlantes' are said to have represented the god and his followers. The remaining four columns were square piers bearing carving in low relief.

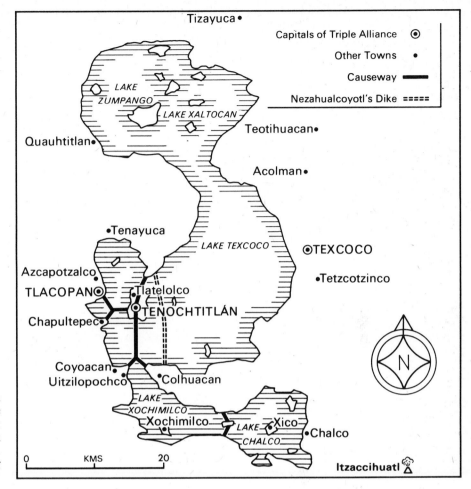

144. Right: map of the Valley of Mexico in Aztec times, showing the location of the three cities involved in the Triple Alliance: Tenochtitlán, (the Aztec capital), Tlacopan (to the west) and Texcoco (to the east). Note the three major causeways linking Tenochtitlán to the mainland.

War was the dominant aspect of Aztec civilization. In the early days in the Valley of Mexico, the survival of the Aztec tribe had depended on the fighting qualities of its people, and this tradition was carefully fostered in later times during the expansion of Tenochtitlán and the development of the Empire. Success in war was a major means of social and political advancement and a young man of humble origins could rise to considerable heights through his prowess as a warrior. War was, however, something more than a physical outlet for the aggressive spirit of the Aztecs. They regarded themselves as a chosen people and war had a deep religious significance for them. As much as anything else, wars were undertaken to capture prisoners who could be sacrificed to the gods, and human sacrifice, including the extraction of the heart, was an integral part of Aztec life and an aspect which particularly horrified the Spanish conquerors.

By the time of the conquest Tenochtitlán covered an area of about four square miles, much of it land reclaimed from Lake Texcoco, and had a population estimated at 350,000, much larger than anything in Europe of that date. It was linked to the mainland by three causeways to the north, west and south. These causeways were prolonged into the city as major thoroughfares and ended at three fortified gateways which gave access to the focal point of Tenochtitlán, the Great Temple Precinct [145]. This precinct, defined by a

145. Imaginative reconstruction of the Great Temple Precinct in the centre of the city of Tenochtitlán. The dominant feature of the precinct was the steep-sided, 300 ft. square pyramid at the left of the picture with two temples, side by side, on its summit, one dedicated to Tlaloc, the rain god, and one to Huitzilopochtli, a war god and tribal god of the Aztecs. The ruins of Tenochtitlán are deeply buried beneath present-day Mexico City.

great stone wall, was some 1300 ft. from north to south and between 1000 and 1200 ft. from east to west. The gateways were in the middle of the northern, western, and southern sides with the major temple group in the eastern half of the precinct. The central feature of this group was a great, steep-sided four- or five-stepped pyramid (c. 300 ft. square at the base) which supported on its summit two temples, side by side. One was dedicated to Tlaloc, the rain god, a cult the Aztecs adopted, ultimately, from the Classic civilizations of Mexico, and the other to Huitzilopochtli, their own tribal and national deity, a war god—ideally suited to be the patron of a warlike nation like the Aztecs. Facing this double temple and roughly in the middle of the precinct was another temple, to Quetzalcoatl, the feathered-serpent, and between this and the western gate was the ball-court in the now standard double-ended T form. The precinct embraced many other temples, as well as the living quarters of the priests, treasure-houses to safeguard the temple riches, monastic schools, and a rack where the skulls of the sacrificed victims were placed.

Outside the main precinct, at the time of the conquest, there were no less than three royal palaces in Tenochtitlán, one of which had only just been completed on the orders of Montezuma II. It was about 660 ft. square and consisted of buildings, some two storeys high, ranged around courtyards and gardens. The royal apartments were on the upper floors while down below were a series of colonnaded halls in which were housed the civil and military courts, police and public treasury, and the supreme council of the country. The royal palace at Texcoco was even larger, 3000 × 2300 ft., and contained over 300 rooms, some of them very large colonnaded halls. A site near Texcoco, Chiconauhtla, exemplifies a more modest form of Aztec dwelling. The basic pattern is that of a series of rooms facing inwards on to a patio or courtyard; the exterior walls were quite blank. Each room was entered separately via a vestibule supported at the front by two columns. The fireplace was against the back wall.

The walls of both temples and secular buildings were richly decorated in relief or fresco painting, but unfortunately not much of this has survived. The same is true of the free-standing, three-dimensional sculpture which was also a prominent feature of Aztec temples and their precincts.

One of the most famous and most striking of all Aztec antiquities is the Calendar Stone, measuring 12 ft. in diameter and weighing 24 tons, from the sacred precinct in Tenochtitlán. Its richly carved surface records the date of the (then) existing creation and of the four previous creations recognized by the Aztecs. It also records the twenty day-signs and the signs of the fifty-two years of the normal calendar cycle. The stone is, in effect, a comprehensive statement of the Aztec chronological system. The stone of Tizoc, an Aztec king, is of the same shape, 8 ft. in diameter. In this case the main feature is the relief sculpture around its rim which, in fifteen scenes, shows Tizoc as a god receiving the submission of fifteen chiefs of conquered regions [146].

In the field of goldwork, featherwork, and woodcarving the Aztecs achieved a very high standard. Unfortunately a great deal of such material was destroyed at the time of the conquest and what remains is only a tiny sample of the original. Similarly large numbers of Aztec books or *codices* (singular *codex*) were destroyed. These were made from the inner bark of fig trees and consisted of a long continuous strip folded concertina-fashion. The paperwork involved in the administration of a great empire was no less than anywhere else in the world, and included diplomatic correspondence, reports, tax accounts, land registers, household accounts, legal records, and royal archives. In addition there were large numbers of religious and astrological works.

With so much spectacular material deliberately destroyed by the Spaniards, there is reason to be thankful that in the more humble sphere of pottery there is a well-defined chronological framework. The Aztecs observed a 52-year religious cycle and on the night of the New Fire ceremony which began each

146. The stone of Tizoc, an Aztec king. The stone, *c.* 8 ft. in diameter, carries a band of relief sculpture on its rim showing Tizoc as a god in fifteen scenes, in each case receiving the submission of the chiefs of conquered regions.

cycle they systematically broke all their pottery. The result is that there are clear divisions in the ceramic sequence and these have been identified for the four cycles or calendar rounds from AD 1299 to 1507, the last one before the conquest. All Aztec pottery is hand-made (as opposed to wheel-made), and although the coarser domestic wares were probably produced in the home, the finer painted wares were almost certainly the work of specialist potters. The typical Aztec pottery was yellow or orange in colour with designs painted on in black. Judging by its wide distribution, it was produced and exported on a very large scale to many cities in the Valley of Mexico. The ware was red-brown in colour with geometric designs in black and white paint. In spite of its massive production, however, Tenochtitlán also imported pottery, notably from the non-Aztec city of Cholula where there was a tradition of fine ceramic ware. This was something of a luxury import, even for Tenoch-titlán, and it is reported that Cholula dishes were used exclusively in the royal household. Certainly, royal patronage may have had a great deal to do with its popularity among the rich and noble. Cholula pottery is polychrome, in red, brown, black, orange, and white, with complex designs of men, gods, animals and abstract motifs.

SOUTH AMERICA

Thinking on South American archaeology tends to be dominated by the Inca civilization, possibly because, like the Aztec civilization in Mexico, it was in being when the Spaniards arrived and was cut off abruptly while still in the process of development. Like the Aztecs again, the Incas had emerged as a dominant force only in the last century or so before the conquest, and before them was more than a thousand years of Andean civilization of a high level, on which they drew heavily when developing their own culture. In fact, the Andean civilization may have developed at a very early date, possibly earlier than in Mexico. Recent Carbon-14 dates have indicated that there were elaborate temples in Peru in the second millenium BC.

For the purposes of this section, the story of South American archaeology begins at the beginning of times AD, with the Mochica and Nazca cultures on the northern and southern sections of the Peruvian coast respectively, and the Tiahuanco culture in the southern highlands of the interior. Among the outstanding (and certainly the best known) products of the two coastal cultures are their pottery, which was produced in enormous quantities for, among others, funerary purposes, and which has now found its way into many museums throughout the world. The best-known types of the Mochica culture are the portrait vases, modelled in the shape of a human head, and the stirrup-spouted pots with a combined handle and spout in the form of a stirrup on top of the vessel [147]. In the field of architecture, the Mochica people erected enormous temple platforms of adobe brick—the largest (the Temple of the Sun) near Trujillo is estimated to contain 130 million bricks. The lower part is 750 × 450 ft. and it rises in five terraces to 60 ft. At the north end of this is an upper section, 340 ft. square and 75 ft. high, approached by a ramp 300 ft. long and 20 ft. wide. Temple platforms and pyramids of smaller dimensions are found at most Mochica sites. For richness of colour, Nazca pottery of the southern half of the coastal region is unsurpassed in ancient America, and indeed anywhere in the world. In some cases as many as eleven colours were used. The two main shapes were open bowls and spherical vessels with twin spouts connected to a bridge [148].

147, 148. Opposite: top, pottery of the Mochica culture (northern sector of the Peruvian coast), showing two of the best-known types: the portrait vases, modelled in the shape of a human head, and the stirrup-spouted pots with a combined handle and spout in the form of a stirrup on top of the vessel. Bottom, pottery of the Nazca culture (southern sector of the Peruvian coast), showing the main shapes: open bowls and spherical vessels with twin spouts linked by a handle. For richness of colour, Nazca pottery is unsurpassed in ancient America, or indeed anywhere in the world, as many as eleven colours being used in some cases.

149, 150. Tiahuanaço, Bolivia. Above: the sunken temple; in the foreground Stela 15 and two smaller stelae; in the background, the stairway to the main entrance of the Kalasasaya Temple, a monumental complex dating from the Inca occupation of the sacred city. Opposite: the monumental gateway known as the Gateway of the Sun. This great monolith was cut from a block of lava $12\frac{1}{2} \times 10$ ft. It bears a carved central figure, depicting the sun god, dominating a frieze of three rows of birdmen attendants.

Tiahuanaco, 13,000 ft. above sea-level, was probably more of a ceremonial than a conventional city. It was built of stone, not adobe brick, and much of the work was megalithic in character, i.e. units carved from single, large blocks of stone, often with great precision [149, 150]. Probably its resident population was comparatively small, the bulk of the people there at any one time being pilgrims from the surrounding area which it can be presumed to have served. As in the coastal cultures, there is a Tiahuanaco pottery style which, like the Nazca, was painted in many colours, most commonly on goblet-shaped vessels, the characteristic design being a puma in profile. It is through the medium of this pottery that it is possible to trace the spread of Tiahuanaco influence from the inland area to the coast. Tiahuanaco is, however, a long way to the south-east of the coastal cultures and its influence seems to have been transmitted via another important site in the central highlands, Huari. This appears to have been a great residential city, as much as four square miles in area. Eventually, during the seventh century, its expansion brought the Nazca and Mochica cultures to an end, replacing them with an Huari Empire. This was, however, short-lived and it collapsed during the eighth century, although Huari influence, in pottery styles for example, survived until the end of the millenium.

The collapse of the Huari Empire was followed eventually by the formation of three coastal states: the Chimu, in the north, the Cuismancu in the centre, and the Chincha in the south, the most important of which was the Chimu. All three were eventually conquered by the Incas and absorbed into the Inca Empire. The Chimu state or Empire embraced a large number of cities, the most impressive of which was Chan-Chan, the Chimu capital, near Trujillo, covering an area of about eleven square miles. The city consisted of nine or ten rectangular enclosures, each with its own surrounding wall, the largest

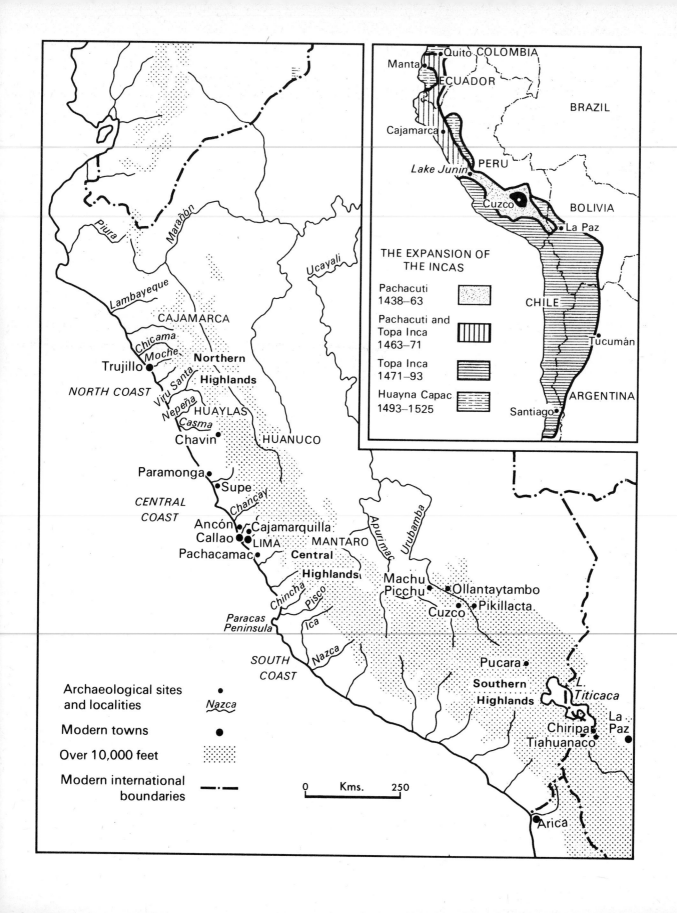

THE EXPANSION OF
THE INCAS

Pachacuti
1438–63

Pachacuti and
Topa Inca
1463–71

Topa Inca
1471–93

Huayna Capac
1493–1525

Archaeological sites
and localities

Nazca

Modern towns

Over 10,000 feet

Modern international
boundaries

0   Kms.   250

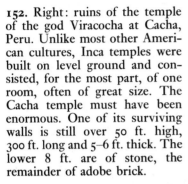

151. Opposite: map of Peru showing archaeological sites and localities and the expansion of the Incas.

152. Right: ruins of the temple of the god Viracocha at Cacha, Peru. Unlike most other American cultures, Inca temples were built on level ground and consisted, for the most part, of one room, often of great size. The Cacha temple must have been enormous. One of its surviving walls is still over 50 ft. high, 300 ft. long and 5–6 ft. thick. The lower 8 ft. are of stone, the remainder of adobe brick.

up to 40 acres in area (*c.* 1100 × 1600 ft.). Each enclosure, probably intended to house a complete clan, contained houses, reservoirs, store-houses, platforms and pyramids—for temples—and palaces, making each a self-contained unit, a city within a city. In the space between the enclosures were cultivated areas, fed by irrigation channels, and cemeteries, together with one or two isolated buildings. In spite of erosion, the enclosing walls are still in many cases over 30 ft. high. Each of the many river valleys running down to the coast seems to have had its city, on similar lines to, though smaller than, Chan-Chan; Pacatnamu and Purgatorio in the northern part of the Chimu area are two of the larger examples.

The Chimu and the other coastal states were eventually brought to an end by the Incas in about 1470, but the Inca story starts some centuries earlier. The traditional list of Inca kings begins with Manco Capac, who reigned *c.* 1200 BC, but information about him and the following seven kings is more legend than fact. Inca history proper begins with the last five kings on the list, headed by the Emperor Pachacuti (1438–1471). With him begins the great expansion of Inca territory which led very quickly to the huge Inca Empire as it existed at the time of the Spanish conquest.

The Inca tribe originated in the Cuzco valley on the eastern side of the central highlands. For over two centuries, from the traditional date of *c.* AD 1200, their activities were limited to the valley and its immediately surrounding area, where they carried on intermittent wars with their neighbours. This long apprenticeship in aggression was, in a sense, the firm base on which the quite dramatic change in Inca fortunes was set. Under the Emperor Pachacuti (according to Sir Clements Markham, 'the greatest man that the aboriginal race of America has produced') and his son Topa Inca, between the years 1438 and 1493 the Inca domain was enlarged from the confines of the Cuzco valley to virtually the full extent of the Inca Empire, from Ecuador in the north to central Chile in the south, a distance of some 3,000 miles—one dimension of an area of about 350,000 square miles. Some minor additions were made under the third Emperor Huayna Capac (1493–1525), and this was the Inca Empire as it existed when the Spaniards arrived in 1532 [151].

In spite of its size this vast empire was administered, from the capital, Cuzco, on highly centralized lines under a divine emperor, with the aid of an hereditary nobility. Nothing illustrates the far-reaching power and control of the capital better than the extensive road system which the Incas established throughout the Empire, in much the same way, and for much the same reasons, as the Romans did in their empire. There were two main north–south roads, one along the coast and one inland through the highlands, linked to each other by transverse roads, so that the whole Empire was linked by a single system, along which relays of messengers could travel 150 miles in a single day. At regular intervals along these roads were *tambos* or official rest-houses. The mountain roads were narrow (*c.* 3 ft. wide) and were often replaced by steps on steep stretches; in the absence of wheeled transport this was no drawback. The coastal roads were wider, up to 15 ft. across, defined be twin lines of posts in the desert area and by continuous walls in the populated valleys.

In the architectural field one of the most noticeable differences betweer the Inca civilization and the pre-Inca, and between it and the various Mexican civilizations, is the absence of temple platforms and pyramids. Inca temples were built on level ground within the cities and appear to have consisted, for the most part, of one great room. The Coricancha in Cuzco, a great ceremonial building, is estimated to have had a main room or hall 93 ft. long and 47 ft. wide. The temple of the god Viracocha at Cacha, built by his namesake the Emperor Viracocha Inca, Pachacuti's immediate predecessor, was, judging by its existing remains, an enormous structure. One of its walls is still standing to over 50 ft. in height and is 300 ft. long [152]. The lower 8 ft. are of masonry, the remainder of adobe brick, and the whole wall is 5–6 ft. thick. Whatever its original layout, it quite clearly represents something different from the widespread tradition of a relatively small temple structure on a high stepped pyramid, and this is true of all Inca temple building.

One of the most spectacular pieces of Inca architecture is a defensive work: the great fortress of Sacsahuaman, overlooking Cuzco, probably built to house the population of the city in times of danger [153]. More than any other structure it illustrates the Inca predeliction for megalithic masonry. The largest stone in the structure is 27 ft. high, 14 ft. wide and 12 ft. thick, and is estimated to weigh 200 tons. The difficulties of transporting such a huge piece of stone can be imagined. The fortress is over 1,800 ft. long and the defences consist of three massive retaining walls arranged in step-fashion up the sides of the hill on which it stands. Each wall is zigzag in plan and the combined height of the three is over 60 ft., the lower one, facing on to a level plaza, being the largest. The interior buildings, to house the refugee population, have been largely destroyed by the robbing of stone for buildings in Cuzco. There is another great stepped Inca fortress at Ollantaytambo, about forty miles north-west of Cuzco.

The commonest, not-to-say, standard forms of Inca pottery were the aryballus (similar to the Greek vessel of that name) and vessels of general

153. Opposite: aerial view of the great Inca fortress of Sacsahuaman, Cuzco, Peru. The main defences (on the left) consist of three zigzag retaining walls arranged step-fashion up the slope of the hill.

154. Group of Inca pottery, illustrating the main shapes and decorative styles.

155. Doll, representing a fisherman and net, with a slit tapestry face and a warp-striped plain weave shirt.

aryballoid shape [154]. The decoration is polychrome (black, white, red, yellow, orange) and the design largely geometric. Other shapes were shallow open dishes and cylindrical vessels with a spout and two loop handles on the side, presumably intended to be used as water bottles, each slung over the shoulder on a cord. Another common form of container was made of wood. The *kero* or *quero* is in the form of a flaring beaker, rather like the earlier form common at Tiahuanaco, painted in bright colours, often showing elaborately dressed human figures. Some such figures are shown in Spanish costume, indicating manufacture after the conquest.

Peru took a leading part in the domestication of plants and many items of (now) staple diet originated there. By Inca times there was a wide range of agricultural produce and an elaborate system of agriculture, based largely on irrigation and terracing. A great deal of the land in the valleys was sloping and this was brought into cultivation by means of terraces, retained by stone walls, stepping up the hillside. The terraces also facilitated irrigation, allowing water to be fed down from top to bottom from some source at the upper level. In many ways the most important Peruvian vegetable was the white or 'Irish' potato, the subsequent importance of which needs no emphasis. Other Peruvian crops included maize, squash, chilli, beans, sweet potato, tomato, peanuts, avocado, manioc, cotton and gourds. The main domestic animals, apart from the dog, were the llama and the alpaca which, although of cameloid type, were not used for draught purposes. They were kept mainly for their wool, which was extensively used in Peruvian textiles. This latter field represents possibly the most outstanding of all Peruvian achievements. It is not an exclusively Inca distinction; weaving was being practised in the area many centuries before Inca times and the Incas inherited and carried on the native tradition, but it would be wrong to conclude even a brief section such as this on South American archaeology without mentioning textiles. According to John Alden Mason 'Textile experts . . . state that the ancient Peruvians employed practically every method of textile weaving or decoration now known . . . Certain of the finer fabrics have never been equalled from a point of view of skill' [155].

In 1525 Huayna Capac died and a dispute between his sons about the succession led to a civil war. It was thus in a country split by internal troubles that the Spaniards under Pizarro landed at Tumbez in 1532, the great Inca Empire falling to a band of only 180 men.

7

European Archaeology

This account of European archaeology begins at the point reached in Chapter 3, where the Upper Palaeolithic cultures were at an end. The progressive retreat of the ice-cap from *c.* 10,000 BC on produced new climatic and environmental conditions and, inevitably, new cultures, grouped under the general heading of Mesolithic or Middle Stone Age. The cold, open tundra of Upper Palaeolithic times gradually gave place, in Europe, to forest conditions, appropriate to the warmer and wetter climate. Much of the game moved north, following the conditions to which it was accustomed, leaving Man to adapt himself as best he could to this new and radically different environment. Habitation was confined for the most part to the margins of the forest (lake and river banks and the sea-shore), and to upland areas above the tree-line. The ways in which Mesolithic man adapted to these conditions are defined by four main groups or cultures, more or less contemporary with each other, in different parts of Europe: the Maglemosian culture, the Tardenoisian culture, the Azilian culture, and what may be termed the Caledonian-Scandinavian group of cultures.

Quite apart from its own intrinsic interest, the European Mesolithic period is important because it provides the setting for the succeeding Neolithic cultures, all derived ultimately from the Near East. The Europe which they moved into was far from being a cultural vacuum and the character of the European Neolithic owed not a little to the widespread and well-established traditions of the preceding Mesolithic period.

The Maglemosian culture is found over an extensive area of the North European plain, from eastern England to Russia, including what is now the southern part of the North Sea, north Germany and Poland and southern Scandinavia; in the first half of the Mesolithic period Britain was still joined to the continent, even if the area between was mostly marshland. Most Maglemosian sites are on lake or river banks and appear to have been quite small, perhaps accommodating fifteen or twenty people in all. Their food supply came from fishing and hunting, the animals involved including elk, deer, wild pig, bear, fox, beaver, and squirrel, as well as small birds. For hunting they had long bows made of elm and arrows up to a metre in length tipped with microlithic flints. For fishing they had bone fish-hooks, nets made from bark fibre and fish-spears with bone points, barbed on one edge, for use in shallow water. They also had dug-out canoes up to 12 ft. long, hollowed out with the aid of substantial flint axes and adzes. These were mounted in a sleeve or socket of wood or antler which was pierced to take a wooden handle. Other Maglemosian equipment included flint scrapers and burins, bone and antler needles and awls, and necklaces and pendants of stone and animal teeth.

The Tardenoisian culture overlaps the southern part of the Maglemosian area and is found widely over central Germany, France and Spain. It was much poorer in its equipment than the Maglemosian, the principal remains being various kinds of microlithic tools. The chosen locations were also different, light soils, with correspondingly light vegetation, and upland areas being preferred, although certain Tardenoisian groups settled on the coast, living on shell-fish, sea-birds and fish. The principal weapon was the bow, with arrows tipped with microlithic points.

On the coasts of Norway, Sweden, Denmark, south-west Scotland, and north-east Ireland there was another distinct Mesolithic group, closely tied to the sea-shore, shell-fish being an important food item. There was also some hunting, and fishing, possibly from skin boats, and they may have exploited stranded whales as a source of food and other raw materials. Their equipment included microliths, some larger tanged flakes, possibly javelin heads, flat bone harpoons and mattocks made of stag antler. A flint adze from north-east Ireland suggests links with Maglemosian people.

The Azilian culture is virtually confined to south-west France and north-east Spain, i.e. the Franco-Cantabrian region where the last Palaeolithic culture, the Magdalenian, flourished. In fact, the Azilian seems to be the Mesolithic successor of the Magdalenian and there is a large measure of continuity between them, particularly in the matter of harpoon heads. The two cultures occupied many of the same sites, Azilian layers occurring immediately above Magdalenian in a large number of cases.

The last word on the Mesolithic period concerns its art. This is confined to the Spanish Levant (i.e. the south-east coast) and appears to have been the work of a local Tardenoisian or some closely related group. Many of the paintings are in rock shelters rather than caves and are on a small scale, often consisting of hunting scenes which show, incidentally, the widespread use of the bow and arrow.

THE NEOLITHIC PERIOD

The Neolithic communities of the ancient Near East were described in Chapter 4. In this section attention will be confined to the arrival and spread of Neolithic people in Europe. The overall picture of their diffusion from the Near East can best be seen from a combination of C-14 dates and a distribution map [156]. It is noticeable that the earliest sites in Europe (pre-5200 BC) are in the southern Balkans, that is, immediately adjacent to Asia Minor and the Near East; it is also perhaps worth noting that agriculture arrived in Europe before it reached Egypt. From south-eastern Europe the main movement indicated by the C-14 dates is north and west via the river valleys, with the Danube as the main axis, as far as the Rhine, which was reached before 4000 BC. Subsequently, between 4000 and 2800 BC, agriculture was extended to southern Scandinavia, the British Isles, France, and Spain in the west and to the north-eastern Balkans and south-west Russia in the east. The whole process of diffusion occupied some 3000 years, a much shorter time than the periods involved in the Palaeolithic, but still incredibly long to our understanding.

SOUTH-EASTERN EUROPE
South-eastern Europe is in many ways an extension of the Near East, perhaps most particularly because its settlements form 'tells'. This is due to the

XVI. Opposite: three columns from the *tholos* at Delphi, considered by the Greeks to be the centre of the world and the seat of the most important temple of Apollo.

156. Map showing the spread of farming from the ancient Near East to Europe and Africa, charted by Carbon-14 dates.

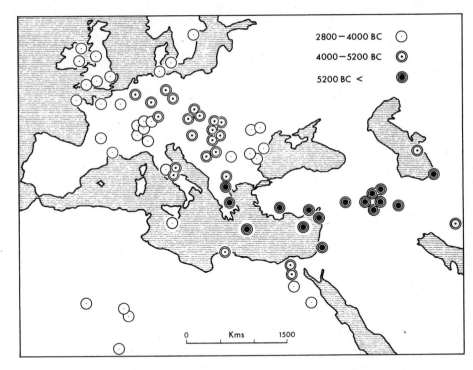

Near-eastern practice of using mud brick for building and to long occupation of the same site, so that successive rebuilding produces a great accumulation of debris which forms the tell on which the settlement sits. The long occupation implies good agricultural practice, which does not exhaust fields and make it necessary to move the whole settlement to a new location at regular intervals, which was, in fact, the pattern in much of the rest of Europe. It is in the architecture of the tell settlements, however, that 'European' characteristics appear, the main difference being that the houses are free-standing. In the Near East the normal pattern was one of contiguous houses with occasional open courts, or the flat roofs, as a means of communication. In Europe each house was a separate entity and was, moreover, covered with a pitched and not a flat roof, a concession to the wetter European climate.

The Neolithic farmers of Greece kept cattle, sheep, goats and pigs and cultivated wheat and barley. They lived in villages of free-standing houses built either of mud brick or of timber uprights with wattle-and-daub filling. Their main equipment consisted of polished stone axes, adzes and chisels, bone awls, needles, and beads and hand-made pottery in globular or jar shapes. The earlier pottery was mostly plain but in the Middle Neolithic (Sesklo) phase a wider range of shapes was introduced together with painted decoration. In the Late Neolithic (Dimini) phase (c. 3500–3000 BC), spiral and meander designs were introduced and these have links with central Europe. At both Sesklo and Dimini enclosing defensive walls were built in the Late Neolithic period. Other important Neolithic sites in Greece include Argissa, Otzaki and Nea Nikomedeia.

From Greece the early farmers spread northwards over much of the Balkan region, probably via the Vardar-Morava and Struma valleys, their tells eventually occupying western Bulgaria, eastern Hungary and Yugo-slavia, and most of Rumania, with the greatest concentration around the

XVII. Opposite: detail of the Alexander Mosaic, showing Darius III, King of Persia (336–30 BC), raised high in his chariot, retreating before the advancing Greeks, led by Alexander.

River Körös in Hungary. As in the Greek communities, goats, sheep, cattle, and pigs were kept and corn was grown in the fields. Houses appear to have been rectangular, one-roomed structures with timber-reinforced mud walls. Pottery was either painted, or decorated with the impressions of finger-nail or shell. Spindle whorls and loom weights indicate that both spinning and weaving were carried on. Among the outstanding sites are Vinča, Karanovo and Starčevo. The expansion from Greece into the Balkan area probably occupied the years *c.* 5000–4500 BC.

THE DANUBIAN NEOLITHIC

North and west of the Balkans developed one of the great Neolithic cultures of Europe, the Danubian. This extended from the Vistula to the Rhine, and from the Danube to northern Europe. Over this extensive region there is a remarkable degree of uniformity in houses, settlements, pottery and other equipment, which suggests that the whole area was occupied relatively quickly in archaeological terms, perhaps in a matter of a few hundred years [157]. Perhaps the two most distinctive features of the culture are its pottery and its houses. The pottery shapes are very simple and are decorated with incised designs of spirals or meanders, and such designs occur throughout the Danubian area. Danubian houses are timber-built and can be 100 ft. or more long and up to 25 ft. wide. Even allowing for livestock, they are still big enough to house an extended family, i.e. three generations, perhaps numbering about twenty people in all, under one roof. Such houses are grouped in villages of twenty to thirty dwellings, implying a population of between 400 and 600 people. These settlements did not form tells, partly because the buildings were mainly of timber, and partly because they were not continuously occupied, probably as a result of their agricultural technique which, without crop rotation, tended to exhaust the land, necessitating

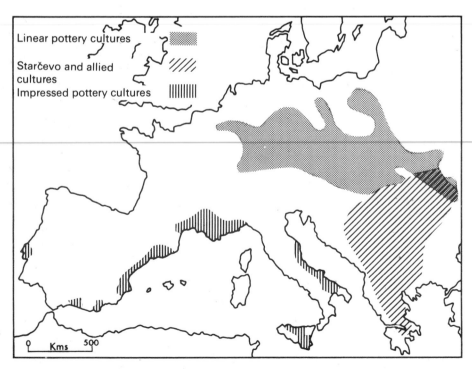

Linear pottery cultures

Starčevo and allied cultures

Impressed pottery cultures

157. Distribution map of agricultural communities in Europe, fifth millenium BC.

a move to a new site. However, there is evidence that Danubian peasants later returned to the same sites and rebuilt their villages, presumably when the land had recovered its fertility. Some Danubian houses are trapezoid in plan, although the reasons for this are not clear. The remaining material equipment included polished stone adzes (a necessary tool in timber building), arrowheads, end-scrapers and flint blades for composite tools. Wheat, barley, peas, beans, and flax were grown and cattle, sheep, goats, and pigs were kept. In European prehistory the Danubian Neolithic occupies a very important place.

THE NEOLITHIC IN THE WEST

Just as the river valleys provided the main highways into the heart of Europe, so the Mediterranean provided a relatively quick and easy means of access to the west. Unfortunately, in this area there is much less information about settlements. For the early period, before 4000 BC, the evidence is virtually confined to pottery and stone tools. These, in many cases in caves, have a noticeably coastal distribution in the Italian Adriatic, Sicily, France, Spain, and North Africa, reflecting their arrival by sea. The pottery, decorated by impressions, is similar to pottery from Syria and Anatolia, and it looks very much as if this Neolithic culture stemmed from some east Mediterranean source. This impressed pottery represents the earliest Neolithic culture in the west and appears to have been well established by *c.* 4000 BC. Subsequently, between *c.* 4000 and 3000 BC, there developed what is often described as the Western Neolithic, characterized by plain, round-based pottery. Just how this culture is related to the impressed-ware culture is not yet satisfactorily established, but it may represent a second wave of migration from some east Mediterranean source. Under various names (the Chassey culture of France, the Cortaillod of Switzerland), Neolithic settlement spread over much of western Europe, reaching the British Isles in the form of the Windmill Hill culture, named after a site in Wiltshire [158]. Details

158. Causewayed camp at Windmill Hill, Wiltshire, *c.* 3000 BC. Windmill Hill is the type site of the Neolithic of southern England (i.e. the Windmill Hill culture), and consists of three roughly concentric rings (now incomplete), each formed by a bank and ditch, with numerous causeways across the ditches (hence the name). Its original function is uncertain. The many causeways make a defensive use unlikely and it may well have been associated with the rounding up and sorting of livestock, perhaps in the autumn, as a prelude to slaughter in order to save winter feed. About a dozen such causewayed sites are known, with from one to four rings of banks and ditches.

of settlements and huts are few and far between except in Switzerland. Otherwise, caves seem to have been much used, although these seem unlikely to represent all the habitation sites, which are probably yet to be found. The Swiss lake-dwellings stood on platforms resting directly on the damp ground at the water's edge, rather than on legs above the open water as they have so often been shown in the past. The timber-built houses were about 24 × 16 ft., much smaller than the Danubian long houses. The damp conditions helped to preserve such normally perishable remains as wooden bows, bowls and troughs, basketry and remains of linen; in addition there were stone and flint axes and arrowheads and reaping knives. The usual domestic animals were kept and crops grown included wheat, peas, beans, lentils, and flax.

The most remarkable aspect of Neolithic culture in western and north-western Europe was the use of elaborate tombs built of very large stones, known as megalithic tombs (Greek, *megas*: large, *lithos*: stone). These were collective burial places, probably for a single important family, and were built in thousands in many parts of western Europe: Spain, Portugal, Sardinia, Corsica, France, England, Ireland, Scotland, Wales, north Germany, Denmark and southern Sweden [159]. Exactly where this tomb fashion began is uncertain but it may have arisen originally from burial in natural caves and then, in the eastern Mediterranean area, from rock-cut tombs imitating caves, the next step being a tomb above the ground built of dry-stone walling covered with a mound of earth, forming a sort of artificial cave. In western Europe the commonest method of building such tombs was by means of large megalithic slabs set on edge for walls and further slabs laid across forming a roof, the whole structure being covered by a mound of earth [160].

Two main types of megalithic tomb can be distinguished: passage graves and gallery graves. A passage grave consists of a burial chamber (round, rectangular, or cruciform) approached by a distinct passage or corridor which is both narrower and lower than the chamber. Passage graves are normally covered by circular mounds. A gallery grave consists simply of a parallel-sided passage or gallery which fulfills both functions. Gallery graves sometimes have side-chambers (transepts) but these are usually smaller and lower than the gallery from which they open. Gallery graves are covered by both long and round mounds. Even within the British Isles a large number of different groups can be distinguished, among them the Cotswold-Severn and Clyde-Carlingford groups (gallery graves under long mounds), and the Boyne group in Ireland (passage graves under circular mounds). Outstanding tombs are New Grange, Ireland, and Maes Howe, Orkney, both passage graves, and West Kennet, Wiltshire, a gallery grave, with transepts, under a long mound [12].

THE NEOLITHIC IN NORTHERN EUROPE

In north Germany and Poland and southern Scandinavia there is another province of Neolithic culture. This formed part of the region previously occupied by the Maglemose culture and it may be that their descendants took over the ideas of agriculture and stock-breeding and little else from the Danubian people to the south, developing their material equipment along their own independent lines. Although they buried their dead in separate graves, these northern people made use of the megalithic technique for the construction of tombs, covering them with circular and long, and, in the

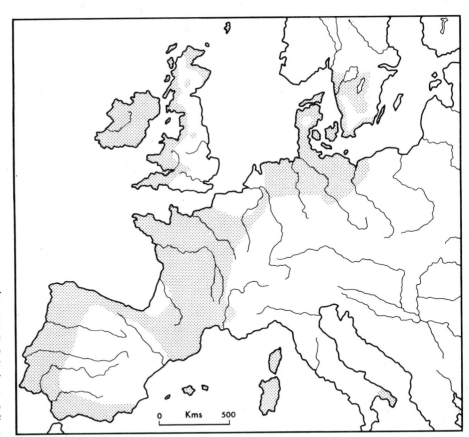

159, 160. Right: distribution map of megalithic chamber tombs in western Europe. The emphasis on western coastal regions is particularly noticeable, from the Atlantic coasts of Spain and France up to the Hebrides, north-east Scotland, Orkney and Shetland. Below: megalithic chamber at Le Bernard, France, *c.* 2500–2000 BC. The tomb has lost its covering mound, allowing the megalithic character of the internal stone structure to be clearly seen.

more easterly regions, wedge-shaped mounds, recalling the trapezoid house plans mentioned earlier (p. 195).

THE NEOLITHIC IN EASTERN EUROPE

To the north-east of the Balkan region, in the western Ukraine, there developed, during the fourth and early third millenia BC, another branch of the European Neolithic: the Tripolye culture. The Tripolye peasants lived in large rectangular wooden houses, up to 100 ft. long, forming villages of up to fifty houses which were sometimes arranged in a circle, presumably to give some degree of protection. Other settlements followed no particular plan but were sited on defended promontaries. Tripolye pottery was of high quality and was mostly a painted ware, red, black, and brown being the predominant colours. The other equipment consisted of flint axes, tools of bone and antler, and looms for weaving. The food supply was based on the growing of wheat, barley, and millet, and on husbandry—cattle and pigs being the most important animals.

North and north-east of the Tripolye area, in the forest zone of Russia, are a whole series of cultures which, although acquiring some of the trappings of Neolithic culture, such as pottery and polished stone tools, remained nevertheless basically Mesolithic in their way of life and only very gradually adopted Neolithic economy long after it was established in the rest of Europe.

This completes a brief survey of European Neolithic culture. In fact, in most cases, only the first or principal stage has been considered. According to area, the Neolithic lasted from two to three thousand years and during such a period change was inevitable. The Danubian, as described earlier, represents only the early part of the period and there was, subsequently, a long development which cannot be followed here. The same is true of the Neolithic in other parts of Europe.

THE BRONZE AGE

The change to metal-working was a very gradual one and stone tools remained in use for many centuries alongside the, presumably, expensive metal tools and weapons. The full Bronze Age was preceded, in many areas, by a Copper Age. Copper was known in the Neolithic, but it had been treated as a form of malleable stone by cold hammering into such things as beads and pins. No metallurgical knowledge was involved. Such knowledge was possibly first discovered in Anatolia, where copper had long been used in its cold-hammered form. By about 3000 BC copper-smelting and casting were fairly widespread in the Near East, in Anatolia, Mesopotamia, Egypt and even in the Aegean area. On the technological side the knowledge of metallurgy represented an enormous breakthrough. Hitherto, technology had been of the simplest, manual kind, involving flaking, scraping, grinding, etc. No chemical change took place in the raw material. Copper- and bronze-working, however, represented a technology of a new and advanced kind in which one substance, of limited use, was transformed chemically into another of the very greatest use. In fact, some understanding of chemistry is already implied in transforming soft clay into hard pottery by the application of heat, and it may be that this knowledge was applied, either accidentally or by design, to copper ores. Into a world of static raw materials such a stone or bone had come the knowledge that Man could transform an apparently useless lump of copper ore first of all into a liquid and then into a solid, and this knowledge had profound effects on the whole pattern of Neolithic Europe.

Technology was further advanced by the move from copper- to bronze-working. Copper is relatively soft as a material for tools and weapons and is difficult to cast. An alloy of ninety per cent copper and ten per cent tin, however, produces a metal (bronze) which is both harder and more manageable in casting, and within a couple of centuries of the first copper-working the properties of a tin/copper alloy were discovered, probably somewhere in the Anatolian region where copper-working was itself discovered.

As far as Europe is concerned, perhaps the most important fact is that neither tin nor copper is very common. Both occur in widely scattered localities (Hungary, Spain, and Cornwall, for example), which means that they have to be sought for and traded over long distances. One of the effects of this ever-increasing trade was to 'open-up' a Europe which had hitherto consisted largely of self-contained communities with little need of outside contact. The bronze trade also formed contacts with the more advanced civilizations of the Aegean and the Near East. These inevitably had an almost insatiable demand for the new tools and weapons and the metal prospecting which opened up Europe was part of the attempt to supply the necessary raw materials. The Bronze Age is not so much significant because its tools and weapons were better than their stone equivalents, but more because with it came into being a whole organized system of manufacturing and trade in which it was difficult for any one region of Europe to remain entirely isolated. Sooner or later all communities were involved, and once that happened the self-sufficient Neolithic world was at an end.

Outside the Aegean area the two earliest centres of copper-working in Europe were in Spain and in Transylvania. These were almost certainly the result of prospecting from the eastern Mediterranean region and both centres would appear to have been established by about 2500 BC. In southern Spain and Portugal, six early copper-using sites are known which closely resemble sites in the Aegean. In particular, the defences of Los Millares in Spain and Vila Nova de Sao Pedro in Portugal are virtually identical to defences in the Cycladic islands, and there are further close parallels in tool and pottery forms. Another parallel was the use of closed moulds for casting, a technique which was lost in the west in the succeeding period. This began about 2000 BC, when the colonies came to an end, in some cases apparently by violence. They were succeeded by the Beaker people, so-named after their characteristic pottery, who represent one of the most unusual episodes in European prehistory and were responsible, among other things, for spreading the knowledge of metal-working over much of western Europe.

The Beaker people, whose pottery, heavily decorated with impressions, suggests that they might have been descendants of the impressed-ware people mentioned earlier (p. 195), seem to have developed on the coasts of Spain and Portugal. From there they spead north and east to France, southern Britain, the Low Countries and central Europe, carrying with them the knowledge of copper-working. Thereafter they appear to have spread back westwards (carrying with them certain central European traits) into eastern England, France, and back into Spain. Over this region there is such a remarkable uniformity in Beaker pottery that the whole movement probably took place very quickly, perhaps during a couple of generations. Their other

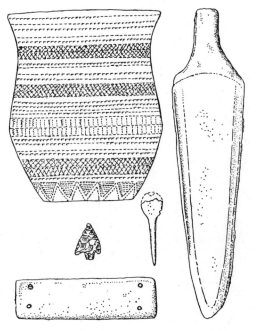

161. Group of material from a Beaker culture burial at Roundway, Wiltshire, c. 1800 BC. The culture takes its name from its very characteristic pots which are usually termed beakers, on the assumption that they were drinking vessels. The other items, apart from the beaker, are a tanged copper dagger, a flint arrowhead, a copper pin and a rectangular stone wrist-guard for an archer, to protect his wrist from the snap-back of the bow-string.

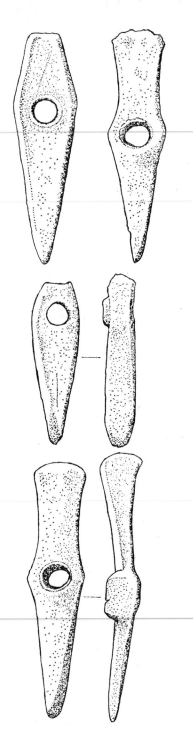

162. Copper shaft-hole axes and axe-adzes from Czechoslovakia, c. 2750 BC.

equipment included copper axe blades, copper knives or daggers, tanged and barbed flint arrowheads and rectangular archer's wrist-guards made of stone [161]. Gold and silver were now in use, mostly for objects of personal adornment such as ear-rings. The Beaker people buried their dead, accompanied by Beaker pottery, in single graves, as opposed to the collective burials of the preceding Neolithic people, and covered them with circular mounds or barrows. In its very rapid diffusion of copper metallurgy over such a large part of western Europe, the Beaker people effectively prepared the way for the full Bronze Age which was to follow.

In Spain and Portugal the Beaker period is followed, c. 1700 BC, by the El Argar culture which represents the Iberian Bronze Age. New trade routes across south-western France now left Spain somewhat isolated, but its Bronze Age was not substantially different from that of the rest of Europe. Its equipment included flat bronze axes with splayed blades, daggers with riveted handles, some of which were developed into short swords or rapiers, and halberds fixed by rivets to wooden hafts, types which were common in central Europe.

The second great centre of early copper-working was the Transylvanian area of Hungary, Rumania and Slovakia, where the implements themselves form the bulk of the evidence. Outstanding among these are the copper axes and axe-adzes, hafted by means of a shaft hole [162]; other products included flat copper axes, dress pins, beads and spiral arm-rings. These copper-working activities seem to have been brought to an end shortly before 2000 BC by the incursions of people from the east, ultimately, it seems, from the area north of the Black Sea. The movements were on a massive scale and affected also the Aegean world, Anatolia, Mesopotamia, and even Egypt, the events in the last two being recorded in official documents.

In the area north of the Black Sea, another copper-using culture had developed between 2500 and 2000 BC. Much of the evidence comes from its single graves, each covered by a circular mound with, in some cases, a timber mortuary house to contain the body. Other diagnostic features are stone battle-axes and globular pottery with cord-decoration. Under a variety of names (Globular Amphorae people, Corded Ware people, Battle-Axe people and Single-grave people), there developed in much of Europe a wide series of cultures which were almost certainly the result of a massive and fairly rapid expansion of people from the south Russian region in the centuries just before 2000 BC. This expansion brought the Danubian Neolithic world to an end, as well as ending the Transylvanian copper-working centres. In central Europe it encountered the Beaker peoples from the west, and it was from this contact that the latter acquired the single-grave practice and stone battle axes, both of which they brought into Britain in the Reflux movement. In the Aegean and the Near East the same expansion seems to have brought the Mycenaeans into Greece and the Hittites into Anatolia. Both Mycenaeans and Hittites spoke Indo-European languages, to which group most European languages belong. It seems likely, therefore, that it was the expansion of the Single-Grave/Battle Axe/Corded Ware/Globular Amphorae people which first brought into Europe, c. 2000 BC, the languages ancestral to those of the present day.

These disturbances seem to have had an effect on trade and trade routes. Shortly after 2000 BC new types of copper objects appear in central Europe. These included riveted, instead of tanged, daggers, ingot torcs, beads, and dress pins, some of which appear to be of Syrian type. These are all interesting because they are ancestral to the full bronze types which were to follow. The Syrian–central Europe link appears to have been via the Adriatic and the Alpine passes, possibly indicating that long-established routes through the Balkans were no longer available.

It was no doubt the demands from the east Mediterranean world, and particularly from the rapidly developing Mycenaean civilization, that stimulated the European metal trade [163]. From the new copper types just described there developed very shortly, and before 1500 BC, the full European bronze-working tradition—which is perhaps best seen in the Ụnetice (German Aunjetitz) culture, although similar products appear in many other parts of Europe. The Ụnetice culture developed in the western half of Czechoslovakia and the adjacent areas of Poland and Germany, with closely related groups nearby in south-west Germany, Poland, and Hungary. Other groups, further removed, include a north Italian group, significantly at the head of the Adriatic, the El Argar culture of Spain and the Wessex culture of southern England. The outstanding Ụnetice product was the triangular bronze dagger with riveted handle. This later developed into a much slimmer form and was gradually increased in length until it could be described as a rapier, and this is one of the standard bronze types in the years between 1500 and 1000 BC. Another Ụnetice type was the halberd, a dagger-like blade fixed at right angles to a wooden or bronze shaft. In addition to daggers, rapiers and halberds, Bronze Age warriors now had bronze spears and, perhaps for more

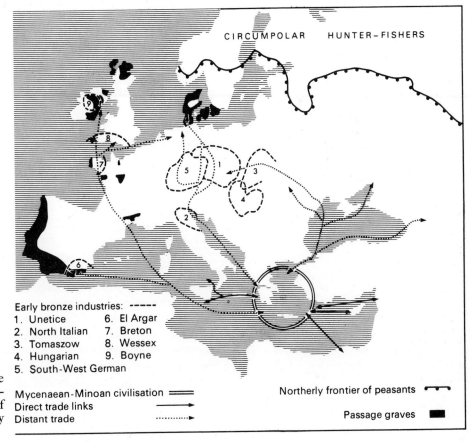

163. Map of Europe *c*. 1500 BC, showing the Minoan-Mycenaean world, the major contemporary Bronze Age groups, and some of the trade links between them, attested by archaeological finds.

Early bronze industries: -----
1. Unetice 6. El Argar
2. North Italian 7. Breton
3. Tomaszow 8. Wessex
4. Hungarian 9. Boyne
5. South-West German

Mycenaean-Minoan civilisation ===
Direct trade links →
Distant trade ·········►

CIRCUMPOLAR   HUNTER-FISHERS

Northerly frontier of peasants
Passage graves

utilitarian purposes, bronze axes with cast flanges for greater strength. Bronze ingot torcs were perhaps a convenient way of carrying and trading the basic raw material of the industry.

Most of the evidence for this Bronze Age civilization comes from graves. The contents of these graves are so rich (numerous weapons of the types mentioned above, gold, jewellery, pottery, stone battle axes, etc.) that they must surely represent the graves of a special warrior class—a separate and higher social class than the ordinary peasants. This is a provincial reflection of the spectacular warrior aristocracy of the Mycenaean civilization, and in fact both patterns stem ultimately from the same south Russian source.

There remain two developments to be described. Individual burial under a tumulus now gives way to the practice of cremation, with the cremated remains placed in a pot and buried in a flat urnfield. This new fashion seems to have begun in east central Europe about 1500 BC and, by 1000 BC, urnfield cultures covered much of southern and central Europe, including the area north of the Alps (the North Alpine Urnfield culture) which was to prove so important for the beginnings of the European Iron Age.

The second development was in the field of weapons. The bronze swords described earlier were suited to a thrusting technique, hence the term rapiers. However, c. 1500 BC, there developed in east central Europe a new type of heavy sword more suited to a slashing action. These leaf-shaped swords have the blade and the tang (for the handle) cast in one piece, and appear to have been invented in Europe rather than in any of the centres of higher civilization. They spread widely over Europe, but perhaps their most dramatic appearance was in the Aegean at about the time when the Mycenaean civilization collapsed (c. 1150 BC), probably as a result of invasions from the north by people bearing such swords. At about the same time the North Alpine Urnfield culture, a link between the Bronze Age and the Iron Age, was in process of formation.

THE IRON AGE

The change to iron-working was a gradual one which, for central Europe, began some time after 700 BC. However, iron-working among the Hittites in Anatolia seems to have begun shortly after 1500 BC. Thereafter it spread generally over the Near East and the Aegean before 1000 BC and by the ninth century it had reached south Italy. It was not, however, until c. 700 BC that it was used on any considerable scale in Europe north of the Alps, the region with which we are most concerned in this section.

Iron was, in fact, known from the third millenium BC, but was treated as more of a curiosity than anything else. Presumably it was the discovery of an effective technology by the Hittites which enabled iron-working on a commercial scale to begin. In Europe, iron ore is relatively abundant, so that the possibilities of rapid expansion were good. On the other hand, iron-working is rather more complex than bronze; iron (except under modern conditions) cannot be cast and has to be forged or hammered into shape, and this is by no means the only process involved. However, once the technology was mastered by a sufficient number of iron-workers, then the conditions existed for the production of cheap and effective tools and weapons on a large scale.

For reasons of space attention in this section will be confined to the Iron Age as exemplified by the Hallstatt and La Tène periods of Celtic civilization. The Celts, who are first identified by name as a nation in this period (Greek,

164. The spread of the Iron Age Hallstatt culture, *c*. 700–500 BC, in central and western Europe, including, towards the end of the period, eastern and south-eastern England. The distribution of the (earlier) Hallstatt C and the (later) Hallstatt D wagon graves shows the westward shift in the presumed centre of power represented by these rich burials.

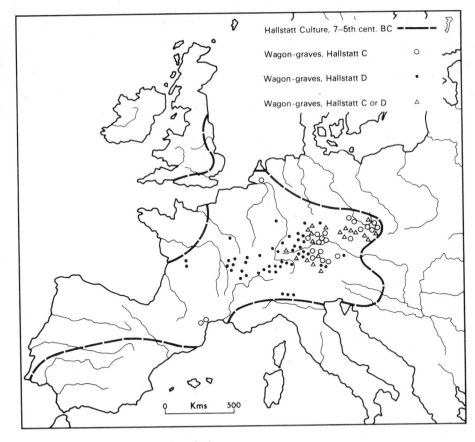

Hallstatt Culture, 7–5th cent. BC ———

Wagon-graves, Hallstatt C ○

Wagon-graves, Hallstatt D ·

Wagon-graves, Hallstatt C or D △

0 Kms 500

Keltoi), spread considerably beyond their original homeland north of the Alps, so that the survey will still embrace much of central, western, and north-western Europe, including Britain.

THE HALLSTATT CULTURE

It was in the North Alpine area that the Hallstatt culture first developed [164]. In spite of the advent of iron-working around 700 BC, there seems to have been a continuous development by substantially the same people from as early as 1200 BC, when the North Alpine Urnfield culture began, and it seems likely that we can already regard the Urnfield people as Celts. The arrival of iron technology was not by itself the great distinguishing feature of the Hallstatt culture. For the factors which did produce it, we must again look eastwards, to the Russian steppe.

In south Russia, the historically recorded Scythians buried their dead in timber-chambered barrows and by 1000 BC had developed a remarkable animal art in metalwork, wood, leather and textiles. They had a high regard for horses and their equipment (bridle and harness fittings), which were buried with or close to their owner. Scythian expansion during the ninth–eighth centuries BC caused the displacement of the Cimmerians (Greek, *Kymmeroi*), a people with a culture closely allied to that of the Scythians. The latter expanded south into eastern Anatolia and west into the Carpathians and the Hungarian plain. It is, however, the dispersal by the Scythians of the Cimmerians over wide areas of Europe which is most significant for the emergence of the Hallstatt culture.

During the eighth–seventh centuries BC, and presumably as a result of Cimmerian migrations or raids, or both, there appear in many parts of Europe, including the North Alpine region, a series of bronze horse trappings which are quite clearly of eastern, ultimately Russian steppe, origin. They appear in graves which are presumably those of warriors to whom mounted warfare is now the normal pattern. These burials are succeeded, shortly after 700 BC, in the North Alpine region, by much more elaborate burials, in wooden mortuary houses or chambers, sunk in the ground or covered by a mound, or both. The most outstanding items in them are the remains of four-wheeled wagons or carts, possibly acting as hearses and perhaps reflecting their owner's nomadic way of life. Also included are the bronze trappings for two draught horses and frequently a third set, presumably for the warrior's riding horse. The form and content of these burials indicate a very powerful influence on central Europe from the east. It was this influence on the late North Alpine Urnfield culture which brought into being the Hallstatt culture of central Europe. Iron swords were now in use, so that the Hallstatt culture stands at the beginning of the Iron Age in central Europe, but the most significant change is represented by the wagon burials, which must be those of very powerful chiefs and would appear to indicate profound social and political changes. The iron swords reflect the wealth and power of the Hallstatt chiefs but they appear, in fact, to have been derived not from the east but from the south, from the head of the Adriatic.

Between 700 and 500 BC the Hallstatt culture expanded to occupy much of central and western Europe, including, by the end of the period, eastern and south-eastern England. In the outlying parts, and beyond, bronze-using cultures continued, in many cases making bronze versions of Hallstatt iron swords. The heart of the Hallstatt region, however, appears to have been southern Germany and eastern France where, judging by the rich range of imports, the Hallstatt people seem to have been in close trade contact with the Greeks and Etruscans, via the Greek colony at Massilia (modern Marseilles) and the Rhone valley. Wine, and Graeco-Etruscan pottery to contain it, seems to have flowed in one direction, and salt, very important to the Hallstatt economy and now mined on a large scale, in the other.

Wagon burials have been found in a great east–west band from Czechoslovakia to central France. It is noticeable, however, that the earliest burials are in the east and the latest in the west, perhaps indicating a progressive shift westwards in the centre of power. The graves appear to be too numerous to be those of a single royal family and the pattern may be that of a royal tribe which had assumed the leadership of the Hallstatt peoples and which, perhaps, through its prestige, gave its name (*Keltoi*) to the whole confederation of tribes involved in the culture.

THE LA TÈNE CULTURE

Around 500 BC Hallstatt culture gave way to La Tène to which it had, in a sense, served as a prelude. The homeland of the La Tène culture, continuing the pattern noted already, is to the west and north-west of the bulk of the Hallstatt wagon burials, in the area between the middle Rhine and the Marne. There is also a noticeable change in burial practice. Instead of the four-wheeled wagon there is now a two-wheeled vehicle, almost certainly a chariot. This indicates also a change in the technique of war. The warrior aristocrat now rides a chariot into battle instead of a horse and, as the object

165. Opposite: detail of the lower terminal of a flagon handle from Basse-Yutz, Lorraine, early La Tène period, fifth century BC. The La Tène period, the second part of the European Iron Age, from *c.* 500 BC on, is notable among other things for its superb, curvilinear decorative art, applied to such things as bronze mirrors, shields, armour, weapons, etc., as well as to pottery and wood.

of his greatest pride, his chariot is buried with him. Other martial equipment included long iron swords in bronze scabbards, shields, spears, helmets, and daggers, often richly decorated in the distinctive La Tène style. From its Rhine/Marne development area, La Tène culture spread outwards in all directions during the next two or three centuries, eventually to embrace, by c. 250 BC, virtually the whole of France, the Low Countries, the British Isles, Switzerland, western and southern Germany, Czechoslovakia and the middle and upper Danube regions, with large-scale raiding beyond, notably into Italy and Greece where the unwelcome presence of Celts is recorded c. 400 BC and c. 279 BC respectively.

The art style of the La Tène culture is recognized as a major contribution to the repertoire of world art, regardless of date or area. Art is always difficult to analyse, but some of the formative elements of the La Tène style are reasonably clear. Not unexpectedly there is evidence of Scythian influence, but not to any overwhelming extent. Scythian art developed along its own distinctive lines and forms a second great province of Iron Age art outside the Classical world. No doubt, also, the preceding Hallstatt and Urnfield traditions played their part in the La Tène style, but the most potent influence was the range of Greek decorative motifs which the Celts became familiar with through trade, mostly the wine trade and the vessels associated with it. These they adapted freely to their own decorative needs without regard to, indeed without knowing, what they were meant to represent. The results are much easier to illustrate than describe but, in its virtually complete rejection of a representational approach, it is completely different from contemporary Greek art which during the fifth–fourth centuries BC was at its peak. Human and animal figures rarely appear in La Tène art. It is an art of curvilinear lines and shapes with a freedom that allows it to adapt without difficulty to all sorts of surfaces, from a sword scabbard to the back of a bronze mirror, and from the curving surface of a pot or a wooden bowl to the head of a spear. In spite of its debt to the sources mentioned above, it is an entirely new and original art, begun by the native Celts from about 500 BC onwards [165].

FORTIFICATION

The most common field monuments in the Celtic world, from Spain to the Balkans and from the Alps to Scotland, are the fortified enclosures known as hillforts. These first appeared around 1000 BC in the North Alpine Urnfield culture and may well have been based on knowledge derived from the Mediterranean world, either by trade or through mercenary service there by Urnfield warriors. They continued to be built and used throughout Iron Age times, their construction being terminated by the Roman conquest at whatever date it took place locally (58–50 BC in Gaul, AD 43 onwards in Britain). In spite of the term hillfort, not all such enclosures are situated on hills. Celtic forts were built also on promontories, either coastal or inland, with part of the defences formed by natural features (cliffs or very steep slopes), and (less frequently) on ridges, cliff or plateau edges, and in low-lying situations. The term fort suggests a permanently manned military site, but this was certainly not the case in the Celtic world. The thousands of forts which exist were probably built for a number of different purposes, some, for example, as temporary refuges in times of danger, others as fortified villages or towns, possibly some form of local or tribal capital.

166. Iron Age hillfort on the Herefordshire Beacon. The small, innermost enclosure is a medieval feature and is therefore nothing to do with the Iron Age defences. These consist of the larger central enclosure, representing the original Iron Age fort, and the enclosures or annexes to the north and south, which are later extensions, presumably to increase the space within the ramparts. Hillforts are widespread in Europe—there are well over two thousand of them in Britain alone.

Very large enclosures, 50 or 100 acres in area, could well have been intended for cattle, while very small enclosures (an acre or less) may well have been fortified farmsteads for a single family unit [166].

The defences of these forts are now a series of grass-grown banks and ditches (or a bank of loose stones in the case of stone-built ramparts), but such remains conceal a variety of original structures. The simplest defence was a bank of earth, derived from a V-shaped ditch, forming a continuous slope from the ditch bottom to the crest of the bank where the defenders would stand. The alternative form of rampart had a vertical, rather than a sloping, outer face and was built in a variety of ways: with a timber front (and rear as well in many cases) and a core or filling of earth in between, or a stone front with either stone or mixed stone and earth filling. To resist the outward thrust of the core, cross-timbers running from front to back were used, although evidence for these is not often found. A very special form of this practice (timber lacing) was developed in Gaul at the time of the Roman conquest, involving a complex timber framework, with iron nails at the intersections, contained in the core, and outer and inner faces of stone. Such ramparts were thought to be resistant to attack by fire or by battering ram.

Special attention was paid to the entrances. In the widely-used inturned type the ramparts turn inwards, parallel to each other, to form a narrow entrance-corridor or roadway, with timber gates near the inner end. Rectangular guard chambers were often placed immediately inside the gates.

Other types involved out-turned, or inturned/out-turned ramparts, overlapping ramparts and various forms of outworks.

While these events were taking place in most of Europe, events in the southeast, in the Aegean world, were taking a noticeably different course, leading eventually to the rich achievements of the Classical (i.e. Greek and Roman) world. To see how this separate development began, it is necessary to go back in time to *c.* 2500 BC and the Minoan civilization of Crete.

THE MINOAN CIVILIZATION

The story of Classical civilization begins in the island of Crete, around 2500 BC, when bronze was first introduced, possibly from Asia Minor. Until recently many people would have chosen a much later initial date, within the Greek Dark Age (1100–700 BC), but modern research has shown that people speaking the Greek language first entered Greece around 1900 BC, i.e. within the Aegean Bronze Age, and it seems legitimate, therefore, to start the story at the beginning of this period, 2500 BC. The existing population of Crete consisted of simple, agricultural village communities at a Neolithic (New Stone Age) level of civilization. Crete forms the southern flank of the Aegean world, the world of Classical Greece, and was ideally situated for contact with the higher civilizations of the ancient Near East; these contacts must be responsible for the very rapid development of Minoan civilization which took place from 2000 BC onwards.

The term Minoan (after the legendary King Minos of Crete) was coined by Sir Arthur Evans, excavator of Knossos, to denote the island's Bronze Age civilization. In the Early Minoan (E.M.) period (2500–2000 BC), quite a lot is known about pottery and other small finds, but very little about architecture. The Middle Minoan (M.M.) period, on the other hand, is

167, 168. Below: drawn reconstruction of the palace of Minos at Knossos, Crete. As far as can be ascertained from the remains [37], the formal State rooms were to the west (left) of the courtyard in the area marked A, while the Royal private apartments were to the east (right), in the area marked B. To the south of these were what appear to have been guest suites for important visitors. Opposite: the Queen's megaron, the richly decorated main room in what are generally regarded to be the Queen's private apartments.

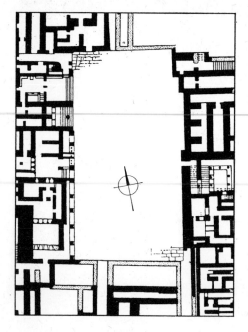
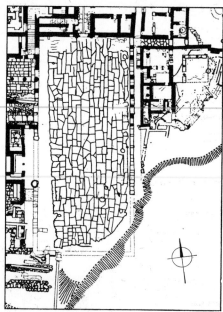
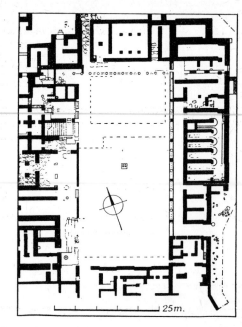

rich in architecture, particularly in its palaces at Knossos, Phaistos, Mallia and Kato Zakro. Palaces of such size (Knossos covers over three acres) must indicate the existence of powerful rulers with diplomatic and economic contacts with the other major powers of the east Mediterranean world (the Egyptians, Hittites, etc.), and the comparatively quick appearance and development of such monumental architecture in Crete must be due in part at least to such contacts. As a result of earthquakes *c.* 1650 BC, there was a major rebuilding on most Minoan sites and it is in this reconstructed form that the palaces are visible today, albeit as ruins.

Knossos, the first discovered and largest of the palaces, was excavated by Sir Arthur Evans between 1899 and 1934. The most notable feature of the plan is the large courtyard (*c.* 170 × 80 ft.), around which the major blocks of buildings are ranged [37, 167]. Similar central courts appear in the three other palaces. Other features in common are storage magazines, impressive stairways and formal, monumental entrances. The Grand Staircase at Knossos, some 20 ft. wide, was quite clearly the formal approach to the State apartments which must have existed on the first floor. The visible remains are, of course, those of the ground floor only. They include a range of magazines which once housed perhaps as many as 400 huge storage jars, up to 6 ft. high, capable of storing up to 15,000 gallons of oil or wine. The thickness of the magazine walls may indicate the presence immediately above of the State apartments. The remaining visible rooms in the west block appear to be shrines and religious buildings, including the so-called throne room in which an actual stone throne or formal seat was found in position. On the east side of the court, the very thick walls in the workshop area may again indicate the former existence of an important room or hall immediately above. The rooms to the south appear to have been the private quarters of the royal or noble family living in the palace and include the so-called Queen's apartment [168], with an impressive bathroom and lavatory. There were two further bathrooms in the rooms to the south which may have formed the accommodation for royal guests.

169. The central courts and the immediately surrounding areas at the four Cretan palaces: Knossos (opposite, far left), Phaistos (opposite, centre left), Mallia (opposite, left) and Kato Zakro (right), all to the same scale. The similarity in size (except for Kato Zakro) is striking, as is the position occupied by all four at the heart of their respective palaces. Quite clearly the central courtyard was a very important part of the whole palace complex.

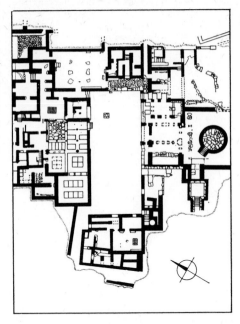

The other three palaces at Phaistos, Mallia, and Kato Zakro are somewhat smaller but are obviously of exactly the same type [**169**]. The most striking similarities are in the central courtyards, all of which have their long axes more or less north and south, all of which are paved with flagstones, and three of which (Knossos, Mallia and Phaistos) are identical in size (170 × 80 ft.). Kato Zakro is somewhat smaller (100 × 40 ft.). These courts are quite clearly a very important part of the whole building complex and there is now little doubt that they were intended for the bull games which may have had some religious or ritual significance. These are well illustrated in wall-paintings, seals and figurines, and are not bull fights. They are mainly gymnastic in content, the most spectacular manœuvre being a full somersault over the bull's head from the front, perhaps (although this is not certain) using its horns as a hand-hold.

In addition to the four major palaces there are remains of what may be minor palaces and a considerable number of very large houses or villas, seven of which, including the Little Palace and the Royal Villa, cluster around the main palace at Knossos. The two Minoan towns of Gournia and Palaikastro have the same narrow winding streets with small houses crowding between.

THE MYCENAEAN CIVILIZATION

The most splendid period of Minoan civilization (c. 2000–1500 BC) saw also the gradual development of a rival centre of wealth and power on the Greek mainland. By about 1600 BC, the Mycenaeans were already sufficiently powerful to constitute a threat to Minoan power, and by about 1450 BC this threat appears to have become a reality, with the centre of power shifting decisively to the Greek mainland. One of the most noticeable differences between the Minoan and Mycenaean civilizations is the warlike character of the latter. There is no evidence of fortification around the Minoan palaces. Tiryns and Mycenae, on the other hand, have massive defences and carefully contrived entrances and these and the swords and other military equipment found in graves demonstrate very forcibly the more aggressive, martial

170. The Lion Gate at Mycenae. The martial world suggested by these massive defensive walls on the mainland of Greece during the Mycenaean period (1400–1100 BC) is far removed from the peaceful conditions implied by the lack of any sort of defences around the earlier Royal palaces on the island of Crete.

character of the Mycenaean world [2]. This character is evident in the rich contents of the Shaft Graves (gold and silver vessels, gold death masks, jewellery, and richly decorated weapons) which date from about 1600 BC, and which appear to have been the burials of the Royal House of Mycenae [35]. These consisted of rectangular shafts cut down into the rock, lined with stone walls and roofed with timber and stone slabs. The circle of upright stone slabs in which the group is enclosed is a later addition, added when the main Mycenaean citadel was built. In recent years a second circle enclosing a group of graves has been found.

Something of the wealth and power of the Mycenaeans is evident in the powerful citadels they erected in the period from 1400–1100 BC, particularly at Tiryns and Mycenae, both originally excavated by Schliemann. Both strongholds are characterized by powerful walls (up to 22 ft. thick), and by cleverly contrived entrances, including the famous Lion Gate at Mycenae [170]. The purpose of such citadels, in a warlike environment, was to house the palaces of the ruling Mycenaean kings or princes. From the point of view of later developments in architecture, particularly temple architecture, by far the most important feature of the internal buildings was the megaron, which at this stage was simply the main room of the palace, and it was presumably in this impressive hall that the ruling king or prince lived and held court. Equally impressive are the burial chambers of the Mycenaean princes which from 1400 BC onwards replaced the earlier Shaft Graves. These consist of domed, circular stone chambers approached by long passages, the whole structure being buried in a covering mound of earth.

It is this Mycenaean world which is depicted in the poems of Homer, written, as far as we know, in the eighth century BC, but describing events of some centuries earlier. Homer's *Iliad* tells the story of the siege of Troy (Ilium) on the north-west coast of Asia Minor, the third major site excavated by Schliemann. No less than nine successive cities existed on the site and it was the sixth city which (*c.* 1200 BC) was sacked by the Mycenaean powers.

THE GREEK DARK AGE (1100–700 BC)

Less than a century later the glittering Mycenaean world was itself at an end. One of the factors involved, perhaps the major one, was a further invasion or migration from the north of Greek-speaking peoples (the Dorian invasion). The resultant pressure led to the movement overseas of some of the existing population, notably to the western coastal region of Asia Minor, which henceforward was an integral part of the Greek world. At a later stage various Greek cities sent out colonies to overseas territories, including Sicily and southern Italy which likewise became part of the Greek world. The Dorian invasion was a necessary pause, during which new ideas were absorbed (including the knowledge of iron-working) and fresh strength gathered, in anticipation, as it were, of the great advances which were to follow. The Greece which emerges into the light of history around 700 BC is recognizable as Classical Greece, even if it had not yet reached the heights it was to achieve some two and a half centuries later.

ARCHAIC AND CLASSICAL GREECE

This section covers the four centuries from the end of the Greek Dark Age to the death of Alexander the Great in 323 BC. What are today recognized as the greatest achievements of Greek civilization took place in the fifth century. The two preceding centuries, when this civilization was not yet fully developed, are known as the Archaic period (700–475 BC). As a result of widespread trade contacts with the east Mediterranean world, the Archaic Greeks were subject to a great deal of Oriental influence and this is quite evident in their pottery, architecture and sculpture. In the field of pottery, for example, the change from Dark Age to Archaic is marked, in broad terms, by a change from geometric-style decoration to realistic drawings of Oriental subjects (exotic winged lions, for example). The then chief trading centre of Greece, Corinth, was very much influenced by all this and gradually developed its own characteristic Corinthian pottery; and as it developed, Oriental subjects were progressively replaced by purely Greek subjects, from mythology and everyday life. In its turn Corinthian pottery gave rise to the great Archaic pottery tradition, the black-figure style which began *c.* 625 BC [21]. It was produced mainly in Corinth and Athens and exported widely in the Mediterranean world. The technique consisted of painting the design in black silhouette on the light red clay of the pot, the reverse of the classic red-figure style of the fifth century to which black-figure eventually gave rise.

Oriental influence is equally evident in Archaic sculpture, virtually a new subject in the Greek world since none appears to have existed in the Dark Age period. The two main types were the male *(kouros)* and female *(kore)* standing figures which first appear *c.* 650 BC [171, 172]. Egyptian influence is quite clearly evident in the pose, the expression and the wig-like hair. The

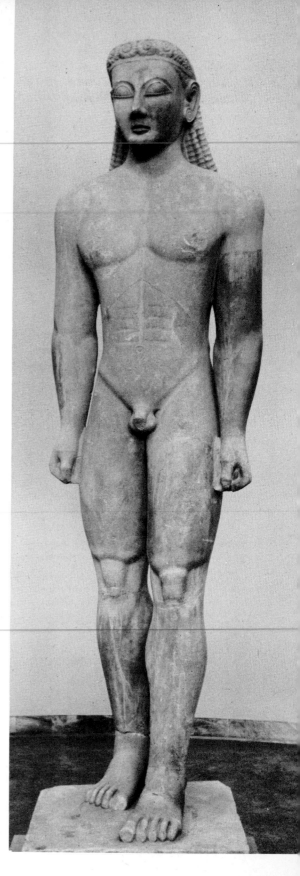

171, 172. Male and female standing figures of the Archaic period of Greek sculpture (650–475 BC). Left: female figure (Greek *kore*), probably by the sculptor Antenor, *c.* 530–25 BC. Right: male figure (*kouros*), from Sunium, *c.* 615–590 BC. In the earlier, male figure in particular, the influence of Egyptian sculpture can be clearly seen in the wig-like hair and the stiff, formal posture.

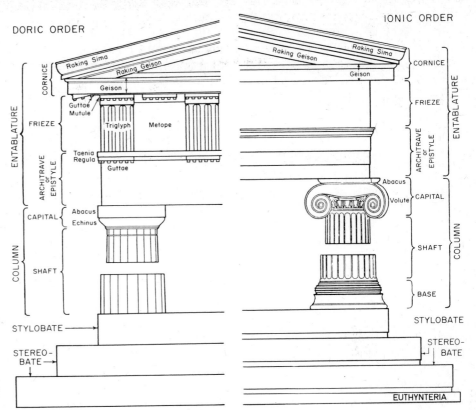

DORIC ORDER

IONIC ORDER

173. The Doric and Ionic orders, the two main styles used in Greek architecture. The third Classical style, the Corinthian, was not used much by the Greeks and flourished mainly in Roman architecture. Although the column is the most noticeable feature of each style, the diagram makes it clear that the whole order consisted of much more than just the column, embracing everything from ground level to cornice.

achievement of the Archaic period was, eventually, an intimate knowledge of human anatomy and a complete mastery of even the most difficult postures. In the latter half of the period relief sculpture, as opposed to sculpture-in-the-round, made its appearance, as did the technique of hollow-bronze casting, in which the figure is first made in clay, giving the artist much greater freedom in modelling.

In architecture, the main element in the Greek temple (the megaron) seems to have been derived from the old, native Mycenaean tradition where it was the principal room of the royal palace. As such it was the only room suitable to house a god in human form, and it remained the basis of the Graeco-Roman temple for the next thousand years, until the end of the Roman Empire. The addition of the colonnade transformed the megaron into what we now recognize as a Classical temple, and this again may represent influence from Egypt, where columns and colonnades were long-established architectural features. Although basically conforming to the same plan, Graeco-Roman temples differ in appearance according to the three great orders of Classical architecture, Doric, Ionic and Corinthian, although the latter was used more by the Romans than by the Greeks. Broadly speaking, the Doric style predominated in mainland Greece, southern Italy, and Sicily, while the Ionic predominated in western Asia Minor [173]. The heyday of the Doric style was the period *c.* 600–400 BC. Its distinctive features were the absence of a separate base to the column, the very plain capital and the frieze consisting of alternating triglyphs (decorative stone versions of the original timber beam ends) and metopes (square panels of relief sculpture). In plan, the majority of Doric temples were six columns

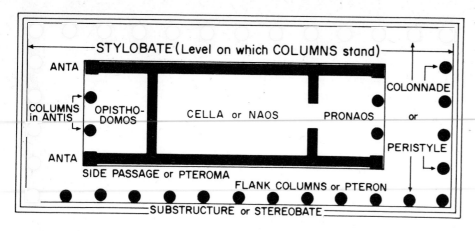

wide and twelve to fifteen columns long. In the Ionic order the column was slimmer than the Doric, with a well-defined base, more elaborate fluting and a more ornate capital in which the volutes were the characteristic feature. The Ionic frieze was a continuous band of relief sculpture, although the frieze was sometimes omitted altogether. The Corinthian order was similar to the Ionic except for its capitals, which represent a clump of acanthus leaves. Many Ionic temples were of enormous size with great ranks of columns at the front, perhaps again reflecting Egyptian influence, where massed columns had been used in much the same way.

In the early part of the fifth century the Greeks finally achieved the mastery in pottery, sculpture, and architecture which they had been working towards during the two previous centuries. In mainland Greece and in the west, the Doric temple reached the peak of its development [174]. Three temples illustrate what must be regarded as the standard Doric type: the temples of Zeus at Olympia, of Hephaestus in Athens, and of Poseidon at Sunium. In plan all are six columns wide and thirteen columns long and internally the temples at Sunium and Athens are almost identical. The latter, the temple of Hephaestus, is one of the best preserved of all Greek temples and some of its sculptured metopes are still in position [1]. The temple at Olympia was begun in about 470 BC, the temple of Hephaestus around 450 BC, and the Sunium temple about 440 BC. The temple of Hera at Paestum, in southern Italy (c. 460 BC), also belongs with this group. It is somewhat longer (6 × 14 columns), but is otherwise not dissimilar to the temple at Olympia, having a double row of columns inside the cella. Of the same layout (6 × 14 columns) is the unfinished temple at Segesta (Sicily) which consists of the platform and colonnade only. The columns are still unfluted and the blocks forming the platform still have the projecting bosses, which were left on for handling purposes and removed only when the stone received its final dressing.

Externally the temple of Apollo at Bassae follows the Doric formula but internally it has both Ionic columns and a single Corinthian one. The ten Ionic columns are engaged or attached to the sides of the cella by short spur walls. More unusual is the single Corinthian column, one of the first uses of the type in Greece. The position of the door in the east wall may be a result of the unusual north–south orientation of the temple, enabling the cult statue still to face to the east.

The Doric temple of Zeus at Agrigentum in Sicily (begun c. 480 BC) was enormous (360 × 170 ft.), comparable with the Ionic temples of Greek

175. Opposite: view of the Acropolis in Athens showing the Propylaeum or formal entrance (left), the Erechtheum, a temple of very unusual plan (centre), and the Parthenon, perhaps the most famous of all Doric temples (right). The Acropolis is a natural knoll of rock which has been further strengthened by the retaining wall that can be clearly seen below the Parthenon.

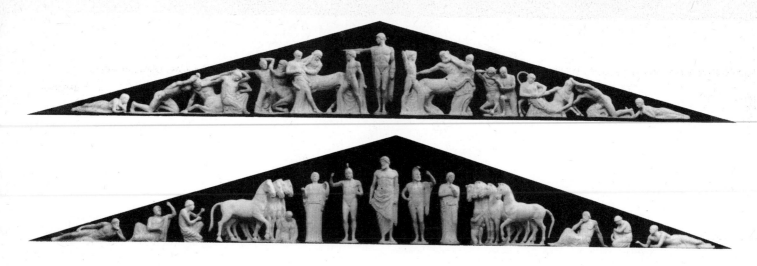

176, 177. Conjectural arrangement of sculptural figures in the west (top) and east pediments of the temple of Zeus at Olympia. Of all the positions in Greek architecture where sculpture was used, this was the most difficult to fill satisfactorily because of the diminishing height and sharply angled outer corners. Part of the solution was to make the central figure, a god, larger than the other figures, and to place these progressively in seated, kneeling, reclining and finally prone positions.

178. Opposite: the Diskobolos, by the sculptor Myron, c. 460–50 BC. Compare this with the stiff Archaic figure from Sunium, some 150 years earlier [172]. Nothing better illustrates the Greek mastery of anatomy and natural posture than this figure of a discus-thrower in the act of winding up for the throw.

Asia Minor. Externally it had half-columns linked by a continuous curtain wall, with square pilasters on the inside. The structure included huge male and female figures, some 25 ft. high, between the external half-columns. The interior was divided into three parts by two rows of square pillars, again linked by a continuous curtain wall. To allow for the admission of light, the curtain wall probably reached only half the height of the pillars.

The Parthenon on the Acropolis in Athens does not conform to the normal Doric pattern [175]. It is, unusually, seventeen columns long and eight wide. Internally the arrangement is even more unusual, with the cella divided into two separate parts. The cella proper (c. 95 × 60 ft.) has a two-tier colonnade on the two long sides and across the back, within which stood the great gold-and-ivory statue of Athena, by the sculptor Phidias, which unfortunately has not survived. The western chamber was much smaller, with its roof supported by four Ionic columns. The whole of the temple was of marble, even the roof tiles. Many of the Parthenon sculptures were brought back to England by Lord Elgin in 1816 (the Elgin Marbles) and are now in the British Museum [27].

Both in plan and general appearance the Erechtheum (begun 421 BC), also on the Acropolis, is the most unusual of all Greek temples. The plan is basically rectangular, with the addition of porches to north and south. A cross wall cuts off the eastern portion of the interior and this part is at a higher level and faces east in the usual way. The western portion is at a lower level and is further sub-divided into a vestibule and two smaller chambers. A central doorway at the back of the north porch gave access to the vestibule but, because of the difference in level, by means of a staircase. The style of the temple is Ionic with a frieze of figures in white marble on a background of black limestone.

In sculpture, the Greeks had, by c. 475 BC, completely mastered the anatomy of the human figure and were able to render virtually any posture they wished. Unfortunately, apart from a few bronzes, not many original works have survived and it is at second hand, from the surviving Roman copies, that we have to study this aspect of Greek achievement. In spite of this, the splendour of the Greek work is unmistakable.

One splendid original work (c. 460 BC) is a bronze figure of Poseidon (Neptune), or Zeus, found in the sea near Cape Artemisium. The pose and

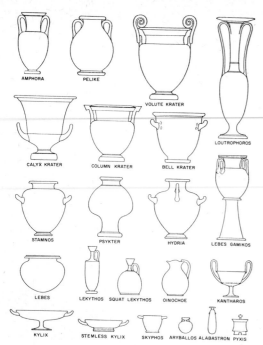

AMPHORA   PELIKE

VOLUTE KRATER

LOUTROPHOROS

CALYX KRATER   COLUMN KRATER   BELL KRATER

STAMNOS   PSYKTER   HYDRIA   LEBES GAMIKOS

LEBES   LEKYTHOS   SQUAT LEKYTHOS   OINOCHOE   KANTHAROS

KYLIX   STEMLESS KYLIX   SKYPHOS   ARYBALLOS   ALABASTRON   PYXIS

179, 180. Above: the main shapes of Greek pottery from *c.* 550 to *c.* 350 BC, and their Greek names. Opposite: detail of a red-figure oinochoe, *c.* 425 BC, showing a reveller pounding at a door. Among many other topics, scenes from everyday life, such as this, formed the subject matter of Greek red-figure painting on pottery.

the perfectly rendered anatomy are a far cry from the stiff, upright poses of the Archaic figures of the previous century. This figure alone is eloquent testimony of fifth-century achievement in sculpture. The famous Diskobolos (Discus-thrower) by the sculptor Myron (*c.* 460–50 BC) perhaps more than any other figure illustrates the complete mastery which had now been achieved [178]. The athlete is both crouching and turning at the same time, caught in the momentary pause between winding up for the throw and actually launching the discus. Another famous athletic figure is by the sculptor Polykleitos. The Doryphoros (the spear-holder) is the figure of a well-developed young man in a very relaxed standing pose with the left hand holding a lance and the right hanging easily by the side.

The fifth-century female figure shows a mastery in the rendering of drapery which reveals rather than conceals the anatomy. Figures of Amazons, one attributed to Polykleitos, are common female types with the many folds of the clothing rendered with perfect naturalism.

The nature of fifth-century architectural sculpture is exemplified in the temple of Zeus at Olympia. In the west pediment the centre is occupied by the figure of Apollo. On either side are scenes of Lapiths and Centaurs fighting, in progressively more crouching postures to fit in with the available space [176]. The east pediment has Zeus in the centre, and preparations for the race between Pelops and Oinomaos in progress on either side [177].

Apart from pediment sculpture, the other great area of architectural sculpture was the metope of the Doric temple. A normal 6 × 13-column Doric temple would have sixty-eight such panels, so that quite clearly this part of the temple alone represented a very considerable output of sculpture. Many of the metopes from the Parthenon are in the British Museum. Each panel is about 4 ft. square and the subjects include fights between Lapiths and Centaurs, gods and giants, and Greeks and Amazons, all popular subjects in Greek art.

The frieze, a continuous band of relief sculpture, is more usually associated with the Ionic order, although there is a frieze on the Parthenon, placed inside the colonnade, high on the outside of the cella wall. Its subject is the procession which took place every four years as part of the Panathenaia, the religious festival held in Athens in which a new robe was presented to a much venerated image of Athena on the Acropolis. The frieze of the temple of Apollo at Phigaleia has the same subjects as the Parthenon metopes: fighting between Greeks and Amazons and Lapiths and Centaurs. Another well-preserved frieze is that of the temple of Hephaestus in Athens, which is still popularly (though erroneously) known as the Theseum, because the frieze shows the exploits of Theseus.

In the field of pottery the change to the red-figure style was complete by about 500 BC, and shortly thereafter perfect mastery in form and decoration had been achieved [179]. Athens was the major centre of production and Athenian red-figure pottery was exported to most parts of the Mediterranean world. Red-figure technique was a reversal of black-figure: the figures were now left or reserved in red and the background was painted black, and instead of incision the internal details were now painted in black lines, allowing the artist much greater freedom. Scenes and figures from Greek mythology still formed an important part of the subject matter, but increasingly in the fifth century scenes from everyday life were represented: athletes exercising, people feasting and women performing household

chores, etc [180]. Some of these scenes are briefly described in the inscriptions that appear on some vessels (he runs, he is going to jump); sometimes the words are those of a figure on the pot (look, a swallow), or else they form a greeting (I greet you). Occasionally artists' signatures appear. They show that normally two artists were involved, one to fashion the pot and one to paint it, although sometimes one man did both. Through these signatures the names and works of a number of Athenian artists are known (e.g. Epiktetos, Euphronius, Euthymides, Phinthias, and Makron).

Coinage, the practice of stamping a piece of metal of given size with a recognizable mark, appears to have originated in the Ionian cities of Asia Minor about 650 BC, probably as a result of commercial needs in the major trading centres there. At first only very simple designs were used, but quite quickly the Greeks began to produce designs specially adapted to the circular field. The results are some of the most splendid coins the world has ever seen. The chief metals used were gold, silver, an alloy of the two (electrum), and bronze.

The method of production was laborious, two dies being required. The designs were carved in intaglio, i.e., in the reverse of relief. One die was attached to the top of the anvil and the other to the end of a metal punch. A metal disc, heated to make it malleable, was then placed between the two dies and the punch was struck with the hammer, forcing the soft metal into the intaglio portions and producing the design in relief on the two faces of the coin [22].

In the fourth century, in spite of a dozen or so Doric temples, the outstanding architectural works were the Ionic temples of western Asia Minor. The great fourth-century temple of Artemis at Ephesus, originally begun about 550 BC, was burnt down in 356 BC, but was rebuilt almost immediately on the same plan, but with the Ionic order brought up to fourth-century style. Another temple of Artemis, of similar dimensions, was built about the same time at Sardis. Its cella was sub-divided into two more or less equal parts, presumably to provide two sanctuaries, one entered from the west, the other from the east. The temple of Apollo at Didyma was begun late in the fourth century, but the bulk of the construction belongs to later centuries so that it falls outside the buildings being considered here. It was not actually completed until AD 41. Of smaller dimensions was the Ionic temple of Athena Polias at Priene, which was dedicated by Alexander the Great in 334 BC. It followed the classic plan except that it was somewhat broader in relation to its length (6 × 11 columns) than the majority of fifth-century temples.

One other fourth-century Ionic structure which is not a temple may be mentioned here. This is the monumental tomb of King Mausolus of Caria at Halicarnassus (the Mausoleum). Only part of the structure survives and the arrangement of the upper portion is a matter of considerable dispute [181]. The tomb was completed by the King's widow, Artemisia, soon after 353 BC.

By the time it had emerged as a clearcut architectural form, in the fourth century BC, the Greek theatre had three main parts: the auditorium, the *orchēstra* and the *skēnē* [182]. The auditorium normally made use of natural slopes, covered with tiers of stone seats, and in plan was slightly larger than a semi-circle. The *orchēstra* was the circular area where, at least in the fifth and fourth centuries, the actual performance took place. Behind the *orchēstra* was the third element, the *skēnē*, which originally was probably

181. Reconstruction by H. W. Law of the Mausoleum or tomb of Mausolus, King of Caria, at Halicarnassus, completed by his widow, Artemisia, soon after 353 BC. This reconstruction is only one of many, but in its main lines it is probably fairly close to the original.

just a building for housing the actors, scenery, and the administrative side of the theatre. The *proskenion*, attached to the front of the *skēnē*, consisted of a row of columns supporting a flat roof. By about 150 BC this had almost certainly become the stage on which the action took place. When the entire action took place in the *orchēstra*, the *skēnē* must have simply acted as a backcloth; the *proskenion* may have been added originally to provide a more varied background.

Places of assembly (council chambers, for example) were important in Greek cities. The Telesterion at Eleusis had a long and complex structural history, but basically it consisted of a square hall (*c.* 170 × 170 ft.) with seating on all four sides and a forest of columns supporting the centre. On the east, the main front, there was a Doric porch, twelve columns wide and two columns deep. In the same general category were the Thersilion at Megalopolis, the Ecclesiasterion at Priene, the Bouleuterion at Miletus and the Hypostyle Hall at Delos.

In close association with the *agora* or market-place was the *stoa*, a long colonnade designed to provide protection from either rain or heat, where people could meet informally and where business could be transacted. The *stoa* of Attalos in Athens (*c.* 150 BC) has been splendidly restored by the American School of Classical Studies [183].

The best examples of Greek houses of the fifth and fourth centuries have been found at Olynthus and Priene. In general the Greek house was of one storey and faced inwards on to a small courtyard. The external walls were largely blank, and were pierced only by small windows, placed high, and the street entrance. The rooms opened on to the courtyard, either

182. General view of the theatre at Epidauros, *c.* 350 BC. The Greek theatre consisted of three main parts, which can be seen here: the auditorium or seating area (in the background), the *orchēstra* or circular acting area (centre), and the *skēnē* or stage-building (stone foundations in the foreground). The two entrances, one of which can be seen on the right, were between the stage-building and the ends of the auditorium.

183. The *stoa* of Attalos in the *agora* or market-place in Athens, with the Acropolis in the background. The *stoa* was originally built *c.* 150 BC and in recent years has been restored to its original state by the American School of Classical Studies.

directly or by means of a porch or portico. In some cases the latter existed on all four sides of the courtyard, forming a peristyle which would allow access from one room to another under cover. Greek hotels employed the same principle, one or more large courts being surrounded by peristyles with the guests' rooms ranged round on all four sides.

In fourth-century sculpture the female nude became an important type, exemplified by such famous figures as the Aphrodite of Knidos, the Aphrodite of Arles, and the Capitoline Aphrodite (all Roman copies) [184]. The nude male athletic type also continued although certain changes are now noticeable. The figures are slightly less austere, slightly less remote and majestic. There is a more gentle, sentimental feeling, seen best perhaps in the figure of Hermes with the infant Dionysius, a group with an almost playful air, which would have been completely out of place in the fifth century. In the same spirit are the Apollo of Belvedere, and the Pothos figure, a youth leaning on a pillar gazing wistfully upwards (both Roman copies).

The three centuries between the death of Alexander the Great (323 BC) and the beginning of the Roman Empire (27 BC) are known as the Hellenistic period, indicating the diffusion of Greek or Hellenic-type culture (hence the term Hellenistic) over a great part of the east Mediterranean and Near-eastern world as a result of Alexander's conquests. Alexander's empire did not survive his death, which was followed by a scramble for power among his generals. Eventually, by the early part of the third century, three kingdoms emerged: Egypt under the Ptolemies; a varying portion of the Near East, centred on Syria, under the Seleucids; and Macedonia, the homeland of the empire, under Antigonus and his heirs. These countries and the many new Greek cities perpetuated the forms and traditions of Greek culture until they were eventually incorporated in the Roman Empire.

In Italy the formative period of Roman civilization goes back to the Etruscan civilization of northern Italy. The Etruscans appear in the archaeo-

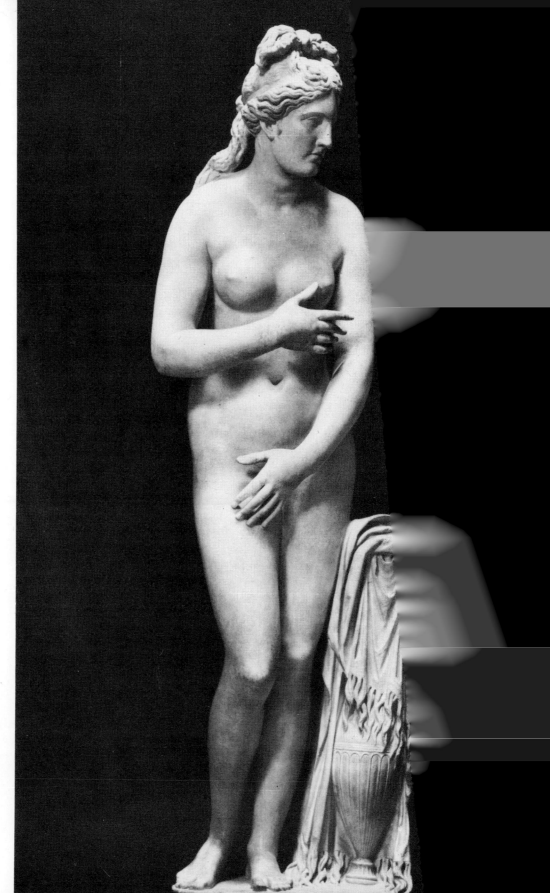

184. The Capitoline Aphrodite, *c*. 320–280 BC, known to us, like so many other pieces of Greek sculpture, only through this Roman copy. In the fourth century BC, Greek sculptors devoted a great deal of their attention to the nude female figure, in contrast to the male, athletic figures which had occupied so much of their time in the fifth century BC.

logical record in the eighth century BC and had close contacts with the Archaic and Classical Greek world. In the early centuries (eighth-sixth centuries BC) Rome itself was part of the Etruscan domain and therefore absorbed elements of Greek civilization. In 510 BC Rome threw off Etruscan domination and gradually the Roman Republic supplanted Etruria as the main political power in Italy. More direct Greek influence on Rome was represented by the Greek cities to the south in southern Italy and Sicily (Magna Graecia). These were as much a part of the Greek world as Ionia (Asia Minor) or Greece itself and their relative proximity to Rome made Greek influence inevitable. These were absorbed into the territories of the expanding Roman Republic, perpetuating Greek civilization beyond the termination of their political power.

The Hellenistic period, the Etruscan civilization and Rome in the Republican period (510–27 BC) are each major archaeological topics. Their brief treatment here is no reflection of their importance in the ancient world. Without them the civilization of the Roman Empire would have been vastly different and its inheritance from Greece greatly diminished.

THE ROMAN WORLD

At the Battle of Actium in 31 BC Mark Anthony was defeated by Octavian who, in 27 BC, became the first Emperor (Augustus), and it is with the archaeology of the Imperial period that this section is concerned.

185. The Maison Carrée, Nîmes, in southern France, a Roman temple begun *c.* 19 BC during the reign of the first Emperor, Augustus. This is an excellent example of the smaller type of Roman temple displaying the main Roman characteristics: a high podium or platform, a deep porch, and engaged, rather than free-standing, columns along the sides and the back.

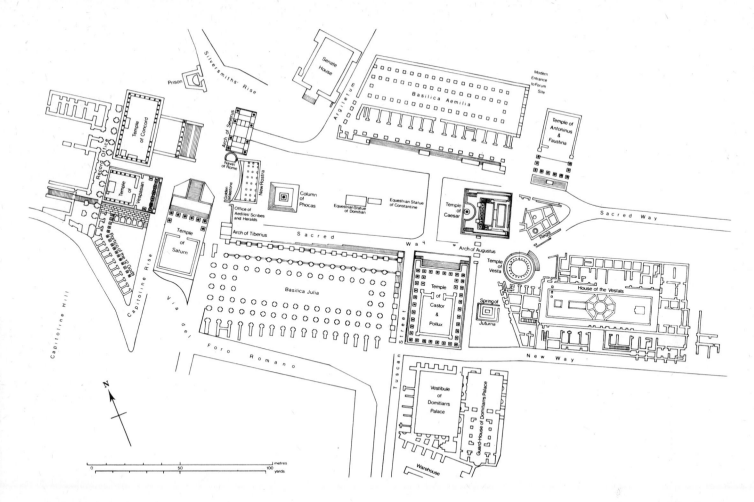

In the field of architecture Roman technique differed from Greek in two main respects. For building walls the Greeks relied mainly on masonry blocks locked together with clamps, and for spanning spaces they used the flat lintel formed from a single length of stone or timber. The Romans, on the other hand, made great use of brick and concrete and, in the spanning of space, of the semi-circular arch, the vault and the dome, none of which had been used to any great extent in the Greek world.

Temples form an important part of Roman architecture and the family resemblance to Greek temples is quite clear. Equally clear, however, are the differences which developed in the centuries between. One of the most noticeable is the use of a high podium or base (an Etruscan inheritance) which can be seen very clearly in one of the best-preserved Roman temples, the Maison Carrée at Nîmes in southern France [185]. The same temple illustrates most of the other differences between Greek and Roman temples. The order is Corinthian, a style known to the Greeks but only used to any great extent in Hellenistic and more particularly Roman (Imperial) times. The approach is from the front only, by means of a flight of steps rising between two bastion-like projections of the podium, and this emphasis on the frontal aspect is another typically Roman feature. This is further emphasized by the absence of free-standing columns along the sides and at the back. There are, instead, half-columns engaged or attached to the cella

186. Plan of the main Forum in Rome, the Forum Romanum. Other Forums were added to the north and north-west by Julius Caesar and by successive Emperors —Augustus, Vespasian, Nerva and Trajan.

walls, so that the cella, in fact, occupies the full width of the podium. Another Roman feature is the deep porch, three columns deep in the Maison Carrée, but with all the internal columns omitted.

The Maison Carrée belongs to the reign of Augustus. The temple of Antoninus and Faustina (c. AD 142) resembles it closely both in size and plan. In this case, however, the free-standing Corinthian columns of the portico are unfluted shafts of green and white marble from Greece. This is one of a number of temples closely associated with the Forum in Rome [186]. Two of them, the temples of Vespasian and of Saturn, are of the same general plan. The three remaining temples are those of Julius Caesar, Castor, and Concord. The temple of Julius Caesar marks the spot where he was assassinated. The temple of Castor has free-standing Corinthian columns at the sides and across the back. The whole structure was over 150 ft. long and 95 ft. wide, with a podium 22 ft. in height. It was rebuilt by Tiberius, under Augustus, and dedicated in AD 6. The temple of Concord (originally fourth century BC) was rebuilt by Tiberius between 7 BC and AD 10. Its unusual plan was due to pressure of space at the western end of the Forum. The large cella (148 × 82 ft.) had its entrance in the middle of the long eastern wall, fronted by a very deep porch. The whole structure stood on a podium nearly 20 ft. high.

The temple of Mars Ultor, one of the most splendid in Rome, occupied one end of, and dominated, the Forum of Augustus and was completed in AD 2. It had free-standing fluted Corinthian columns on three sides, a deep porch, and an almost square cella with a semi-circular recess at the back, all standing on a podium which was backed against the high enclosing wall of the Forum, separating it from the slums beyond. The temple of Venus and Rome was unusual in that it consisted of two cellas, back to back, and was built originally by Hadrian in AD 135, although the surviving remains above the podium date from a rebuilding by Maxentius in AD 307. It had a complete peristyle of Corinthian columns (20 × 10 columns). There were steps on all four sides and the temple stood within an enclosing wall which had a colonnade on its inner side, the whole structure resting on an enormous podium, c. 541 × 337 ft.

The Pantheon, a circular temple in Rome, was one of the most remarkable buildings of antiquity [187]. It dates substantially from the time of Hadrian (AD 117–38), although the portico probably belongs to an earlier building. The circular portion is over 180 ft. in external diameter and the walls are 20 ft. thick. The most remarkable feature of all is the great dome, probably of concrete, spanning the interior space (over 140 ft. in diameter) without any internal support and with a central opening nearly 30 ft. across which provides the only source of light. This building, without any substantial addition or alteration, is still in use today as a church, a remarkable tribute to the quality of its building. There are other, smaller circular temples of similar construction in Rome (of Vesta), Tivoli (also of Vesta), and at Baalbek.

In Roman theatres the three fundamental parts of the original Greek structures are integrated into a single unit. In plan the building is now D-shaped with the *orchēstra* reduced to a semi-circle immediately in front of what is now quite clearly the stage. The stage-building occupies most, if not all, of the straight side of the D, and is as high as the highest part of the auditorium. This too is reduced to a semi-circle and its ends abut the stage-building. Perhaps the most striking feature of the latter is the elaborate

187. Opposite: the interior of the Pantheon, Rome, c. AD 130, which is still in use as a church, after an eighteenth-century painting by G. P. Pannini. The dome spans some 140 ft., and the central opening is nearly 30 ft. across, providing the only source of light apart from the doorway.

architectural façade *(scaenae frons)* which forms a backcloth to the stage. When the terrain allowed, the Romans, like the Greeks, made use of a natural hollow or slope to form the auditorium but, because they were built inside cities, their theatres frequently had to stand on level ground, with the auditorium supported on an elaborate sub-structure.

Only three theatres will be considered here. The theatre of Marcellus (*c.* 500 × 350 ft.) is the only surviving example of a Classical theatre in Rome, although its stage-building has not been preserved. The substructure of the auditorium and the two lower storeys of its outer wall are the best preserved portions. The theatre at Aspendus in Asia Minor is in a much better state although it is somewhat smaller (325 × 230 ft.); its auditorium is hollowed out of the slope of a hill. The stage-building is well-preserved, enabling the *scaenae frons* to be reconstructed with a high degree of accuracy. Above it was a sloping wooden roof. The stage-building did not extend to the full width of the theatre, the difference being made up by two wing-like walls against which the seats of the auditorium abutted. The latter could accommodate about 7,000 people, with room for another 500 in the *orchĕstra*. The theatre at Orange, in southern France, is also well preserved. The *scaenae frons* appears to have been even more elaborate than that at Aspendus, with three tiers or storeys of architectural decoration. The dimensions of its back (outer) wall (340 ft. long and 120 ft. high) give some idea of the scale of Roman theatres [188].

Unlike the theatre, the amphitheatre was a type of Roman building without a Greek prototype, used to stage gladiatorial contests and other savage spectacles. Probably the outstanding example of the type is the Colosseum in Rome, which could accommodate some 45,000 people [189].

188. The Roman theatre at Orange in southern France. This is one of the best preserved of all Roman theatres and is typical of the normal Roman layout (cf., the Greek theatre at Epidauros—182). In the Roman theatre, the circular *orchĕstra* of the Greeks has been reduced to a semi-circle, there is now a stage with an elaborate architectural 'backcloth' (*scaenae frons*), and all the separate elements have been integrated into a single building.

It is oval in plan (617×512 ft.) with an arena 289×180 ft. The outer wall rested on eighty massive piers, linked by arches, with two further tiers of arcaded wall above; above these is a section of solid wall with flat pilasters, bringing the total height of the external wall to over 160 ft. Perhaps more than any other type of monument the amphitheatre, and the Colosseum in particular, exemplifies the Roman skill in structural engineering. There are other well-preserved amphitheatres at Verona in Italy, at El Djem in North Africa and at Arles and Nîmes in southern France.

Space does not permit the description of other aspects of Roman architecture which cover a wide range of buildings, spread over the huge geographical extent of the Roman Empire. These include such types as baths (from the huge Imperial constructions in Rome to the humble bathhouse outside a Roman fort in the provinces), basilicas, palaces, houses, triumphal arches, aqueducts and bridges, granaries and town walls and gates, to mention only some of the more obvious types.

Rome's debt to Greece is equally marked in sculpture, an enormous amount of which was produced during the Roman Empire. It would, however, be a mistake to assume that Roman sculpture was simply a pale imitation of Greek; while the family likeness is quite clear, so also is a very considerable Roman element. In two types of sculpture in particular, portrait sculpture and relief sculpture, the Romans made a great native contribution to the repertoire of Classical art.

The Greeks of the fifth and fourth centuries produced very little that could be termed true portrait sculpture, i.e. sculpture which represented the subject realistically. For the most part they produced idealized versions, types rather than individuals; the end product was often great sculpture but not necessarily a realistic representation of the subject. The Romans, on the other hand, had a largely uncompromising attitude towards portraiture and attempted to show people as they were, 'warts and all'. There is a con-

189. The Colosseum, Rome, the greatest of all the amphitheatres in the Roman Empire. In its layout, a central arena surrounded on all sides by a steeply-raked auditorium, it is very similar to the present-day Spanish bull-ring which must ultimately, in fact, be derived from the Roman amphitheatre.

siderable range of surviving Roman portrait sculpture, including members of the Imperial family and portraits of humbler people, which display the basic Roman qualities of hard work, self-discipline and common-sense. The Imperial portraits of the first century AD show very vividly the personalities of the Caesars, while those of later centuries display clearly the cosmopolitan nature of the Empire, with Emperors drawn from many different races and backgrounds. Imperial female portraits are interesting for the wealth of incidental detail, particularly with regard to the hair, which shows great elaboration.

The Ara Pacis (Altar of Peace), completed in 9 BC by Augustus to celebrate the establishment of peace in the Roman world, contained a large amount of relief sculpture, including a frieze showing the Imperial family and important state officials walking in procession, presumably in connection with the ceremony dedicating the altar in 13 BC. The essence of this relief is the deliberate, public association of the Emperor with the benefits of Roman rule and the Roman way of life. It was a form of propaganda, carried on even more intensively by means of the Roman Imperial coins, each of which was, in a sense, a piece of relief sculpture in miniature, furthering the same message. The Ara Pacis consisted of a large sacrificial altar on a podium, surrounded by a high enclosure wall, the inner and outer faces of which carried the procession frieze and large areas of floral relief decoration [190].

One of the traditional vehicles for official Imperial relief sculpture was the triumphal arch, and two panels from the Arch of Titus illustrate this. In one scene, the captured booty from the sack of Jerusalem (AD 70), including the Jewish seven-branched candelabrum, is borne in triumph [191], and in the other the triumphant Emperor rides in a four-horse chariot and is crowned by Victory. The composition of the scene involving the Emperor is not absolutely realistic and is obviously dominated by an official formula for such a piece of work, concentrating on projecting the Emperor rather than any artistic ideal.

One of the most celebrated, and most unusual, pieces of all Roman relief sculpture is Trajan's column, erected in AD 113 to celebrate and, very vividly, commemorate the Emperor Trajan's campaigns against the Dacians on the Danube frontier in AD 101–2 and 105–6. The column (12 ft. in diameter

190. The Ara Pacis or Altar of Peace, Rome, now reconstructed. It was originally completed in 9 BC by the first Emperor Augustus to celebrate the establishment of peace in the Roman world, after the long period of civil war which followed the assassination of his uncle, Julius Caesar, in 44 BC.

191. Relief sculpture from the Arch of Titus, Rome, showing a triumphal procession celebrating the sack of Jerusalem in AD 70. Note in particular the Jewish seven-branched candelabrum borne aloft as part of the booty.

and 120 ft. high) is decorated with a band of low-relief sculpture which winds around in a spiral from bottom to top. It contains very detailed evidence of the Roman army in action, although it is not, in fact, a strict diary of events, but rather a series of selected scenes. In keeping with official practice, the Emperor appears regularly throughout, quite clearly being associated with this triumph of Roman Imperial civilization.

The most striking relief sculptures of the Hadrianic period (AD 117–38) are the eight circular panels re-used on the Arch of Constantine (AD 312–37), but known to belong originally to the earlier period. All show scenes connected with the hunt and may have belonged to a monument erected by Hadrian to his favourite Antinous.

The column of Marcus Aurelius (AD 161–80), commemorating his victories on the Danubian frontier in AD 172 and 175, was closely modelled on the earlier column of Trajan. Unlike the latter, however, its sculpture is much less complex in composition. In the scenes showing the Emperor, for example, there is a tendency for the figures to be shown in full frontal view rather than in profile, resulting in sculptures which look stiff and formalized as compared with works of the earlier part of the Empire.

Only a few of the more important works of the first two centuries AD have been mentioned here, but this brief survey is no reflection of the very rich field of relief and portrait sculpture which was produced.

The characteristic black– and red–figure pottery of the Greeks is matched by the equally characteristic but very different pottery of the Roman Empire, known variously as Terra Sigillata, Samian ware or red-glazed ware. Its immediate ancestor appears to be a type of pottery produced at Arretium (Arezzo) in Italy in the first century BC known as Arretine ware, which in turn appears to have developed from an earlier type of pottery common in the east Mediterranean area which had moulded decoration, possibly in imitation of metal vessels, and a red or black glaze. Arretine ware was an Italian version of this tradition and was produced in both black-glazed (earlier) and red-glazed (later) forms, and it is the latter which stand at the beginning of the long tradition of Roman red-glazed ware.

Although it began in Italy, the main manufacturing centres of red-glazed pottery were in Gaul. In the first century AD there was large-scale production in south Gaul, particularly at La Graufesenque, where surviving tally-lists

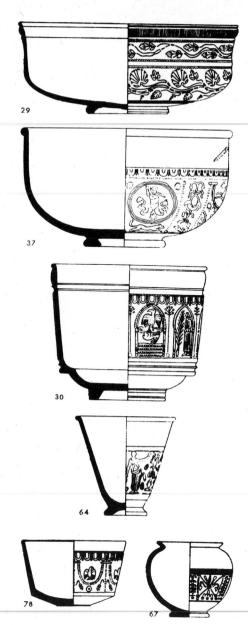

192. Forms 29, 30, 37, 64, 67 and 78, the main forms used in the relief-decorated, red-glazed Roman pottery, popularly known as Samian ware.

show that thirty-four workmen from a particular workshop (that of Castus) produced no less than 409,315 vessels. By about the middle of the century factories had been established in central Gaul, one of the most important being at Lezoux. During the second century AD production was on an enormous scale, exports from the central Gaulish factories largely displacing those of south Gaul. The third main production centre was in east Gaul, where there were many small factories with only one, Rheinzabern, of any considerable size. The principal period of production was the second half of the second century AD. Some Samian ware was produced in Britain at about the same time at Colchester in Essex.

Decorated Samian ware was produced in a limited number of shapes [192]. Form 29 is a carinated bowl, i.e., one with a sharp angle in the profile, while Form 37 is much more rounded, almost hemispherical in shape. A hybrid, intermediate type is known as Form 29/37. Form 30 is a deep cylindrical bowl on a narrow base. Form 64 is a conical cup or beaker, while Form 78 is a small cup or bowl in the form of a truncated cone. Form 67 is a small globular jar. Plain Samian ware was made in a much wider variety of shapes which included a wide range of shallow open dishes and bowls.

The relief decoration on Samian ware was usually produced by means of moulding. With the aid of a series of clay stamps, the potter impressed the desired decoration on the inside of the clay mould prepared for whatever shape was being produced. This was baked hard and could then be used to make any number of vessels. More rarely the relief decoration was produced by applying separately moulded figures to individual pots.

In addition to Samian ware, a vast amount of what is known as coarse, more utilitarian pottery was produced, in a wide variety of regional forms, in the different parts of the Roman Empire. One very special type of Roman coarse ware was the mortarium, a vessel used for mixing and crushing food. The mortarium was a shallow, bowl-shaped vessel, usually about twelve inches in diameter, with a heavy rim and an interior studded with particles of hard gritstone to aid the grinding process and to lengthen the life of the pot.

Coinage, an invention of the Greek Archaic period (p. 222), was developed on an enormous scale by the Romans who used four main metals: gold, silver, copper, and brass. The standard gold coin of the Roman Empire was the *aureus* (strictly the *denarius aureus* or gold *denarius*) which was fixed by Augustus at a rate of forty-two to the Roman pound weight of gold. The *aureus* remained in use during the next three centuries although it was progressively reduced in value: to forty-five to the pound weight by Nero (AD 54–68), fifty to the pound by Caracalla (AD 198–217), and sixty to the pound by Diocletian (AD 284–305). Under Constantine (AD 306–37) a new gold coin, the *solidus*, was introduced (at seventy-two to the pound) and this became the standard Roman gold coin. Both *aureus* and *solidus* were produced in smaller denominations, principally the half-*aureus* or *quinarius aureus* and the half-*solidus* or *semis* [193].

The gold *aureus* was worth twenty-five of the principal Roman silver coin, the *denarius argentus* or silver *denarius*, known simply as the *denarius*. Under Augustus there were eighty-four *denarii* to the pound weight of silver, although under Nero it was devalued to ninety-six to the pound. There was also a half-*denarius* or *quinarius*. Nero included at least ten per cent of copper into the composition of the coin, and during the next century and a half the percentage increased to as much as sixty per cent. In AD 215

Caracalla introduced a new silver coin, the *antoninianus*, which eventually drove the *denarius* out of circulation, and by AD 242 the *antoninianus* was the only silver coin in circulation. Some fifty years later Diocletian introduced a new silver coin, the *argentus*, at ninety-six to the pound, the same as the *denarius* had been under Nero. An equivalent coin was introduced by Constantine, the *siliqua*, as well as another new silver coin, the *miliarense*, at seventy-two to the pound weight.

In the baser metals there were four coins at the beginning of the Empire, two of brass and two of copper. The two brass coins were the *sestertius* (four to the silver *denarius*) and the *dupondius* (eight to the silver *denarius*). The two copper coins were the *as* (sixteen to the silver *denarius*) and the *quadrans* (sixty-four to the silver *denarius*). Nero, again, introduced changes involving no less than five brass coins (*sestertius, dupondius, as, semis, quadrans*) and three copper coins (*as, semis, quadrans*), but as compared with the previous system this was unnecessarily complicated and after Nero the old system was resumed, eventually without the *quadrans*, so that the smaller denomination coins for the next couple of centuries were the *sestertius, dupondius* (in brass) and the *as* (copper). During the third century there were great variations in the composition and weight of these coins and eventually in AD 294 Diocletian introduced a new copper coinage (which in fact contained some silver) in three denominations known as *follis, radiate* and *denarius communis*. The follis was the standard copper coin of the first half of the fourth century. Around the middle of the century (AD 348) a new large copper coin, the *centionalis* or *pecunia maiorina* was introduced.

During the four centuries of the Roman Imperial coinage a number of mints in different parts of the Empire were in use. Under Augustus, at the beginning of the Empire, the gold and silver coins were struck at Lyons (Lugdunum), while the bronze and copper coins were struck principally at Rome, although by the middle of the century (*c.* AD 50) the gold and silver were being struck there as well, and Rome remained the source of Imperial coinage until the end of the second century. During the next two centuries many mints were in use, not all at the same time, including London, Trier, Lyons, Arles, Rome, Ticinum and Aquileia. The various places of origin were shown by the mint marks which appeared on the coins: thus coins from the mint in Rome were marked either R, RM, ROM, or sometimes in full, ROMA, coins from London, L, LN, LON, coins from Lyons, L, LD, LG, LVG, LVGD, and so on. Other mint marks indicated the particular workshop within the mint in which the coin was struck—I, II, III, etc., or PRIMA or P (first), SECUNDA or S (second), TERTIA or T (third) and so on—the value of the coin, and the quality of metal used.

Although much of the sculpture, architecture, etc., referred to in the previous paragraphs has been in Rome there have also been references to other places which give some hint of the wide extent of Roman civilization. The Roman Empire, in fact, embraced the whole Mediterranean basin, as well as a great area of western Europe, each part of which (Roman Britain, Roman Africa, etc.) is a complete archaeological subject in itself. Despite the passage of some 2000 years, the former Roman presence in many of these regions is still marked by impressive architectural remains. Nowhere is this perhaps more true than in Roman Africa.

Although Rome became involved in Africa with the destruction of Carthage in 146 BC, it was not until the beginning of the Empire that really significant

193. Gold medallion (10 aureus piece) of Constantius Chlorus (Emperor AD 293–306) found at Arras, and minted after AD 296. This commemorative medallion was struck after Constantius Chlorus finally defeated the usurper Allectus and recaptured Britain. On it is the inscription REDDITOR LUCIS AETERNAE (Restorer of the Eternal Light), and it depicts London at the Emperor's feet.

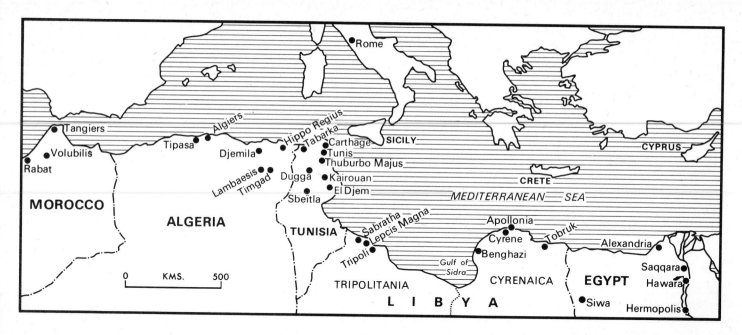

194. Map of Roman Africa.

progress was made in the establishment of Roman towns and cities and the Roman way of life [194]. In Tripolitania there are extensive structural remains at Sabratha and Lepcis Magna, including two splendid theatres together with temples, basilicas, baths, triumphal arches, colonnaded streets, market halls, etc. The third city of the trio, Oea, is now buried under modern Tripoli. Further west in Tunisia there are extensive remains of Roman cities at Carthage (rebuilt, mainly by Augustus), Dugga, Thuburbo Majus and El Djem. The buildings include theatres, temples, baths, etc., as well as a particularly well-preserved amphitheatre at El Djem, with an arena 214 × 130 ft., comparable in size with the Colosseum in Rome. Of the three major Roman establishments in Algeria (Timgad, Lambaesis and Djemila), the most striking is Timgad, from its plan (c. 1100 ft. square) quite clearly the work of a military engineer following the pattern of a Roman fort, with rounded corners, entrances at the middle of each side, and a regular grid-pattern of streets. The most important site in Morocco was Volubilis which, like many other African sites, enjoyed its period of greatest prosperity in the early third century under the Severan emperors. One of its main surviving monuments is the Arch of the Emperor Caracalla, son of Septimus Severus.

Roman remains in Syria/Palestine, at Palmyra, Ba'albek and Jerash, rival those of North Africa. At Palmyra dozens of standing Corinthian columns, spread over a wide area, are the surviving evidence of great colonnaded main streets of the city, providing shade and shelter from the elements. At Ba'albek the outstanding structure is the great temple standing within an enormous colonnaded enclosure with a monumental entrance. There is another, only slightly smaller, temple alongside, just outside the enclosure wall. Jerash is noted for its oval forum with a surrounding colonnade.

In western Europe the Maison Carrée and the amphitheatre at Nîmes, the amphitheatre at Arles and the theatre at Orange, all in southern France, have been mentioned already. In addition there are two well-preserved town gateways at Nîmes, considerable remains of a theatre, a palace, and baths at Arles and of a temple and a triumphal arch at Orange. Nearby is

195. Opposite: double-arched aqueduct at Segovia, Spain, c. AD 10. This and the Pont du Gard in southern France are the two most famous examples of Roman water engineering. The Roman achievement in supplying water over long distances by means of aqueducts was not to be equalled until comparatively recent times.

one of the most celebrated of all Roman engineering feats, the aqueduct across the river Gard (the Pont du Gard), bringing water to the town of Nîmes. There is an equally impressive aqueduct at Segovia in central Spain [195]. In Germany the most impressive standing remains are in Trier and include the famous Porta Nigra, a town gateway, the huge basilica, still in use as a church, and a well-preserved amphitheatre. In Britain, in the realm of still visible Roman monuments, Hadrian's Wall quite clearly takes pride of place although the remains of many of the later Roman forts along the south and east coasts (the so-called forts of the Saxon shore) are equally impressive. The palace at Fishbourne, about which much has, justifiably, been heard in recent years, is not a standing monument. Although most of what survives is now visible, the site was discovered by accident and only revealed as a result of extensive excavation.

MEDIEVAL ARCHAEOLOGY

Medieval archaeology spans the thousand or so years in Europe from the break-up of the Roman Empire (*c.* AD 475) to the beginning of the Renaissance. The Medieval period has its own particular problems. Its cities, towns, and villages are largely buried beneath their modern counterparts, which greatly limits the possibilities of excavation, although in recent years the recon-struction of town centres and the building of by-passes and motorways has alleviated the situation somewhat. A second problem has been the con-centration on the architecture of the second half of the period (cathedrals, abbeys, castles, etc.), to the detriment of the more everyday material. Again the balance has now been redressed to some extent by a more objective approach to the subject. Christian burial practice creates a third problem. The depositing of material with the dead was frowned on by the Church and the archaeologist is thereby deprived of an important body of evidence.

The commoner types of Medieval artefact are exemplified by the London Museum collection. London was one of the great cities of Medieval Europe and its material remains were probably similar to those of other European cities. The *Medieval Catalogue* of the London Museum includes the following headings: swords, knives, daggers, axes, arrowheads, spearheads, maces, horse-bits, bridle bosses, stirrups, spurs, horseshoes, heraldic pendants and badges, ploughs, sickles, pruning knives, flesh-hooks, spoons, keys, scissors, shears, purses, steelyard weights, candlesticks, lanterns, bronze jugs, cooking vessels and mortars, wooden vessels, pottery, floor tiles, pilgrim badges, dress fittings, lead mortuary crosses, bone, ivory and horn objects, whet-stones and seals. Behind virtually all of these headings is a wide range of sub-types and variations. Axes, or more strictly axe-heads, for example, are divided into six groups based on shape. Arrowheads and spearheads also embrace a wide variety of shapes and sizes. As benefits an age when the horse was an important means of transport, spurs, stirrups, and bridle fittings form a considerable part of the collections, as do the pilgrim badges or medals made of lead, pewter or brass, worn around the neck or on the hat [196]. Medieval pottery was produced in enormous quantity, common types being tall handled jugs, large barrel-like storage jars, and squat, cylindrical cooking pots [197]. Also in the ceramic field are floor tiles, used widely in Medieval times in religious and, less commonly, civil buildings.

The Vikings constitute a very special aspect of Medieval archaeology. From Scandinavia, by means of trade, raiding, and settlement, their influence

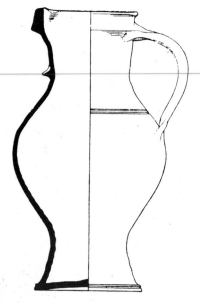

196, 197. Above: medieval pewter pilgrim badges. Pilgrim badges or medals, made of lead, pewter or brass, were worn around the neck or on the hat by pilgrims making the journey to Canterbury or other pilgrimage centres. Below: a fifteenth-century jug from London.

198. The Gokstad ship, a Viking long-boat, *c.* AD 900, discovered in a burial mound in Vestfold, Norway. In such ships, *c.* 70 ft. long, the Vikings ranged widely around the coasts and up the rivers of Europe, trading, raiding, and, in some cases, settling down to a more peaceful existence in their new-found homes.

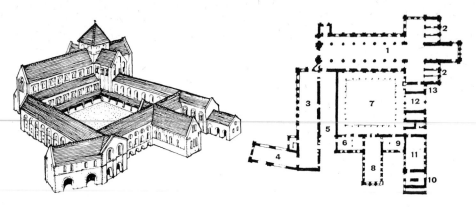

199. Reconstruction and plan of Kirkstall Abbey, Leeds, Yorkshire, *c.* AD 1190. Key: 1, church; 2, chapels; 3, lay brothers' dormitory (over); 4, lay brothers' WCs; 5, passage; 6, buttery; 7, cloisters; 8, dining-hall or Frater; 9, kitchen; 10, monks' WCs; 11 and 12 (over), monks' dormitory or Dorter; 12 (below), Chapter House; 13, Sacristy.

reached many parts of Europe during the eighth to eleventh centuries. As befits a warlike people, much of the surviving material is of a military character—richly decorated swords, helmets, and metal fittings for (presumably) leather belts, straps, harnesses, etc. On a larger scale are the Viking longboats with their intricately carved prows, many of which have been found, in spite of their size (*c.* 70 ft.), in Viking graves [**198**]. The famous Sutton Hoo ship burial in Suffolk is of the same general type. The most spectacular Viking sites are the fortresses such as Trelleborg, circular in plan, with the internal barrack blocks laid out in strict military fashion.

The buildings of the last four or five centuries of the Medieval period represent the largest body of monumental evidence surviving from any period, and many of them are still in use for their original function. The great outburst of building in the latter part of the Medieval period was a general European phenomenon, with the same basic styles (Romanesque and Gothic) and the same basic types (castles, cathedrals, abbeys, and parish churches) prevailing everywhere.

The richest heritage of the Medieval period are the cathedrals, which are not only great architecture in themselves but are also great repositories of the other arts: sculpture, stained glass, woodcarving, monumental brasses, etc. There are several hundred Medieval cathedrals in Europe.

Abbeys or monasteries on the other hand are numbered by thousands, and because of this and, in many cases, because of their great size, they represent a very important economic aspect of the Medieval period. Virtually all monasteries were laid out in accordance with a standard formula in which the main buildings were grouped around a rectangular cloister which normally abutted the south side of the church [**199**]. These buildings included the Chapter House, where the monks met to discuss monastic affairs, the Dorter (monks' dormitory), and the Frater (or dining-hall), together with kitchens, store-rooms, infirmaries, guest houses, etc. British monasteries form a rather special group in that their existence was ended at a single stroke when they were all suppressed by Henry VIII in 1540. In Europe they continued, but by this time the whole monastic movement was in decline anyway, so that eventually most of the European monasteries fell into disuse as well.

The most numerous of all Medieval monuments are the parish churches, humble versions of the great cathedral or abbey churches. In England alone these number some eight thousand, and the numbers in Europe must be in the tens of thousands. In spite of many additions and alterations, these are substantially original Medieval constructions. They represent a rich field of study and they have the advantage of being so widespread that they are within reach of virtually anyone wishing to study them.

Castles, like abbeys, are a widespread European phenomenon. In Britain, many of the best examples are in the care and guardianship of the Ministry of the Environment. Two special groups can be mentioned here. In 1066 the Normans brought with them castles in the form of a 'keep', a great square tower, and many such were built here, including the central part of the Tower of London (the White Tower) and the great keeps at Dover, Rochester and elsewhere [200]. The second group are the castles built by Edward I from 1277 onwards to subdue North Wales. These represent the culmination of European castle-building in the form of the concentric castle (Rhuddlan, Harlech and Beaumaris), and also provide two of the best surviving examples of Medieval walled towns in Europe (Conway and Caernarvon), built by Edward I as part of his pacification policy.

Cathedrals, castles, abbeys, and parish churches represent the greater part of the monumental remains of the Medieval period. There are others, but these alone provide a very rich field of interest and study.

POST-MEDIEVAL ARCHAEOLOGY

The centuries following the end of the Medieval period (c. 1475) are no less rich archaeologically than those described in earlier sections. Much of the interest in the last two centuries of this period (from c. 1750 on) has crystallized in the last decade or so into the subject of Industrial archaeology, leaving some three centuries (c. 1475–1750) which have been more recently, in Britain at least, crystallized into the subject of post-Medieval archaeology: the Society for Post-Medieval Archaeology was formed only in 1966. In both cases interest in the subjects was of long standing. What has happened in recent years is that they have been formally recognized, and clearly defined, as integral parts of the whole subject of archaeology.

By the end of the Medieval period the cathedrals, abbeys, and churches had been long established, and in the following centuries there was much greater emphasis on secular building, both public and private. The post-Medieval period was, in fact, a great period of domestic architecture involving houses both large and small, built in stone or in the timber-framed technique, the so-called black-and-white houses. It would, however, be a mistake to assume that all post-Medieval archaeology is concerned with domestic architecture, however grand. With a growing population the demand for such things as pottery was no less great than in earlier periods. Study of the large volume and variety of post-Medieval pottery can still tell us a great deal about trade and economy which research in written records may not reveal, just as the excavation and study of pottery kilns can tell us about the technical and organizational side of the industry. The same is true in other fields, glass-making for example, or iron-working, or the manufacture of clay pipes, to mention just a few of the many areas of post-Medieval archaeological research. In a period long dominated by the historian, the development of post-Medieval archaeology has opened up a new and rich field of endeavour which can make a tremendous contribution to an understanding of all aspects of life in the post-Medieval period, many of them outside the scope of written records and revealed only by the techniques of modern archaeology.

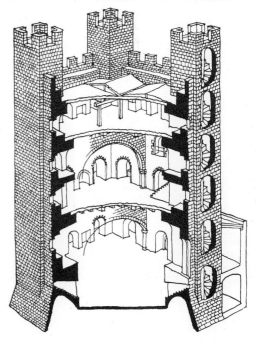

200. Reconstruction of Castle Hedingham, Essex, 1130–40, an example of the great square tower or keep which formed the basis of castle-building during the century or so after the Norman Conquest of 1066.

INDUSTRIAL ARCHAEOLOGY

The subject of industrial archaeology is not so new as the term Industrial Archaeology which was coined only in the postwar period. Remains of early industry have long been of interest to economic historians, to mention only one group, but in the last two decades there has been a great surge of general interest in this field. The Industrial Revolution began in Britain in the mid-eighteenth century and after some two hundred years of progress and change many of the original buildings, and much of the equipment, on which this profound economic change was based were in danger of being destroyed without record. There was also a great danger of valuable documentary evidence being destroyed through ignorance of its potential value to historians, sociologists and archaeologists. Happily, the crystallization of this widespread but hitherto unco-ordinated interest in industrial remains into the subject of Industrial Archaeology has produced a great new impetus, with the participation of many more people, and while there are still many problems and much work to be done, the subject is now very firmly established within the broad framework of archaeological studies.

Industrial archaeology brings to an end this introduction to the subject of archaeology. An introduction usually leads to some sort of long-term relationship. It is, hopefully, a starting-point, the means to an end rather than an end in itself, a way of promoting a mutually beneficial exchange between the two parties concerned. This is no less true of the two parties involved here: archaeology and its would-be student—or, more realistically, the student of some of its branches, for what should now be clear is the vast extent of the subject. This fact alone would make a wide-ranging introduction a necessity. Without it, it would be difficult for the reader to decide just what aspect, period, area, etc., of archaeology he wishes to pursue. The aim of this introduction, therefore, has been to open a series of doors to the major departments of the subject and, without going much beyond the threshold in each case, to look round very briefly at the contents, so that at the end of the process the amateur (in the strict sense here—one who loves the subject) of archaeology should have a fairly clear picture of its extent in time and space. With this information, a choice can be made and a relationship established between the reader and subject, to the benefit of both. The benefit to the reader is clear and direct: the satisfying of a developing curiosity. The benefit to the subject is less obvious but nonetheless real. All academic subjects depend ultimately on a broad base of popular interest. Without such support they become a barren and fruitless exercise. In satisfying his own curiosity, the interested reader is widening the popular base of archaeological studies by adding to the number of the informed general public, and in doing so is in his own way rendering a significant service to the subject. This service is, of necessity, less extensive than that rendered by the full-time, professional archaeologist, but both types of service, and the whole range of contributions in between, are needed for the continuing development of the subject. If this book has in any way added to the essential foundation of general interest in the subject of archaeology, then it can be regarded as having achieved at least a moderate success in performing the preliminary introduction.

Further Reading

CHAPTER 1
Atkinson, R. J. C., *Field Archaeology*, London 1946.
Clark, J. G. D., *Archaeology and Society*, London 1957.
Cookson, M. B., *Photography for Archaeologists*, London 1954.
Corcoran, J. X. W. P., *The Young Field Archaeologist's Guide*, London 1966.
De Laet, S. J., *Archaeology and its Problems*, London 1957.
Kenyon, K. M., *Beginning in Archaeology*, London 1952.
Piggott, S., *Approach to Archaeology*, London 1959.
Webster, G., *Practical Archaeology*, London 1963.
Wheeler, Sir Mortimer, *Archaeology from the Earth*, Oxford 1954.

CHAPTER 2
Ceram, C. W., *A Picture History of Archaeology*, London 1958.
Daniel, G. E., *The Three Ages*, Cambridge 1943; *A Hundred Years of Archaeology*, London 1950; *The Origins and Growth of Archaeology*, London 1967.
Leakey, L. S. B., and Goodall, V. M., *Unveiling Man's Origins*, London 1970.
Lloyd, S., *Foundations in the Dust*, London 1947.
Pope, M., *Ancient Scripts and Modern Scholarship*, London 1973.
Willey, G. R., and Sabloff, J. A., *A History of American Archaeology*, London 1973.

CHAPTER 3
Breuil, H., *Four Hundred Centuries of Cave Art*, Montignac, Dordogne 1952.
Campbell, B. G., *Human Evolution: an Introduction to Man's Adaptations*, London 1966.
Clark, J. G. D., *World Prehistory, A New Outline*, Cambridge 1969.
Coates, A., *Prelude to History*, London 1951.
Coles, J. M., and Higgs, E. S., *The Archaeology of Early Man*, London 1969.
Grand, P. M., *Prehistoric Art: Palaeolithic Painting and Sculpture*, London 1967.
Kühn, H., *The Rock Pictures of Europe*, London 1956.
Leakey, L. S. B., *Adam's Ancestors*, London 1953.
Roe, D., *Prehistory: An Introduction*, London 1970.
Steveking, A. and G., *The Caves of France and Northern Spain*, London 1962.
Ucko, P. J., and Rosenfeld, A., *Palaeolithic Cave Art*, London 1967.

CHAPTER 4
Albright, W. F., *The Archaeology of Palestine*, 5th ed., London 1960.
Bittel, K., *Hattusha*, Oxford 1970.
Blegen, C., *Troy and the Trojans*, London 1963.
Cottrell, L., *The Land of Shinar*, London 1965.
Frankfort, H., *Art and Architecture of the Ancient Orient*, London 1969.
Garbini, G., *The Ancient World*, London 1966.
Ghirshman, R., *Iran*, London 1954.

Gurney, O. R., *The Hittites*, London 1952.

Harden, D. B., *The Phoenicians*, London 1952.

Kenyon, K. M., *Digging up Jericho*, London 1957; *Archaeology in the Holy Land*, London 1970.

Kramer, S. N., *The Sumerians*, Chicago 1963.

Lloyd, S., *Early Anatolia*, London 1956; *Early Highland Peoples of Anatolia*, London 1967.

Mallowan, M. E. L., *Twenty-five Years of Mesopotamian Discovery*, London 1959.

Mellaart, J., *Earliest Civilizations of the Near East*, London 1965; *Catal Hüyük: A Neolithic Town in Anatolia*, London 1967.

Moortgat, A., *The Art of Ancient Mesopotamia*, London 1969.

CHAPTER 5

AFRICA

Aldred, C., *The Egyptians*, London 1961; *Egypt to the End of the Old Kingdom*, London 1965.

Alimen, H., *The Prehistory of Africa*, London 1957.

Baumgartel, E., *The Cultures of Prehistoric Egypt*, Oxford 1947.

Cole, S., *The Prehistory of East Africa*, London 1964.

Clark, J. D., *The Prehistory of Southern Africa*, London 1959.

Davies, O., *West Africa before the Europeans*, London 1967.

Desroches-Noblecourt, G., *Tutankhamen*, London 1963.

Edwards, I. E. S., *Guide to the Egyptian Collections, British Museum*, London 1964; *The Pyramids of Egypt*, London 1967.

Emery, W. B., *Archaic Egypt*, London 1961; *Egypt in Nubia*, London 1965.

Forde-Johnston, J., *Neolithic Cultures of North Africa*, Liverpool 1959.

Fox, P., *Tutankhamun's Treasure*, London 1951.

Gardiner, A. H., *Egypt of the Pharaohs*, Oxford 1961.

Glanville, S. R. K., *The Legacy of Egypt*, London 1947.

Kees, H., *Ancient Egypt*, London 1961.

Lange, K., and Hirmer, M., *Egypt: Architecture, Painting, Sculpture*, 4th ed., London 1968.

MacBurney, C. B. M., *The Stone Age of Northern Africa*, London 1960.

Mertz, B., *Temples, Tombs and Hieroglyphs*, London 1964.

Murray, M., *The Splendour that was Egypt*, London 1951.

Smith, W. Stevenson, *The Art and Architecture of Ancient Egypt*, London 1958.

INDIA

Allchin, B. and R., *The Birth of Indian Civilization*, London 1968.

Allchin, F. R., *Neolithic Cattle-keepers of South India*, Cambridge 1963.

Fairservis, W. A., *The Roots of Ancient India*, London 1971.

Piggott, S., *Prehistoric India*, London 1950.

Wheeler, Sir Mortimer, *Ancient India and Pakistan*, London 1959; *The Indus Civilization*, 3rd ed., Cambridge 1968.

CHINA

Chang, K. C., *The Archaeology of Ancient China*, New Haven, Conn., 1963.

Cheng, T. K., *Archaeology in China*, Vol. I, 'Prehistoric China', Cambridge 1958; Vol. II, 'Shang China', 1960; Vol. III, 'Chou China', 1963; *New Light on Prehistoric China*, Cambridge 1966.

Watson, W., *Archaeology in China*, London 1960; *China before the Han Dynasty*, London 1961.

CHAPTER 6

Bennett, W. C., and Bird, J. B., *Andean Culture History*, New York 1949.

Bray, W., *Everyday Life of the Aztecs*, London 1968.

Bushnell, G. H. S., *Peru*, 2nd ed., London 1963; *The First Americans*, London 1968.

Griffin, J. B., *Archaeology of the Eastern United States*, Chicago 1952.

Kidder, A. V., *An Introduction to the Study of South-western Archaeology*, New Haven, Conn., 1962.

Kubler, G., *The Art and Architecture of Ancient America*, London 1962.

Martin, Quimby and Collier, *Indians Before Columbus*, Chicago 1947.

Mason, J. A., *The Ancient Civilizations of Peru*, London 1957.

Meggers, B., *Ecuador*, London 1966.

Morley, S. G., *The Ancient Maya*, Stanford University Press, California 1947.

Reichel–Dalmatoff, G., *Colombia*, London 1965.

Soustelle, J., *Arts of Ancient Mexico*, London 1967.

Thompson, J. E. S., *The Rise and Fall of Maya Civilization*, Oklahoma 1954.

Vaillant, G. C., *The Aztecs of Mexico*, London 1951.

Willey, G. R., *An Introduction to American Archaeology*, Vol. I, 'North and Middle America', New Jersey 1966; Vol. II, 'South America', New Jersey 1971.

Wormington, H. M., *Ancient Man in North America*, Denver, Colorado 1957.

CHAPTER 7
THE BRITISH ISLES

Ashbee, P., *The Bronze Age Round Barrow in Britain*, London 1960; *The Earthen Long Barrow in Britain*, London 1970.

Ashe, G., *The Quest for Arthur's Britain*, London 1968.

Atkinson, R. J. C., *Stonehenge*, London 1956.

Beresford, M. W., and St. Joseph, J. K., *Medieval England: An Aerial Survey*, Cambridge 1958.

Brailsford, J. W., *Guide to the Antiquities of Roman Britain*, London 1964; *Later Prehistoric Antiquities of the British Isles*, London 1953.

Bruce, J. Collingwood, *Handbook to the Roman Wall*, 12th ed., Newcastle-upon-Tyne 1965.

Bruce-Mitford, R. L. S., *Recent Archaeological Excavations in Britain*, London 1956.

Clark, R. R., *East Anglia*, London 1960.

Collingwood, R. G., and Richmond, I. A., *The Archaeology of Roman Britain*, London 1969.

Daniel, G. E., *Prehistoric Chamber Tombs of England and Wales*, Cambridge 1950.

Evans, E., *Prehistoric and Early Christian Ireland: A Guide*, London 1966.

Feachem, R., *The North Britons*, London 1965.

Forde-Johnston, J., *Hillforts of the Iron Age in England and Wales*, Liverpool 1974.

Foster, I., and Daniel, G. E., *Prehistoric and Early Wales*, London 1965.

Fox, Aileen, *South West England*, London 1964.

Fox, Sir Cyril, *Life and Death in the Bronze Age*, London 1959.

Frere, S. S., *Brittania: A History of Roman Britain*, London 1967.

Grinsell, L. V., *The Ancient Burial Mounds of England*, London 1953; *The Archaeology of Wessex*, London 1958.

Jessup, R. F., *The South-East*, London 1970.

Knowles, D., and St. Joseph, J. K., *Monastic Sites from the Air*, Cambridge 1952.

Leeds, E. T., *Early Anglo-Saxon Art and Archaeology*, Oxford 1936.

Liversedge, J., *Britain in the Roman Empire*, London 1968.

Margary, I. D., *Roman Roads in Britain*, London 1955.

Nash-Williams, *The Roman Frontier in Wales*, 2nd ed., Cardiff 1969.

O'Riordain, S. P., *Antiquities of the Irish Countryside*, 3rd ed., London 1953; *New Grange and the Bend of the Boyne*, London 1964.

Piggott, S., *Neolithic Cultures of the British Isles*, Cambridge 1954; *The Prehistoric Peoples of Scotland*, London 1962.

Rivet, A. L. F., *Town and Country in Roman Britain*, London 1958.

Stone, J. F. S., *Wessex*, London 1958.

Thomas, A. C., *The Early Christian Archaeology of North Britain*, Oxford 1971.

Thomas, N., *Guide to Prehistoric England*, London 1960.

Wilson, D. M., *The Anglo-Saxons*, London 1960.
Wilson, D. R., *The Roman Frontiers of Britain*, London 1967.

EUROPE

Alexander, J., *Jugoslavia*, London 1972.
Berciu, D., *Romania*, London 1967.
Brea, L. B., *Sicily*, London 1957.
Childe, V. G., *The Dawn of European Civilization*, 6th ed., London 1957.
Clark, J. G. D., *Prehistoric Europe: The Economic Basis*, London 1952; *World Prehistory: A New Outline*, 2nd ed., Cambridge 1969.
Daniel, G. E., *The Megalith Builders of Western Europe*, London 1958; *The Prehistoric Chamber Tombs of France*, London 1960.
De Laet, S. J., *The Low Countries*, London 1958.
Evans, J. D., *Malta*, London 1959.
Gimbutas, M., *The Prehistory of Eastern Europe*, Harvard 1956; *Bronze Age Cultures in Central and Eastern Europe*, The Hague 1965.
Giot, P. R., *Brittany*, London 1960.
Hudson, K., *A Guide to the Industrial Archaeology of Europe*, Bath 1971.
Jazdzewski, K., *Poland*, London 1965.
Klindt-Jensen, O., *Denmark*, London 1957.
Megaw, J. V. S., *Art of the European Iron Age*, Bath 1970.
Mongait, A., *Archaeology in the U.S.S.R.*, Moscow 1959.
Neustupný, E., and J., *Czechoslovakia*, London 1961.
Piggott, S., *Ancient Europe*, Edinburgh 1965.
Powell, T. G. E., *The Celts*, London 1959.
Rice, T. T., *The Scythians*, London 1957.
Savory, H. N., *Spain and Portugal*, London 1968.
Stenberger, M., *Sweden*, London 1967.
Sulimirski, T., *Prehistoric Russia: An Outline*, London 1970.
Wilson, D. M., *The Vikings and their Origins*, London 1970.

THE CLASSICAL WORLD

Bloch, R., *The Etruscans*, London 1958.
Boardman, J., *Greek Art*, London 1964.
Boardman, J., and others, *Art and Architecture of Ancient Greece*, London 1967.
Boethius, A., and Ward-Perkins, J. B., *Etruscan and Roman Architecture*, London 1970.
Graham, J. W., *The Palaces of Crete*, Princeton 1969.
Grant, M., *The Roman Forum*, London 1970.
Hutchinson, R. W., *Prehistoric Crete*, London 1962.
Kahler, H., *Rome and Her Empire*, London 1963.
Kurtz, D. C., and Boardman, J., *Greek Burial Customs*, London 1971.
Lane, A., *Greek Pottery*, 3rd ed., London 1971.
MacKendrick, P., *The Greek Stones Speak*, London 1962.
Pendlebury, J. D. S., *The Archaeology of Crete*, London 1939.
Richter, G. M. A., *A Handbook of Greek Art*, 6th ed., London 1969.
Robertson, D. S., *Greek and Roman Architecture*, Cambridge 1969.
Schefold, K., *Classical Greece*, London 1967.
Strong, D. E., *Roman Imperial Sculpture*, London 1961; *The Classical World*, London 1965.
Taylour, Lord William, *The Mycenaeans*, London 1964.
Toynbee, J. M. C., *Roman Burial Customs*, London 1971.
Wheeler, Sir Mortimer, *Roman Art and Architecture*, London 1964.
Wood, R., and Wheeler, Sir Mortimer, *Roman Africa in Colour*, London 1966.
Wycherley, R. E., *How the Greeks Built Cities*, London 1962.

List of Illustrations

The author and publishers are grateful to the many official bodies, institutions, and individuals who kindly supplied illustrative material.

BLACK AND WHITE ILLUSTRATIONS

Sterkfontein, Transvaal. Photo: by courtesy of the Trustees of the British Museum (Natural History).

40 The Swanscombe skull. Photo: by courtesy of the Trustees of the British Museum (Natural History).

41 Cro-magnon Man. Photo: by courtesy of the Trustees of the British Museum (Natural History).

42 Neanderthal Man. Photo: by courtesy of the Trustees of the British Museum (Natural History).

43 Pre-Chellean tool of the Oldowan culture. After Leakey.

44 Levalloisian flake and tortoise-shaped core. After Leakey.

45 Mousterian point and side-scraper. After Leakey.

46 Acheulean hand-axe. Photo: Peter Clayton.

47 Upper Palaeolithic family group. Photo: by courtesy of the Trustees of the British Museum (Natural History).

48 Tool types of the Châtelperronian culture. After Leakey.

49 Tool types of the Aurignacian culture. After Leakey.

50 Tool types of the Gravettian and Magdalenian cultures. After Leakey.

51 A leaf-shaped blade of the Solutrean culture. After Leakey.

52 Spear-thrower representing a bison licking its flank, from the cave of La Madeleine, Dordogne, Château de Saint-Germain-en-Laye, Yvelines. Photo: Musée des Antiquités Nationales.

53 Engraving of a reindeer on a schist plaque. Photo: Collection Musée de l'Homme, Paris.

54 Steatite figurine of a woman, from Grimaldi. Château de Saint-Germain-en-Laye, Yvelines. Photo: Musée des Antiquités Nationales.

55 Female statuette modelled in a mixture of clay and powdered bone, from Dolní, Věstonice, Moravia. Photo: by courtesy of the Moravské Museum, Brno.

56 Bison, modelled in clay and set firmly against the sloping ground, from Le Tuc D'Audoubert. Begoven Collection. Photo: J. Vertut. © S.P.A.D.E.M. Paris 1974.

57 Head of a bronze statue of Naram-Sin (?), from Nineveh, height 14¼ in. Iraq Museum, Baghdad. Photo: by courtesy of the Directorate General of Antiquities, Baghdad.

58 Distribution map of Mesolithic and proto-Neolithic sites in the Near East. Drawn by M. Ely.

59 Neolithic portrait head, from Jericho, Pre-Pottery Neolithic B period. Photo: by courtesy of Kathleen M. Kenyon.

60 Plan of building-level VIB at Çatal Hüyük, c. 6000 BC. Drawn by J. Wickman after Mellaart.

61 Reconstruction drawing of a funerary rite, Çatal Hüyük, Shrine E.VII, 21. By courtesy of The Illustrated London News. Photo: L.E.A.

62 Isometric drawing of a group of houses from Haçilar VI, c. 5600 BC. From James Mellaart, *Earliest Civilizations of the Near East*, Thames & Hudson, London 1965.

63 Map of ancient Mesopotamia. Drawn by M. Ely.

64 Reconstruction of the Ubaid temple in level XIII at Tepe Gawra. Drawn by Patrick Leeson after Herget.

65 Aerial view of the Temple Oval at Khafaje. Photo: Peter Clayton.

66 Isometric restoration of the Temple Oval at Khafaje. After the University of Chicago, Oriental Institute Publications 53, Pl. V. Photo: Verlag M. Dumont Schauberg.

67 Plan of the main level of the Shara Temple at Tell Agrab. From the University of Chicago, Oriental Institute Publications 58, fig. 203.

68 Gypsum statuette of a man, from Tell Asmar, height 19⅛ in. Iraq Museum, Baghdad. Photo: by courtesy of the Directorate General of Antiquities, Baghdad.

69 Plan of the palace of Naram-Sin at Tell Brak. After Iraq 9, Pl. LX.

70, 71 View and reconstruction of the ziggurat of Ur-Nammu at Ur. Photo: Hirmer Fotoarchiv, Munich. Reconstruction: from Moortgat, *The Art of Ancient Mesopotamia*, London 1969.

72 Sumerian statuette, from Lagash, c. 2500 BC, height 11¾ in. Photo: by courtesy of the Trustees of the British Museum.

73 Top of the diorite stele inscribed with the law code of Hammurabi, from Susa. Musée du Louvre, Paris. Photo: Service de Documentation Photographique de la Réunion des Musées Nationaux.

74 Reconstructed façade of the temple of Innin at Uruk. Photo: by courtesy of the Staatliche Museen, Berlin-DDR.

75 Limestone *kudurru*, from Susa, height 21¼ in. Musée du Louvre, Paris. Photo: Service de Documentation Photographique de la Réunion des Musées Nationaux.

76 Plan of Khorsabad. After the University of Chicago, Oriental Institute Publications 40, Pl. 69.

77 Colossal winged and human-headed bull, with attendant winged figure, from a doorway into the palace of Sargon II. Photo: by courtesy of the Trustees of the British Museum.

78–80 Alabaster mural reliefs from the North-west Palace of Ashurnasirpal II at Nimrud, 885–859 BC. Photos: by courtesy of the Trustees of the British Museum.

81, 82 Detail and model of the Ishtar Gate at Babylon. Photos: by courtesy of the Staatliche Museen, Berlin-DDR.

83 Sophia Schliemann, wearing 'Priam's Treasure'. Photo: Peter Clayton.

84 Sphinx carved on the gate at Alaca Hüyük. Photo: Jean Bottin.

85 Plan of the city area of Hattusas. Drawn by M. Ely after Bittel.

86 Ritual figure on the top of a staff, from Alaca Hüyük. Photo: Hirmer Fotoarchiv, Munich.

87 Vessel in the shape of a two-headed duck, from Boghaz Köy. Photo: Hirmer Fotoarchiv, Munich.

88 The Lion Gate at Boghaz Köy. Photo Hirmer Fotoarchiv, Munich.

89 Plan of the city of Sinjerli. Drawn by Patrick Leeson after Akurgal.

90 The succession of Early Bronze Age walls, site M, Jericho. Photo: by courtesy of Kathleen M. Kenyon.

91 Pottery from Jericho, beginning of the Early Bronze Age III period. From Kenyon, *Archaeology in the Holy Land*, London 1960, fig. 19. Reproduced by courtesy of Kathleen M. Kenyon.

92 Reconstructed section of the Middle Bronze Age II rampart at Jericho. From Kenyon, *Archaeology in the Holy Land*, London 1960, fig. 43. Reproduced by courtesy of Kathleen M. Kenyon.

93 Map of Egypt from the Nile Delta to the 2nd Cataract. From Lange & Hirmer, *Egypt*, 4th ed., London 1968.

94 Dynasty I mastabas. Drawn by Patrick Leeson after Edwards.

95, 96 Longitudinal section and view of the step pyramid of King Zoser at Saqqara, by Imhotep, dynasty III. Section: from J-Ph. Lauer, *La Pyramide à degrés*,

COLOUR PLATES

Index

Numbers in *italic* refer to black-and-white illustrations and their captions. Roman numerals refer to colour plates and their captions.